The Martyrdom of St. Paul

Historical and Judicial Context, Traditions,
and Legends

by

H. W. Tajra

WIPF & STOCK · Eugene, Oregon

Wipf and Stock Publishers
199 W 8th Ave, Suite 3
Eugene, OR 97401

The Martyrdom of St. Paul
Historical and Judicial Context, Traditions, and Legends
By Tajra, Harry W.
Copyright©1994 Mohr Siebeck
ISBN 13: 978-1-61097-006-8
Publication date 10/8/2010
Previously published by Mohr Siebeck, 1994

To His Excellency

The Most Reverend Pierre Duprey M.Afr.,

Bishop of the Titular See of Thibar
and Segretarius of the Pontificium Consilium
ad Unitatem Christianorum fovendam,

without whose kind help this book
could not have been written.

Table of Contents

Chapter I: Paul's Condemnation and Martyrdom: Juridical Aspects ... 1
  I. Paul's Roman Citizenship and its Effect on His Martyrdom 1
  II. The Juridical Foundation for Paul's Condemnation to Death 4
    1. The Modification and Extension of the Laws governing the
      Crimen laesae maiestatis 4
    2. The Ruler-Cult 7
  III. Imperial Jurisdiction: Paul and Nero 12
  IV. The Imperial Tribunal: Penal Procedure 18
  V. Execution of the Capital Sentence 20
  VI. Regulation and Disposition of the Condemned's Corpse 24
    1. The *ius sepulcri* 24
    2. *Violatio sepulcri* 26
  VII. Paul's Martyrdom and its Relationship to the Christian
      Persecution of 64 A.D. 27

Chapter II: Paul's legal Situation at the Close of Acts 33
  I. Acts 16–28: Luke's Narration of Paul's judicial History 33
  II. Luke's Omission of Paul's Martyrdom 37
  III. Acts 28: Luke's Account of Paul's two-year Captivity 39
    1. Acts 28,16: Paul in *custodia militaris* 40
    2. Acts 28,30–31: Paul exercises his Ministry at Rome
      sine prohibitione 46
  IV. The Witness of the Captivity Epistles I 51
    1. The *Epistle to the Colossians* 52
    2. The *Epistle to Philemon* 55
    3. The *Epistle to the Ephesians* 57
  V. The Witness of the Captivity Epistles II: The *Epistle
    to the Philippians* 58
    1. *In omni Praetorio* 59
    2. The Saints of Caesar's Household 65
    3. "My desire is to depart and be with Christ, for that is far better" . 68
    4. "That I may share his sufferings, becoming like Him
      in His death" 70

Chapter III: Paul in Rome: the final Period 73
  I. Paul's two Roman Captivities 73

Table of Contents

    II. Were Roman Judeo-Christians Responsible for Paul's Death? ... 76
        1. The nascent Roman Church: a divided Community 76
        2. The Christians as Paul's accusers: Cullmann's Theory
           re-visited 79
   III. The Pastoral Epistles: the beginnings of the Pauline Tradition ... 84
        1. The Image of the martyred Paul as depicted by an early
           Paulinist: the Pastor 84
        2. The Theme of Abandonment: "At my first defence ... all
           deserted me" 86
        3. 2 Tim. 4,6: Paul's Death as a Sacrifice 94
   IV. Excursus 1: Paul and the Mamertinum Prison 98
   V. Excursus 2: *'Usque ad ultimum terrae'*: Did Paul visit Spain
      between his two Roman Captivities? 102
        1. The Westward Thrust of Paul's later Ministry 102
        2. Spain as a missionary Objective 104
        3. N.T. Evidence 105
        4. Patristic Witness to a Spanish Journey 108
        5. Paul's Journey to Spain in the early Christian Apocrypha 115

Chapter IV: Narratives of Paul's Martyrdom in Christian
                Apocryphal Literature 118
   I. The *Acta Pauli:* from the historical Paul to the Paul of faith 118
   II. The *Martyrion tou hagiou Apostolou Paulou* and the
      Passio Paul fragmentum   121
        1. The text 121
        2. The commentary 126
        3. Historical value 131
   III. The *Martyrion tou hagiou Apostolou Paulou:* Versions 134
        1. The Syriac Version 134
        2. The Armenian Version 136
        3. The Coptic Version 137
   IV. The *Passio Sancti Pauli Apostoli* (Pseudo-Linus) 138

Chapter V: Paul's Martyrdom in later Christian Apocryphal Literature . 143
   I. The Pseudo-Marcellus re-working of the tale of Paul's Martyrdom 143
        1. Introduction 143
        2. The *Acta Petri et Pauli:* Text 144
        3. Commentary 150
   II. Excursus 1: The Aquae Salviae as Paul's *locus passionis:* a late
      adjunction to the Paul legend 151
   III. The *Passio Apostolorum Petri et Pauli* (Pseudo-Hegesippus) 154
   IV. The *Historiae Apostolicae* of Pseudo-Abdias:
      Vol. II: The Passion of St. Paul 157

Table of Contents

    V. Excursus 2: Lucina buries Paul 160
   VI. Later accounts of Paul's Martyrdom from the Eastern
       Christian Tradition 162
       1. An Armenian *Martyrium* 162
       2. A Syriac *Chronicle:* Fragments pertaining to the Legend
          of Paul's Head 164

Chapter VI: Paul's Martyrdom in Patristic Literature 166

    I. The Apostolic Fathers 167
      1. Clement of Rome 167
      2. Ignatius of Antioch 170
      3. Polycarp of Smyrna 171
   II. The Fathers from Tertullian to the First Nicene Council 172
      1. Tertullian 172
      2. Peter of Alexandra 175
      3. Lactantius 176
  III. Eusebius of Caesarea: The *Tropaeum* of St. Paul 178
  IV. Paul's Martyrdom in the Nicene and Post-Nicene Fathers 183
      1. John Chrysostom 183
      2. Asterius Amasenus 187
      3. Jerome 188
      4. Augustine of Hippo 189
      5. Sulpicius Severus 190
      6. Orosius 192
      7. Paul's decapitation and the milk-theme: Macarius Magnes
         and Gregory of Tours 193
   V. The Flowering of the Roman Tradition: Leo the Great:
      In Natali Apostolorum Petri et Pauli 194

Chapter VII: An Afterword 198

Bibliography 201

    1. Reference Works 201
    2. Bibliography of Works cited 202

Indexes 209

   Passages 209
   Modern Authors 222
   Subjects 224

New Testament Textual Apparatus

I. *Codices*
   D — Codex Bezae Cantabrigiensis
   E — Codex Laudianus

II. *Versiones Antiquae*
   vg. — Vulgate
   vg.^{codd} — Vulgate codices (excluding the *Sixtina* and the *Clementina*
   g — Codex Gigas
   p — Codex Perpinianus
   tepl — Codex Teplensis

   sy^p — Syriac Peshitta
   sy^{h*}— Asterisked additions to the Harclean readings

   prov. — Provençal Version
   eth. — Ethiopic
   sa. — Sahidic

   Ambst — Ambrosiaster
   δ — indicates Western Text consensus
   614 — miniscule (δ — text), Milan

Abbreviations

Anal. Boll.	*Analecta Bollandiana*, Brussels.
ANL	*Ante-Nicene Library*, T. & T. Clark, Edinburgh.
AC	*Antiquité Classique*, Brussels.
Arndt & Gingrich	Arndt, W.F. and Gingrich, F.W., *A Greek-English Lexicon of the New Testament and other Early Christian Literature* (a translation and adaptation of Walter Bauer's *Griechisch-Deutsches Wörterbuch zu den Schriften des NT und der übrigen urchristlichen Literatur*), University of Chicago Press, Chicago, 1957.
ANRW	*Aufstieg und Niedergang der römischen Welt*, Walter de Gruyter, Berlin/New York, (from) 1972.
BC	Foakes-Jackson, F.J. and Lake, K., (edd.), *The Beginnings of Christianity*, MacMillan & Co., London, in 5 volumes, 1920-1933.
BGU	*Berliner griechische Urkunden* (Ägyptische Urkunden aus den königlichen Museen zu Berlin), Berlin, (from) 1895.
BHG[3]	*Bibliotheca Hagiographica Graeca*, Société des Bollandistes, Brussels, 3rd. Edition in 3 volumes, 1957.
BHL	*Bibliotheca Hagiographica Latina*, Société des Bollandistes, Brussels, in 3 volumes, 1898-1911.
BHO	*Bibliotheca Hagiographica Orientalis*, Société des Bollandistes, Brussels, 1910.
BZ	*Biblische Zeitschrift*, Paderborn.
BCH	*Bulletin de Correspondance Hellénique*, Athens/Paris.
Bull. J.R. Lib.	*Bulletin of the John Rylands Library*, Manchester.
Bull. Litt. Eccl.	*Bulletin de Littérature Ecclésiastique*, Toulouse.
BAC	*Bulletino di Archeologia Cristiana*, Rome.
CAH	*The Cambridge Ancient History*, University of Cambridge Press, 1926-34.

CR	*Classical Review London.*
Corp.Christ.-Ser.Lat.	*Corpus Christianorum, series Latina*, Brepols, Turnhout.
CII	J.B. Frey, (ed.), *Corpus Inscriptionum Iudaicarum*, Rome; Vol. I, 1936; Vol. II, 1952.
CIL	*Corpus Inscriptionum Latinarum*, Berlin, (from) 1863.
DACL	*Dictionnaire d'Archéologie chrétienne et de Liturgie*, Letouzey et Ané, éditeurs, Paris, in 15 volumes, 1907-1953.
DB	*Dictionnaire de la Bible*, Letouzey et Ané, éditeurs, Paris, in 5 volumes, 1895-1912. *DB-Suppléments* start in 1926.
Dict.Théol.Cath.	*Dictionnaire de la Théologie catholique*, Letouzey et Ané, éditeurs, Paris, in 15 volumes, 1909-1972.
Digesta	*The Digest of Justinian*, Corpus Iuris Civile, Vol. I; Latin text edited by Th. Mommsen, 1886. English translation by A. Watson, University of Pennsylvania Press, Philadelphia, in 4 volumes, 1985.
ET	*The Expository Times*
GCS	*Die griechischen christlichen Schriftsteller der ersten Jahrhunderte*, Leipzig/Berlin, (from) 1897.
HTR	*The Harvard Theological Review*, Cambridge, Massachusetts.
HDB	Hastings, James, (ed.) *A Dictionary of the Bible*, Edinburgh, in 4 volumes, 1898-1902.
ICUR	*Inscriptiones Christianae Urbis Romae*, Rome, in 3 volumes, 1857-1861; *Nova Series* in 9 volumes, 1922-1985.
IG	*Inscriptiones Graecae*, Berlin, (from) 1873.
IGR	*Inscriptiones Graecae ad Res Romanas pertinentes*, Paris, (from) 1911.
JOeBG	*Jahrbuch der Osterreichischen Byzantinischen Gesellschaft*, Vienna.
JBL	*Journal of Biblical Literature*, Philadelphia.
JRS	*Journal of Roman Studies*, London.
JTS	*Journal of Theological Studies*, Oxford.
LP	Duchesne, L. (ed.), *Le Liber Pontificalis*, Ernest Thorin, éditeur, Paris, Vol. I, 1886; Vol. II, 1892, Vol. III, 1957.

LCC	*The Library of Christian Classics*, Westminster Press, Philadelphia.
LNPF	*A Selected Library of Nicene and Post-Nicene Fathers*, The Christian Literature Co., New York.
LS^9	Liddell, H.G., and Scott, R.A., *A Greek-English Lexicon*, Clarendon Press, Oxford, 9th. Edition, 1940.
Lipsius	Lipsius, R.A. (ed.), *Acta Apostolorum Apocrypha*, Hermann Mendelssohn Verlag, Leipzig, Vol. I, 1891; Vol. II, 1898, (Bonnet, M., ed.).
Loeb	*The Loeb Classical Library*, W. Heinemann, Ltd., London/Harvard University Press, Cambridge, Mass.
MEFRA	*Mélanges de l'Ecole française de Rome*
Mombritius	Mombritius, B. (ed.), *Sanctuarium seu Vitae Sanctorum*, Fontemoing et Cie., éditeurs, Paris, in 2 volumes, 1910.
NTS	*New Testament Studies*, Cambridge.
NBAC	*Nuovo Bulletino di Archeologia Cristiana*, Rome.
OGIS	*Orientis Graeci Inscriptiones Selectae*, Leipzig, 1903-1905.
P	Papyri
P.Amh.	Amherst Papyri
P. Bodmer	Bibliotheca Bodmeriana, Cologny-Geneva
P.Fay	Fayûm Towns and their Papyri
P. Lille	Papyrus grecs: Institut papyrologique de l'Université de Lille
P. Lips.	Griechische Urkunden der Papyrussammlung zu Leipzig
P. Lond.	Greek Papyri in the British Museum
P. Oxy.	The Oxyrhynchus Papyri, London
P. Ryl.	Catalogue of the Greek Papyri in the John Rylands Library, Manchester
P. Thead.	Papyrus de Théadelphie, Paris
Patr.Gr.Lex.	Lampe, G.W.H., (ed.), *A Patristic Greek Lexicon*, Clarendon Press, Oxford, 1961.
PG	*Patrologia Graeca* (J.P. Migne), Paris.
PL	*Patrologia Latina* (J.P. Migne), Paris.
PLSuppl.	*Patrologia Latina-Supplements*, Paris, (from 1958 on)
PO	*Patrologia Orientalis*, Paris, (from 1907).

PROLEGOMENA	Moulton, J.H., *A Grammar of New Testament Greek*, T. & T. Clark, Edinburgh, 2nd. Edition, 1906: Vol. I, *The Prolegomena*.
RE	*Paulys Real-Encyclopädie der classischen Altertumswissenschaft*, herausgegeben G. Wissowa, Stuttgart/Munich, (from) 1894.
RSR	*Recherches de Science religieuse*, Paris.
RGG	*Die Religion in Geschichte und Gegenwart*, J.C.B. Mohr (P.Siebeck), Tübingen, 3rd. Edition, 1961.
RB	*Revue Biblique*, Paris.
RHE	*Revue d'Histoire ecclésiastique*, Louvain.
RHPR	*Revue d'Histoire et de Philosophie religieuses*, Strasbourg.
Rev.Hist.	*Revue Historique*, Paris.
ROC	*Revue de l'Orient chrétien*, Paris.
RAC	*Rivista di Archeologia cristiana*, Rome.
RQS	*Römische Quartalschrift*, Rome.
SIG^3	*Sylloge Inscriptionum Graecarum*, (W. Dittenberger, ed.), Leipzig, 3rd. Edition, 1915-1924.
TU	*Texte und Untersuchungen*, Leipzig/Berlin, (from) 1882.
ThWb.	Kittel, G. and Friedrich, G. (edd.), *Theologisches Wörterbuch zum Neuen Testament*. The English edition used in this book is by G.W. Bromiley, *Theological Dictionary of the New Testament*, Wm. B. Eerdmans, Grand Rapids, in 10 volumes, 1964-1976.
Thesaurus Ling.Lat.	*Thesaurus Linguae Latinae*, Leipzig, (from) 1900.
VC	*Vigiliae Christianae*, Amsterdam.
ZK	*Zeitschrift für Kirchengeschichte*, Gotha/Stuttgart.
Zerwick-GB	Zerwick, M., *Biblical Greek*, Rome, 1963 (based on the 4th Latin edition of *Graecitas Biblica*).

Chapter One
Paul's Condemnation and Martyrdom: Juridical Aspects

I. Paul's Roman Citizenship and its Effect on His Martyrdom

In the *Trial of St. Paul*, we reviewed at length the primordial importance of Paul's Roman citizenship in his earlier legal history. Twice in the canonical *Acts of the Apostles*, Paul had solemnly proclaimed his Roman citizenship[1] and this cry of *civis Romanus sum* had substantially modified his legal position over against the Roman magistrates charged with his case. Most importantly of all it was because of his status as a Roman citizen that he was able to avail himself of the *ius provocationis* and thus appeal to Nero's court at Rome for protection against what he felt to be an iniquitous magisterial decision on the part of Festus, Procurator of Judaea[2]. It was thus his Roman citizenship which allowed the Apostle to escape extradition, which Festus had proposed[3], and to escape a certain death sentence at the hands of the very same body which had not hesitated to condemn Jesus and the proto-martyr St. Stephen. Later in Rome, the benevolent treatment which Paul received from the police authorities was due to his citizen status. Although one must keep in mind that Luke's pro-Roman stance in Acts would have led him to emphasize the good relations which Paul enjoyed with the Roman *magistratura*, it is nonetheless indubitable that had Paul been a peregrine, the treatment accorded him would have been quite other than what it was. For his part Paul recognized the Roman Emperor, the Roman magistrates and the Roman police as holding full and legitimate political and juridical authority over him and he submitted willingly to that State power[4].

E. Benveniste notes that the Latin word *civis* invoked links of kinship, friendship and companionship, that is of a common *sharing* of political and

---

[1] Acts 16,37; Acts 22,25.
[2] Acts 25,11.
[3] Acts 25,9.
[4] Rom. 13,1-7. Cf. M. Adinolfi, "San Paolo e le autorità romane negli Atti degli Apostoli", *Antonianum*, Rome, Vol. 53; 1978, pgs. 460-461.

juridical prerogatives as well as duties and of a common *participation* in the life of the State. "The true meaning of civis", writes Benveniste, "is not citizen (*citoyen*) ... but fellow citizen (*concitoyen*)"[5]. From this root, the term *civitas* is derived, meaning as is does, of course, the quality of being a citizen or citizenship, but also the whole of the citizenry and indeed the city itself as a real legal entity. Sharing and participation englobed not only the political but also religious life of the city; these were in fact quite inseparable in ancient urban societies. C. Nicolet is quite correct in pointing out that the Roman citizenship

> "whatever visage it would later take on would always keep this double character of both a sacred and political community resting on a community of rights (the *ius civile* — the rights of citizens) which among other things governed family links very strongly".[6]

The fundamental characteristic of citizenship was the guarantee of the individual's juridical and civil status. The key word here is the word *protection*. Roman citizenship "... protected the individual over against the magistrates or high imperial officials in the straight line of Republican tradition"[7]. In Paul's time, Roman citizenship was the privilege of relatively few people. It was of enormous value as citizens enjoyed "all sorts of civil, military, political, juridical, economic and religious rights, privileges and duties (*iura, honores, munera*)"[8]. The Roman citizen was protected from magisterial abuse by the whole body of the Porcian and Valerian laws promulgated during the Republican régime and by the *Lex Iulia de vi publica et privata* of Augustan provenance[9].

The citizen therefore had a completely different legal status from the peregrine who enjoyed none of the former's juridical and political rights, benefits and privileges. Thus St. Peter, for example, as a peregrine, would have quite woefully lacked the legal protection against magisterial abuse and the right to due process which Paul enjoyed as rights inherent to his citizenship. So whereas Peter could be executed very summarily (perhaps after torture) during the anti-Christian terror which occurred in the wake of the great fire of 64 A.D., Paul was protected from torture and could only be executed subsequent to a proper juridical proceeding[10]. If one speaks purely in juridical

---

5 E. Benveniste, *Le Vocabulaire des Institutions indo-européennes,* Paris, 1969, Vol. I, pg. 337.
6 C. Nicolet, *Le Métier de Citoyen dans la Rome républicaine,* Paris, 1976, pg. 39.
7 *Ibid,* pg. 34.
8 M. Adinolfi, *op.cit.,* pg. 461.
9 Ampler discussion in H. Tajra, *The Trial of St. Paul,* Tübingen, 1989, pg. 25 and 146.
10 Cf. Acts 16,37-38 and 22,24-29. Cf. Eusebius, *HE.* 5,1.44. Eusebius writes in his account of the persecutions of the Christians at Lyons: "The people were very bitter against him [Attalus], but when the governor learnt that he was a Roman, he commanded him to be put

terms, it is absolutely necessary to *de-couple* Peter and Paul, that luminous binary so joined together in later Christian traditions, legend, lore, liturgy and art, because their violent deaths occurred at separate times, with different modes of capital punishment (crucifixion/decapitation), consequent to entirely different legal proceedings (or lack thereof in Peter's case).

As we mentioned earlier, Roman citizenship brought with it not only privileges but also duties of both a political and religious nature. The Roman citizen would be expected to adhere to the national religion and, with the establishment of the Principate, this came to include fidelity to and participation in the ruler cult:

> "A *religio* was *licita* for a particular group on the basis of tribe or nationality and traditional practices, coupled with the proviso that its rites were not offensive to the Roman people or their gods. But, for Roman citizens, loyalty to the national religion precluded participation in the rites of others, unless these had been specifically sanctioned by the Senate. (...) The practice by a Roman citizen of an *externa religio* which had not been accepted could be an insult to the gods and an affront to the greatness of the Roman people. (...) Not for nothing were *maiestas* and *sacrilegium* linked in the minds of Roman lawyers, and the participation of individuals in a *religio externa* condemned. Christianity was certainly among the latter".[11]

Finally, a Roman citizen was expected to be fluent in Latin, the language of his *patria*[12]. Although Rome was a completely cosmopolitan city and many of the early Roman Christians were non-Latins more at home in Greek than in Latin, Paul would not have ignored the city's main language when he preached, worked, received visitors or extended hospitality. The Apostle had already demonstrated a considerable knowledge of Roman institutions and of the Roman legal system and doubtlessly his stay in the empire's capital city had greatly enhanced his fluency in Latin[13]. Moreover, if, as seems likely, the Apostle did succeed in reaching Spain, any mission to that thoroughly

---

back with the rest, who were in jail, about whom he had written to the Emperor and was waiting for the reply" (*trans.* K. Lake, *Loeb*, 1959).

11 W.H.C. Frend, *Martyrdom and Persecution in the early Church,* Oxford, 1965, pg. 106. Cf. *Digesta* 48,4.1.

12 Dio Cassius records an incident in which a Lycian was stripped of his Roman citizenship by Emperor Claudius (year 43 A.D.) when his inadequate knowledge of Latin was exposed: "During the investigation of this affair [the murder of a Roman by some Lycians] which was conducted in the Senate, he put a question in Latin to one of the envoys who had originally been a Lycian, but had been made a Roman citizen; and when the man failed to understand what was said, he took away his citizenship, saying that it was not proper for a man to be a Roman who had no knowledge of the Romans' language." (Dio Cassius 60,17.4; *trans.* E. Cary, *Loeb*, 1961).

13 F.R. Montgomery Hitchcock, "Latinity of the Pastorals", *ET.*, Vol. 39; 1927-1928, writes: "He would not have been slow to seize the opportunity of conversing in Latin with the well-trained and educated Praetorian who was always with him ... We must take into account his

Romanized land would have had to have been conducted in Latin[14]. It would seem reasonable to conclude that the proceedings in Paul's trial in Rome took place in that language and that the Apostle's *apologia* before the imperial court, the final one of his ministry, was delivered in Latin.

II. The Juridical Foundation for Paul's Condemnation to Death

As a Roman citizen, Paul could not have been put to death except after having been found guilty by the imperial court of a very grievous infraction of the law. In view of what is known of the indictment lodged against Paul in the lower courts as recorded in the *Acts of the Apostles* and of the political and juridical situation during Nero's reign, Paul could only have been condemned to death on a charge of *crimen laesae maiestatis*. That is to say that his words and deeds were judged to have directly and indubitably diminished and injured the Emperor's person, station and sovereign authority[15].

II,1. The Modification and Extension of the Laws governing the *Crimen laesae maiestatis*

The establishment of the Principate by Augustus substantially modified the legal definition of *crimen laesae maiestatis*. At the end of the Republican régime, Cicero had described crimes of lese-majesty as those acts diminishing the dignity, high estate or authority of the Roman people or those to whom they had confided authority: *maiestatem minuere est de dignitate aut amplitudine aut potestate populi aut eorum quibus populus potestatem dedit aliquid derogare*[16]. Later on the great imperial jurist Ulpianus (170 ? — 228 A.D.), defined *maiestas* as follows: "The crime of treason is that which is committed against the Roman people or against their safety (*maiestatis autem crimen illud est, quod adversus populum Romanum vel adversus securitatem eius committitur*)"[17]. In the same passage Ulpianus also writes that "closest to

---

Latin studies and the fact that he was hourly, for two years, in the company of an Italian who would not speak Greek and with whom he would have to converse in Latin". (pg. 348)

14 *Ibid*, pg. 348.
15 Cf. R. Jewett, *A Chronology of Paul's Life*, Philadelphia, 1979, pg. 46: *Maiestas* was "in all likelihood ... the actual charge on which Paul was executed".
16 Cicero, *de Inventione* 2,17.53.
17 *Digesta* 48,4.1.

II. The Juridical Foundation

sacrilege is that crime which is called treason (*proximum sacrilegio crimen est, quod maiestatis dicitur*)"[18].

With the founding of the Principate, written or verbal insults or any other sort of denigrating acts aimed at diminishing the dignity, sovereign authority or person of the Emperor became assimilated with crimes against the State:

> "The association of insults to the emperor with treason was productive of many anomalies and inconsistencies. Other legal systems know the crime of lèse-majesté, of injury to the dignity of the sovereign, alongside what is usually known as High Treason, but as a rule the distinction between the two is clear. It was not so in Rome".[19]

This new definition of the law assimilating insults to the Emperor with State treason (thereby effacing the old *perduellio* as a crime distinct from *maiestas*, a separation that was clear under Republican law) was refined and more rigorously applied in the reign of the second Emperor, Tiberius (14—37 A.D.). Tacitus writes rather scathingly:

> "For he had resuscitated the *Lex Maiestatis*, a statute which in the old jurisprudence had carried the same name but covered a different type of offence — betrayal of an army; seditious incitement of the populace; any act, in short, of official maladministration diminishing the 'majesty of the Roman nation'. Deeds were challenged, words went immune (*facta arguebantur, dicta inpune erant*). The first to take cognizance of written libel under the statute was Augustus; ... then Tiberius, to an inquiry put by the praetor, Pompeius Macer, whether process should still be granted on this statute, replied that 'the law ought to take its course' (*exercendas leges esse*). He, too, had been ruffled by verses of unknown authorship satirizing his cruelty, his arrogance, and his estrangement from his mother".[20]

Suetonius provides a parallel account showing how repressive the law was:

---

18 *Digesta* 48,4.1. R.A. Bauman comments: "Etymologically *maiestas* is derived from *maior*. As *maior* expresses not an absolute value but the comparative degree, so *maiestas* is not an absolute quality but a relationship. This fact is fundamental to Roman *maiestas*. The word denotes an unequal relationship, with one component occupying the position of the *maior*, and the other that of the *minor*, but it denotes only a relationship and not a quality or attribute existing in isolation". (R.A. Bauman, *The Crimen Maiestatis in the Roman Republic and Augustan Principate*, Johannesburg, 1967, pg. 1).

19 R.A. Bauman, *Impietas in Principem*, Munich, 1974, pg. 2. C.W. Chilton writes that the *crimen laesae maiestatis* "was extended to include, as well as the abuse of the divinity of Julius, verbal abuse and slander of the Princeps and sometimes even slander of his family. It was this extension of the meaning of *maiestas* by Augustus — showing as it did the shift in the balance of power in the State — that was so significant..." (C.W. Chilton, "The Roman Law of Treason under the early Principate", *JRS*. Vol. 45; 1955, pg. 75). B. Kübler notes: "In der Zeit der Monarchie ... ist das Majestätsverbrechen aus einem Staatsverbrechen zum Verbrechen gegen die Person des Herrschers und seiner Familie, der *domus Augusta*, geworden" (B. Kübler, "Maiestas" *RE*. Vol. 14,1; 1928, col. 550).

20 Tacitus, *Ann.* 1.72 (*trans*. J. Jackson, *Loeb*, 1962).

"It was about this time that a praetor asked him whether he should have the courts convened to consider cases of lese majesty; to which he replied that the laws must be enforced (*exercendas esse leges*), and he did enforce them most rigorously (*et atrocissime exercuit*)."[21]

A passage from Dio Cassius about Tiberius (year 20 A.D.) indicates that not only deeds but even *speech* deemed improper was enough to condemn someone under the expanded *maiestas* law:

"Among other ways in which his rule became cruel, he pushed to the bitter end the trials for *maiestas*, in cases where complaint was made against anyone for committing any improper act, or uttering any improper (ἀνεπιτήδειος) speech, not only against Augustus, but also against Tiberius himself and against his mother".[22]

In Nero's reign, Tacitus notes the case of the Praetor Antistius Sosianus, who was charged with treason in the year 62 A.D. by Cossutianus Capito at the urging of his father-in-law Tigellinus, joint commander of the Praetorian Guard. Antistius had written some verses satirizing Nero and had read them openly at a dinner party. Tacitus notes this case as an ominous revival of the *maiestas* law: *tum primum revocata ea lex* [23].

The sort of political climate engendered by the extension of the law on *maiestas* spawned a whole breed of private accusers (*delatores*) whose denunciations would open a judicial proceeding against a foe. Seneca has given a chilling account of the perversion of the Roman legal system during the Julio-Claudian period:

"Under Tiberius Caesar there was such a common and almost universal frenzy for bringing charges of treason, that it took a heavier toll of the lives of Roman citizens than any Civil War; it seized upon the talk of drunkards, the frank words of jesters; nothing was safe — anything served as an excuse to shed blood, and there was no need to wait to find out the fate of the accused since there was but one outcome".[24]

Indeed this brings us to the question of the punishment meted out to the perpetrator of a crime of lese-majesty. C.W. Chilton notes that in the late Republic death was probably the penalty prescribed for crimes of lese-majesty, but that Roman citizens could avoid the capital sentence by going into exile, i.e. *interdictio* "with or without confiscation, became the actual legal

---

21 Suetonius, *Tib.* 58 (*trans.* J.C. Rolfe, *Loeb*, 1960).
22 Dio Cassius 57,19 (*trans.* E. Cary, *Loeb*, 1961). The adjective ἀνεπιτήδειος, that is improper, mischievous, prejudicial, can also be used in a political sense, i.e. as the unfriendly act or discourse of a political opponent (*LS*^{9}, pg. 134).
23 Tacitus, *Ann.* 14,48.
24 Seneca, *de Beneficiis* 3,26 (*trans.* J.W. Basore, *Loeb*, 1958). Tacitus notes that after the fall of Nero in 68 A.D., the Senate demanded the swift punishment of *delatores* as required by ancestral custom (Tacitus, *Hist.* 4,42). Cf. Suetonius, *Titus* 8.

II. The Juridical Foundation

penalty for *maiestas*"[25]. Under the Julio-Claudian Emperors, *interdictio* as a penalty for *maiestas* soon disappeared: "banishment was made harsher and summary execution became more and more common"[26].

II,2. The Ruler-Cult

In Antiquity political loyalty was almost always inseparable from religious practice. The concept of divine honours being bestowed on a ruler had its roots in the ancient Greek notion of kingship and in the later Hellenistic idea of the god-like king who was the benefactor and protector of his subjects:

> "It is an essential aspect of the ruler-cult in Hellenistic and Roman times that it develops this notion of divine man and is not founded upon the notion of hero. One excellent reason among others, is that the ruler-cult, though interested in past rulers, was basically oriented towards living sovereigns: it was meant to explain, justify, and recognize present, not past power".[27]

It is not surprising then that one of the most important factors in the growth and spread of the imperial ideology was the process of increasing veneration for the Emperor; the conscious propagation of what A.D. Nock has termed a "doctrine of royal divinity"[28]. The imperial cult became quite extensively integrated into the local cults in the diverse cities and provinces with the consequence that "the Emperors were the object of the same cult-acts as the other gods"[29].

Imperial Roman policy strove to promote a common religious faith in the Emperor as the being to whom his subjects looked to satisfy their temporal needs, as the benefactor of mankind, as the giver of peace and defender of security, as the liberator from oppression; all this in order to encourage a sense of unity and bonds of loyalty in the vast and variegated Empire. Cultic forms of Emperor-worship varied in the different parts of the Empire, being rather more intense and developed in the Hellenistic East than in the Latin West. Yet everywhere there was a common veneration for the Empire's ruler. Emperor-worship was one of the major assizes underpinning the whole imperial régime

---

25 C.W. Chilton, *op.cit.*, pg. 75.
26 *Ibid.* pg. 75.
27 A. Momigliano, "How the Roman Emperors became gods", *8º CONTRIBUTO ALLA STORIA DEGLI STUDI CLASSICI E DEL MONDO ANTICO*, Rome, 1987, pg. 301.
28 A.D. Nock, "The Augustan Restoration", *CR*, Vol. 39; 1925, pg. 62. Nock notes in the same passage that religion could in no way be neglected by a ruler "eager to regenerate the national spirit".
29 F. Millar, "The Imperial Cult and the Persecutions", in *LE CULTE DES SOUVERAINS DANS L'EMPIRE ROMAIN*, Vandoeuvres-Geneva, 1973, pg. 164.

as it was a concrete and very visible act in which all the Emperor's subjects could unite. It was as much a political statement as a religious deed.

At Rome itself there was a strong tradition against the actual worship of a living ruler; a factor which the early Emperors were forced to take into account. Octavian tried to maintain the political fiction that he was the providential restorer of Republican traditions. It was thus embarrassingly awkward to attribute divine status to an "alleged Republican leader"[30]. He therefore limited himself to being called, from 42 B.C. on, *divi filius* (i.e. of the deified Julius) and then in 27 B.C. taking on the title Augustus. This title, which had formerly been reserved for the gods or sacred things, gave him "a holy character by raising him above mankind"[31]. Augustus set an example in religious policy which was the model for his immediate successors, especially Tiberius and Claudius, although not for Caligula or Domitian, both of whom applied the title *deus* to their person and consequently sought a more developed worship of their divinity. It was only upon his death in 14 A.D. that the Principate's founder was decreed by the Senate to be *divus Augustus* and to be placed among the other State gods[32]:

> "This inclusion was the culmination of a series of honours given in return for services rendered. It was not an automatic culmination. It was warranted by miracle and approved by the authority which was necessary for any addition to the official circle of worships. Further, it depended on the quality shown by the man and not on the fact of his having held the supreme position. Divinity hedged a princeps around but was not inherent in him however much it might and did so appear to provincials and even to individual citizens. From the constitutional point of view he stood between the mass of citizens and the gods on the godward side but without any loss of his humanity or of his ultimate responsibility before the bar of public opinion".[33]

While never *imposing* imperial worship, Augustus encouraged in many subtle ways an unofficial or semi-official veneration of his person. Indeed the founder of the Principate and his successors all quite eagerly accepted the *fact* of the imperial cult[34]. The titles Saviour (σωτήρ) and Benefactor (εὐεργέτης) were frequently attributed to the Emperor[35], sometimes alongside the title "son

---

30 A. Momigliano, *op.cit.*, pg. 304.
31 L. Cerfaux & J. Tondriau, *Le Culte des Souverains dans la Civilisation gréco-romaine*, Tornai, 1957, pg. 330-331.
32 Tacitus, *Ann.* 1,11.
33 A.D. Nock, "Religious Developments from the Close of the Republic to the Death of Nero", *CAH.* Vol. 10; 1934, pg. 488-489.
34 F. Miller, *op.cit.*, pg. 157.
35 *IGR.* 1,1294; Horace, *Odes* 1,12. Cf. two edicts of Germanicus (19 A.D.) in which he disclaims divine status for himself whilst asserting the divinity of Tiberius Saviour (in V. Ehrenberg & A.H.M. Jones, *Documents illustrating the Reigns of Augustus and Tiberius*, Oxford, 2nd. Edition, 1955, No. 320,b.38. A bilingual inscription from Sagalassos in

of god"[36]. In the Latin West the Emperor gradually promoted the cult of *Dea Roma* and *Augustus*, often assimilated with *Pax* and *Fides* or divinized qualities such as *Victoria, Fortuna Redux*, and *Pax Augustus*, and moulded it into an imperial mystique[37]. The identification of Rome with Augustus was a political masterstroke designed to legitimate the Emperor's exceptional State power and to instill political loyalty in his subjects[38].

> "What meaning did this deification possess, especially for Roman citizens? Of one thing we can be certain, of the enormous impression that Augustus had produced: his deification as *Divus Augustus* corresponded to a widespread feeling that here, in his achievements and benefits, was a being divine."[39]

Nero was never officially deified in Rome during his lifetime (nor was he of course, after his death in 68 A.D.), but official worship of a living Emperor as divine was brought nearer mainly through the exaggerated adulation and sycophancy of the Senate and Court. In the Hellenistic East, of course, the cult of the divine Nero was considerably more developed than in the West. Coins struck in the East called him θέος and his bust on the coins had him wearing the radiate crown of the deified Emperors[40]. Nero was invested with the titles of Saviour and Benefactor[41] and was called "Lord of the whole cosmos"[42]. Significantly the Emperor was equated with the sun-god Helios (Νέωι Ἡλίωι Νέρωνι)[43] as well as with Zeus[44]. The usage of such titling clearly demonstrates that the tendency toward the deification of a living ruler was becoming considerably more normalized. Even at Rome itself where the tradition against the worship of a living ruler was much stronger than in the East, Nero succeeded in assimilating himself with the traditional gods to a much greater degree than his predecessors (except for Caligula). Already at the outset of his reign, in 55 A.D., Senators had proposed placing his statue in the temple of Mars Ultor. This motion was more than an ascription of divine attributes to

---

>   Pisidia, dated 18-19 A.D., is most revealing. Here the Latin *princeps optimus* is rendered in the Greek as σωτήρ Σεβαστός. The same manuscript renders *maiestas* as θειότης (in G.H.R. Horsley, *New Documents illustrating early Christianity*, North Ryde, Australia, 1981, Vol. I, pg. 36-37).

36 *I.G.* 7,1836.
37 *CIL.* 14,2898; *CIL.* 10,820.
38 Cf. Suetonius, *Aug.* 52.
39 M.P. Charlesworth, "Some Observations on Ruler-Cult especially in Rome", *HTR.* Vol. 28; 1935, pg. 29.
40 D.L. Jones, "Christianity and the Roman Imperial Cult", *ANRW.* II,23.2; 1980, pg. 1029. Both the head radiate and the head laureate occur on the Nero coins struck at the Rome mint.
41 *OGIS*, 668. The Greek formula θεὸς Σεβαστός was rather widespread.
42 *SIG*³. 814.
43 *IGR.* 3,345.
44 *SIG*³. 814.

Nero. It was a direct association of the reigning Emperor's image with that of a principal god. The fact that the Nero statue was to be of the same size as that of the temple's titular god was a highly symbolic gesture aimed at equating Nero with Mars Ultor himself [45].

The idea of the divine Nero permeated court life especially in the latter part of that Emperor's reign. The unfortunate poet Lucan divinized Nero in a panegyric which amply manifests the perversion of cultural life by the end of the Julio-Claudian dynasty[46]. Dio Cassius writes that when Tiridates came to Rome to be crowned by Nero as King of Armenia in 66 A.D., he worshipped the Emperor as a god:

"And I come to thee, my god, to worship thee as I do Mithras".[47]

Dio Cassius also provides an account of Nero's triumphal entry into Rome in 68 A.D., his last regnal year. Here the author notes that the population hailed the Emperor as Nero-Hercules and Nero-Apollo[48]. Yet even Nero, with his fearsome political power, could not go beyond certain limits. In the same year,, 68 A.D., when the Consul-designate Anicius Cerialis proposed that a temple be built out of public funds to *divo Neroni*, the project was vetoed:

"His notion, it is true, merely implied that the prince had transcended mortal eminence and earned the worship of mankind; but it was vetoed by that prince, because by other interpreters it might be wrested into an omen of, and aspiration for, his decease; for the honour of divinity is not paid to the emperor until he has ceased to live and move among men."[49]

Religious policy under the Julio-Claudian Emperors was thus characterized by attempts to assure the stability of the régime through a programme of restoring traditional Roman religion into which the ruler-cult was inserted in order to assure the ruler a primordial place within the body politic of the State. Thus an active and visible participation in some sort of cultic devotion to the Emperor had become by the end of the Julio-Claudian period a test of a Roman citizen's loyalty and political conformity.

---

45 Tacitus, *Ann.* 13,8.
46 Lucan, *Pharsalia* 1,45 ff.
47 Dio Cassius 63,5 (*trans.* E. Cary, Loeb, 1961)..
48 Dio Cassius 63,20. The great scholar of Roman numismatics, Harold Mattingly, writes: "One very rare Aureus, with reverse *IUPPITER LIBERATOR*, was probably struck for Nero during his stay in Greece (67 A.D.). (...) The allusion of the reverse is unmistakeable. *IUPPITER LIBERATOR* (Ζεὺς ἐλευθέριος) is but a thin disguise for the Emperor who set Greece free, and was actually acclaimed by the grateful province under that name". (H. Mattingly, *Coins of the Roman Empire in the British Museum*, London, Vol. I, 1923, pg. clxxxiii-clxxxiv).
49 Tacitus, *Ann.* 15,74 (*trans.* J. Jackson, *Loeb*, 1962).

II. The Juridical Foundation

"It had become an organic part of the relation between sovereign and subject: indeed, it indicated the exact point at which the subject felt himself to be a subject".[50]

A Roman citizen who manifested an obvious lack of concern for the imperial cult, who roundly refused to participate in it himself or who encouraged others to abandon this type of worship for the exclusive adoration of another King, was considered to have demonstrated political dissidence to State authority and antagonism to the Emperor's sacrosanct person[51]. The dissident could only expect arrest, trial and swift condemnation.

It was against the political, juridical and religious background outlined above that the legal proceedings against Paul took place. Luke finishes his two volume work with Paul's actively pursuing his apostolic ministry in Rome, preaching the Gospel of Jesus Christ without hindrance. But by ascribing to Jesus the title of King, by believing Him to be the Son of God and Saviour of the world and by the very preaching of another Kingdom, Paul was simultaneously diminishing the majesty of his earthly sovereign who was doing all he could to shore up his political power with pretensions to divinity. Paul's enemies no doubt accused him in the Roman court of political disobedience by noting that he was unsettling the established political and religious order in Rome itself by persuading men to turn away from pagan worship including adoration of the Emperor. Paul had already faced exactly these charges in Philippi and Corinth[52]. Thus the indictment against the Apostle most likely depicted him as being thoroughly animated by a spirit hostile to the Emperor and as a convinced opponent of the official State theology. He was charged with being seditious in that he was rejecting his 'city' to give loyalty to another 'city', in this case an unrecognized religion, Christianity[53]. One cannot imagine a confirmed Christian like Paul reciting an invocation to the pagan gods or bestowing divine titles on the Emperor — much less performing any cultic sacrifices to him. Had there been any sort of loyalty test applied to Paul at his

---

50 A. Momigliano, *op.cit.*, pg. 308.
51 Cf. the indictment made up by Cossutianus Capito (at the instigation of Nero) and lodged against Thrasea Paetus in 66 A.D. Thrasea had a much higher social position and greater political importance than the Apostle Paul so their two cases are not entirely parallel. It is interesting to note, however, that amongst the plethora of charges in the indictment against Thrasea were those that he took no part in the national vows *pro incolumitate principis* and although a priest never offered sacrifice for the Emperor's welfare (*pro salute principis*) or for his *caelestis vox* (Tacitus, *Ann.* 16,22).
52 Acts 16,21; Acts 18,13.
53 In the *Digesta*, there is a passage from the jurist Modestinus who rails against stirrers of sedition (*seditionum concitatores*) and lists them as being among the types of persons that the public authority has interest in condemning and punishing immediately (*Digesta* 49,1.16. Cf. Ulpian, *Digesta* 48,4.1.

trial involving sacrifice to the Emperor, the Apostle would certainly have failed it. He himself, in the utmost irony of all, would have furnished the decisive proof to support his enemies' charge that he was a political dissident who willfully diminished the Emperor's majesty[54]. Paul's perceived dissidence, his role as a leader of a religious group unauthorized by the State, his disregard for established Roman religious tradition and his words and deeds which were disturbing the vital relationship between the Emperor (the *maior*) and his subjects (the *minores*) could only call for the severest and most decisive of punishments.

III. Imperial Jurisdiction: Paul and Nero

The judicial competence of the imperial tribunal, which would have heard Paul's case, lay in the plenitude of the *auctoritas* held by the Emperor. Augustus and his successors had succeeded in concentrating in their hands the power inherent in a number of old Republican magistracies, the sum total of which assured them a position of political and juridical supremacy[55]. The Emperor held both the consular and proconsular *imperium*, the highest civil and military powers, with all the *iurisdictio* inherent in the grant of that *imperium*[56]. From that *imperium* "stems the basic power of criminal jurisdiction designated by the terms *coercere* and *animadvertere*"[57]. He held command

---

54 Cf. Rev. 13,15 where those who do not worship the image of the beast are slain; and especially Rev. 20,4: "Also I saw the souls of those who had been beheaded for their testimony to Jesus and for the word of God, and who had not worshipped the beast or its image and had not received its mark on their foreheads or their hands". Pliny, in his famous letter to Emperor Trajan, wrote that he applied a loyalty test to those accused of being Christians who appeared before him. He discharged from his court all those who invoked the gods, worshipped the Emperor and cursed Christ. Pliny notes that those who were really Christians could not be forced into performing any of these acts (Pliny, *Ep.* 10,96).

55 Tacitus describes how Augustus combined the diverse State powers: "Then step by step he began to make his ascent and to unite in his own person (*in se trahere*) the functions of the Senate, the magistracy and the legislature. Opposition there was none ... " (Tacitus, *Ann.* 1,2; *trans.* J. Jackson, *Loeb*, 1962).

56 Cf. J. Rougé, *Les Institutions Romaines*, Paris, 1969, pg. 106: "He had a double *imperium*, consular and proconsular, which enabled him to intervene as he saw fit, not only at Rome and in Italy, but also in all the provinces".

57 A.N. Sherwin-White, *Roman Society and Roman Law in the New Testament*, Oxford, 1963, pg. 4. Briefly defined the juridical term *coercitio* would signify a legal relationship between two parties whereby the one is subject to the will of the other and constrained to do what his free will would have refused to do under ordinary circumstances. The major party in the relationship would thus be competent to apply legal or police measures to the minor party in order to assure, by constraints, an outward conformity. Animadversion would not only

of the army, being acclaimed as *Imperator* or victorious general. He was the *pontifex maximus*, the chief religious authority in the State. Finally he held the grant of *tribunicia potestas* for life[58]; his person was thus *sacrosanctus* [59].

The fact that the Emperor held both the *imperium* and the *tribunicia potestas* gave him an unlimited legal competence. He was the highest controlling party in the administration of justice as his imperium was *maius* vis-à-vis that of all other magistrates. Enjoying tribunician power meant that the Emperor could function as a court of last instance (court of cassation), hearing and judging appeals without any further recourse being available to the appellant. Thus in Acts 25,11, Paul's appeal to Rome to have his case heard anew there was addressed *ad Caesarem* and not *ad populum* as it would have been under the old Republican régime[60]. Based on the exercise of his own personal power of jurisdiction, the Emperor could also function as a court of first instance, judging cases directly introduced into his court without any judicial antecedent:

> "This authority of the emperor as a high court of voluntary jurisdiction granted apparently to Augustus by a plebiscitum of 30 B.C., did enable him to usurp the jurisdiction of the lower courts ... Its effectiveness as a mode of control rested on the fact that the request [for cognizance of a case] could proceed from prosecutor or accused in a criminal case, as it might from either of the parties in a civil suit, and that the merits of the case would have to be considered before the emperor decided whether he should exercise his own jurisdiction".[61]

The strength of the imperial jurisdiction lay in the fact that it was unlimited and free-working. The Emperor was not astricted to the text of a *lex* in the

---

mean the judicial cognizance of a case, but also any eventual punishment handed down as a chastisement for the crime.
58 Dio Cassius 51,19.
59 J. Bleicken, *Die Verfassung der römischen Republik*, Paderborn, 2nd Edition, 1978, pg. 86.
60 A.H.M. Jones writes: "In capital cases both the Emperor and the Senate exercised a primary jurisdiction against which there was, it would seem, no *provocatio ad populum*. these jurisdictions are well attested under Tiberius and can be traced back to Augustus' reign". (A.H.M. Jones, "Imperial and Senatorial Jurisdiction in the Early Principate", *STUDIES IN ROMAN GOVERNMENT AND LAW*, Oxford, 1968, p. 69).
61 A.H.J. Greenidge, "The Power of Pardon possessed by the Princeps", *CR*. Vol. 8; 1894, pg. 430. I. Buti notes: "What interested the Princeps above all, in fact, was the *political* affirmation of his authority in the judicial field as well. This objective was pursued and realized by the assumption of a legal competence to judge both in the first instance and as a court of appeals and to issue rescripts in order to resolve controversies or to dissipate doubts which were submitted to him". (I. Buti, "La *cognitio extra ordinem* da Augusto a Diocleziano", ANRW. II, 14; 1982, pg. 35. A.H.M. Jones writes: "When Augustus in 19 B.C. received the *consulare imperium* he acquired a power of jurisdiction like that of the consuls. He not only used it regularly in appellate jurisdiction, but, it would seem, occasionally in the first instance". (A.H.M. Jones, *op.cit.*, pg. 84).

exercise of his judicial functions[62]. Nor indeed was his *imperium* inhibited by the *provocatio*. Tacitus, Suetonius and Seneca have all given very specific examples of how the Emperor's personal administration of justice was unconstrained by existing definitions of what constituted a crime. He had free *arbitrium* and could thus be as clement or as severe as he saw fit[63]. The Emperor enjoyed the power of pardon in all criminal cases[64]. He could re-examine and modify decisions taken by a lower court, thus attenuating or aggravating penalties in a very subjective way[65]. The Emperor had the right to refuse to take on a case for judgement after having heard the preliminaries[66]. He could either remit the case to another court or quash the whole proceeding[67]. But as F. de Visscher notes, indictments falling under the subsumption of *maiestas* "could not be officially admitted without the latter's opinion"[68]. It was the Emperor who would have to decide what juridical sequel to give to the indictment; but he was not obliged to hear the case personally. In fact the Emperor's personal *cognitio* was generally employed only in cases involving persons of high rank or in important political matters affecting State security. Less important cases, such as the Apostle Paul's, would routinely be heard by delegated officials. As the juridical power of these magistrates was clearly derived from and dependant on the Emperor's power of jurisdiction, the delegates enjoyed the same latitude of judicial freedom as the Emperor himself when hearing cases and deciding on punishments[69]. As we have seen in an above note, Emperor Claudius tended to take on a fairly large number of cases for his own personal cognizance. His successor Nero, on the other hand, tried to avoid a personal administration of justice whenever possible[70].

The Emperor had a wide choice of people to whom he could delegate his power to hear cases:

---

[62] Cf. Th. Mommsen, *Römisches Strafrecht*, Leipzig, 1899, pg. 262.
[63] Tacitus, *Ann.* 3,24; Suetonius, *Aug.* 33; Seneca, *de Clementia* 1,1.9.
[64] A.H.M. Jones, *op.cit.*, pg. 95.
[65] Suetonius, *Aug.* 51; Tacitus, *Ann.* 3,38; *Digesta* 48,19.13. Writing about Claudius' administration of justice, Suetonius says:" He did not always follow the letter of the laws, but modified their severity or lenity in many cases according to his own notions of equity and justice ..." (*Claudius* 14, trans. J.C. Rolfe, *Loeb*, 1960).
[66] Cf. A.H.M. Jones, *op.cit.*, pg. 84: "The scanty evidence suggests that he did not take cases when the praetor could furnish a remedy by the *ordinarium ius*, but used his jurisdiction to supplement or modify the *ordinarium ius* when it seemed to him to be inequitable or contrary to public policy".
[67] Tacitus, *Ann.* 3,10; cf. A.H.J. Greenidge, *op.cit.*, pg. 436.
[68] F. de Visscher, *Les Edits d'Auguste découverts à Cyrene*, Osnabrück, 1940, pg. 86.
[69] Th. Mommsen, *op.cit.*, pg. 269-270; I. Buti, *op.cit.*, pg. 39.
[70] Tacitus, *Ann.* 13,4.

III. Imperial Jurisdiction

A) Delegation could be conferred by a special mandate of the Emperor enabling the delegate to judge a specific and isolated case[71];

B) Delegation could be conferred by a special mandate of the Emperor for certain categories of cases, e.g. group cases according to their geographical provenance. So Suetonius writes about Augustus:

> "Each year he referred appeals of cases involving citizens to the city praetor, but those between foreigners to ex-consuls (*consularibus viris*), of whom he had put one in charge of the business affairs of each province".[72]

C) Referral of cases to the Senate;

D) Finally, and most importantly for our study, the Urban Prefect could replace the Emperor in the administration of justice when the latter was absent from Rome or otherwise indisposed to take on a case[73]. Under the old Roman monarchy, the office of Urban Prefect had functioned in emergencies in order to provide continuity in government during an absence of the King. Under the Republic, the office of Urban Praetor had overshadowed it, but the ancient office of Urban Prefect was revived and given a permanent character under Augustus and Tiberius[74]. "As for the prefect of the city", writes Dio Cassius, "men should be appointed to that office who are leading citizens and have previously passed through the appropriate offices; ..."[75].

The Urban Prefect was a considerable figure in the political and juridical affairs of Rome. He had the power of *coercitio* and was able to uphold and maintain public order using his own discretion without having to refer to or be restrained by specific legislation. Indeed the fact that the Urban Prefect held both police powers and the right to administer justice helped to facilitate the growth of the arbitrary in the Roman legal system. His authority extended over the whole city of Rome and to some distance outside it and he had the power to judge cases involving both citizens and peregrines. He could hear all types of civil and criminal cases[76] and could decide what punishment to mete out,

---

71 Pliny, *Ep.* 7,6.8.
72 Suetonius, *Aug.* 33 (*trans.* J.C. Rolpe, *Loeb*, 1960).
73 Th. Mommsen, *op.cit.*, pg. 271.
74 Tacitus, *Ann.* 6,11.
75 Dio Cassius 52,21.2.
76 The jurist Ulpian notes that the Urban Prefecture successfully claimed all criminal cases to be under its legal competence, not only those committed at Rome itself but also in Italy: "*Omnia omnino crimina praefectura urbis sibi vindicavit, nec tantum ea, quae intra urbem admittuntur, verum ea quoque, quae extra urbem intra Italiam*" (*Digesta* I,12.1). Ulpian also notes that cases involving people accused of having formed an unlawful association (*illicitum collegium*) were to be accused before the Urban Prefect. (*Digesta* I,12.1.13).

including the death penalty.[77] Dio Cassius describes the Urban Prefect's competences:

> "... it should be the prefect's duty, not to govern merely when the consuls are out of town, but in general to be at all times in charge of the affairs of the city, and to decide the cases which come to him from all the other magistrates I have mentioned, whether on appeal or for review, together with those which involve the death penalty; and his jurisdiction should extend, not only to those who live in the city, except such as I shall name, but also to those who dwell outside the city for a distance of one hundred miles."[78]

In the Apostle's case, the question arises as to whether Nero judged Paul *in propria persona*. On the one hand the evidence in the canonical Acts and in the apocryphal Acts would point in that direction:

A) In Acts 23,11, Luke writes that the Lord said to Paul: "Take courage, for as you have testified about me at Jerusalem, so you must bear witness also at Rome". Insofar as Paul's case is concerned, the verse is inconclusive in that it merely points to a legal procedure at Rome during which Paul made an *apologia* before the competent authorities, who are left unnamed.

B) In Acts 25,12, Festus sanctions Paul's appeal to Caesar: "Then Festus, when he had conferred with his council, answered, 'You have appealed to Caesar; to Caesar you shall go'". In Acts 25,21, Festus says to Agrippa; "But when Paul had appealed to be kept for the decision of the Emperor, I commanded him to be held until I could send him to Caesar". The Procurator adds in Acts 25,25: "... and as he himself appealed to the Emperor, I decided to send him".

C) In Acts 27,24, Luke records the story of a visitation to Paul by an angel, who said to him: "Do not be afraid, Paul; you must stand before Caesar".

D) The *Martyrium Pauli*, the final segment of the apocryphal *Acts of Paul* (late 2nd. Century), has Paul appearing before Nero and engaging in a sharp debate with his Emperor-judge.

On the other hand it is abundantly clear that Nero took much less interest in things juridical and heard many fewer cases than his predecessor Claudius. "He would not constitute himself a judge of all cases", writes Tacitus, "secluding accusers and defendants within the same four walls and allowing the influence

---

77 *Digesta* 1,12.1.10; 48,19.2; 48.19,8; 49,3.1.
78 Dio Cassius 52,21.2 (*trans.* E. Cary, *Loeb*, 1960).

III. Imperial Jurisdiction

of a few individuals to run riot"[79]. This reluctance to hear cases did not mean that crimes of majesty went unpunished[80]. Those suspected of such crimes were pursued and punished very rigorously indeed. What it did mean was that Nero left to his delegates the task of judging his real or suspected enemies in Rome. In 67 A.D., for example, when Nero absented himself for a year from Rome to undertake his celebrated journey to Greece, supreme political and juridical authority over Rome, and indeed over all Italy, was vested in Helius, an imperial freedman:

> "This man had been given absolutely complete authority, so that he could confiscate, banish or put to death ordinary citizens, knights and senators alike, even before notifying Nero".[81]

The historical evidence and what is known of legal practice in Nero's reign would tend to infirm, rather than confirm the old, but nonetheless secondary, tradition of a dramatic confrontation between the Emperor and the Apostle in the imperial courtroom. Although a charge of majesty was no trifling matter for a Roman citizen to be charged with, yet Paul's case involved no major threat to State security, such that Nero would have been induced to have taken personal cognizance of this particular action. Luke's references to Caesar in the passages from Acts cited above ought to be thought of generically, that is to say that the Evangelist was designating the whole imperial tribunal and not necessarily the Emperor personally. The tale related in the *Martyrium Pauli*, while high in drama and colour, is the product of a rich literary imagination, and not a recounting of historical or legal fact. That there was a legal action taken against Paul in Rome which led to his condemnation and execution seems certain, but it is highly improbable that Nero himself heard the case or handed down the verdict. At most Nero might have been informed that there had been a charge of *crimen maiestatis* lodged against a Roman citizen named Paul who was preaching a strange and hitherto largely unknown monotheistic religion and who had had a number of previous encounters with Roman judicial authorities in the provinces, Nero, always reluctant to hear cases himself, is quite likely to have handed over a matter of such scarce political importance to the Urban Prefect for his cognizance.

---

79 Tacitus, *Ann*. 13,4 (*trans*. J. Jackson, *Loeb*, 1962).
80 R. Bauman notes: "The problems that troubled Tiberius did not trouble all of his successors, for rulers like Caligula, Nero and Domitian exploited the institutionalising possibilities of *divina maiestas* with some enthusiasm ..." (R. Bauman, *Impietas in Principem, op.cit.*, pg. 18).
81 Dio Cassius 63,12 (*trans*. E. Cary, *Loeb*, 1960). A little further on (in 63,18), Dio Cassius notes that during Nero's absence from Rome, Helius perpetrated many odious deeds there.

IV. The Imperial Tribunal: Penal Procedure

The form which imperial penal procedure took in cases such as Paul's was that of the *cognitio*, that is a "full judicial trial ... which included the admission of evidence and the handing down of the judgement"[82]. Paul's trial at Rome almost certainly followed this procedural form. Indeed Christians were prosecuted until the middle of the 3rd Century according to the *cognitio extra ordinem*[83], that is "outside the schedule or *ordo* of the older criminal code of the *leges publicae*"[84].

> "Both the Emperor and the consuls exercised their primary jurisdiction only in cases which were not covered by the *ius ordinarium* or where its operation was unsatisfactory or inequitable. Seeing that their jurisdiction was thus *extraordinaria*, they were not bound to observe the cumbrous procedure of the *ordo*, but could employ the simpler and more expeditious *cognitio*".[85]

In practice this meant that the trial was "the personal judgement of the holder of *imperium* sitting formally *pro tribunali* to hear the charges made in due form, and assisted by his *consilium*"[86]. Trial procedure arose from the actions of private accusers (*delatores*) who started the whole process by their written or oral delation. The Roman citizen was protected against vexatious prosecution (*calumnia*); thus accusations, especially those of a capital nature, would have to be well substantiated[87]. In capital cases a Roman citizen could not be condemned in his absence[88]. The accused had to be allowed to make a personal defence (thus the *prima defensio* of 2 Tim. 4,16) so as to try to secure his acquittal. Without this *apologia*, an equitable functioning of procedure (*aequitas*) was not maintained and this was quite contrary to tradition and use within the Roman legal system. The *apologia* was personal, for most often the accused was bereft of the presence and succour of an *advocatus* in cases heard personally by the Emperor or his delegates. Nonetheless this was not an iron-clad rule, for sittings of the imperial court could very well include "considerable sympathizers"[89]. In Paul's particular case, accord-

---

[82] G.H.R. Horsley, *op.cit.*, pg. 49.

[83] J. Beaujeu, "L'Incendie de Rome en 64 et les Chrétiens", *LATOMUS*, Vol. 19; 1960, pg. 303.

[84] A.N. Sherwin-White, "The early Persecutions and Roman Law again", *JTS*. Vol. 3 (N.S.); 1952, pg. 205.

[85] A.H.M. Jones, *op.cit.*, pg. 85.

[86] A.N. Sherwin-White, *The Letters of Pliny*, Oxford, 1966, pg. 695.

[87] R. Taubenschlag, "Il delatore e la sua responsabilità nel diritto dei papiri", *OPERA MINORA*, Warsaw, 1959, Vol. II, pg. 732.

[88] *Digesta* 48,19.5.

[89] H.J. Cadbury, "Roman Law and the Trial of Paul", *BC*, Vol. 5; London, 1933, pg. 321. Cf. *P. Oxy.* 1242 where rival delegations from Alexandria appeared before Trajan accompanied

IV. The Imperial Tribunal

ing to the tradition conserved in the Pastoral Epistles, he seems to have been bereft of an *advocatus*, witnesses for the defence or sympathizers. Paul's terrible solitude could only have unfavourably impressed the judge hearing his case.

The personal administration of justice was one of the Emperor's essential functions. He heard cases both publicly and privately, both within the imperial auditorium and without[90]. Normally he would conduct a preliminary hearing in order to determine the exact legal issue that he was being called upon to judge. He could then convoke and consult his assessors, the *consilium principis* before pronouncing sentence[91]. In the Julio-Claudian period a permanent imperial *consilium* had not as yet come into being. The assessors, often a few of the Emperor's intimate *amici*, were convoked only when he felt it would be helpful or simply better politics[92]. Their opinion about the case, which they could express either orally or in writing, was not binding on the Emperor, nor could it restrict or constrain the freeworking nature of his judicial competence. In the *cognitio* system of penal jurisdiction, the Emperor (or his delegates) was free both "in recognizing *crimina* and determining sentences *extra ordinem*"[93]. The *extra ordinem* jurisdiction

> "... depended on no statutes, and the penalties were at the discretion of the magistrate; even if the defendant was upon a 'statutory' crime, if it was being judged *extra ordinem* and not by a standing jury court (as was increasingly the case under the Principate), the Emperor or Prefect of the City or provincial governor could please himself and inflict penalties greater or less or of a different kind".[94]

With so much arbitrariness in the procedure, the case's outcome depended as much on the judge's personality, psychology, disposition or the political realities of the moment as it did on statutory law. Philo, for example, took note of Caligula's dangerous humour when the megalomaniac Emperor received his delegation:

---

by συνήγοροί. U.E. Paoli notes: "The lawyer assisted his client, he did not represent him. He stood by him during the legal proceedings giving whatever help his suggestions and remarks might afford, but during the proceedings the defendant had to stand by himself". (U.E. Paoli, *Vita Romana*, Florence, 10th Edition, 1968, pg. 450).

90 Cf. *Digesta* 42,1.54.1 where the term *ad maius auditorium* appears. This space was perhaps so designated to contrast it with the *auditoria* of lesser magistrates such as that of the Praetorian Prefect (cf. *Digesta* 12,1.40).

91 Pliny, *Ep.* 4,22; 6,31.

92 Tacitus, *Ann.* 3,10. Cf. Herodian 6,1.2; Philo, *Legat. ad Gaium* 44,349.

93 A.N. Sherwin-White, "Early Persecutions ... ", *op.cit.*, pg. 208.

94 J.A. Crook, *Law and Life of Rome: 90 B.C. - A.D. 212*, Ithaca, New York, 1967, pg. 272.

"The moment we entered we knew from his look that we had come into the presence not of a judge but of an accuser more hostile than those arrayed against us".[95]

Suetonius has described how Nero typically handled cases which he had reserved for his personal cognizance:

"In the administration of justice he was reluctant to render a decision to those who presented cases, except on the following day and in writing. The procedure was, instead of continuous pleadings, to have each point presented separately by the parties in turn. Furthermore, whenever he withdrew for consultation, he did not discuss any matter with all his advisers in a body, but made each of them give his opinion in written form; these he read silently and in private and then gave a verdict according to his own inclination, as if it were the view of the majority".[96]

Paul's trial was most likely conducted by the Urban Prefect using this kind of procedure.

V. Execution of the Capital Sentence

As the tradition in the Pastoral Epistles infers (and all subsequent tradition explicitly states), Paul's trial at Rome ended with his being found guilty on a charge of majesty. As we have seen, *maiestas* was a capital offence; thus the Apostle was sentenced to be executed rather than to be banished.

A) As Paul was a Roman citizen, some official report of the trial proceedings and verdict (*memorandum*) was likely to have been made.

B) It was customary (*ex more*) for the Emperor to ratify a death sentence pronounced on a Roman citizen[97].

C) It was unlikely that Paul was executed on the same day the guilty verdict was handed down. In the year 21 A.D., Clutorius Priscus had been found guilty of transgressing the *maiestas* laws. Immediately after the verdict had been pronounced, Priscus was led *in carcerem* and straightaway executed (*ac statim exanimatus*). Tacitus notes Tiberius' reaction to this hasty execution:

---

95 Philo, *Legat. ad Gaium* 44,349 (trans. F.H. Colson, *Loeb*, 1962). Sometimes there was an opposite psychological dynamic in the proceedings and it was the defendant who was rude, disrespectful or threatening to the imperial judge. Cf. Suetonius, *Claud.* 15; *P. Oxy.* 1242 (Hermaiscus of Alexandria defies Trajan); *P. Oxy.* 33 where the Alexandrian gymnasiarch Appianus deeply insults an unnamed Emperor, (probably Marcus Aurelius) even though he is on trial for treason.

96 Suetonius, *Nero* 15 (*trans.* J.C. Rolfe, *Loeb*, 1959).

97 Suetonius, *Nero* 10.

"This promptitude drew a typically ambiguous reprimand from Tiberius in the Senate. He commended the loyalty of members, who avenged so sharply insults, however slight, to the head of the state (*principis iniurias*), but deprecated such a hurried punishment of a verbal offence.(...) It was therefore resolved that no senatorial decree should be entered in the Treasury (*aerarium*) before the lapse of nine full days, all prisoners under the sentence of death to be reprieved for that period".[98]

D) The condemned was led out to the place of execution by a military escort composed of both officers and soldiers. The escort's size was variable and depended on the particular circumstances attending the case or the notoriety of the condemned[99]. The execution would be consummated outside the city proper.

It was customary for the condemned to go to the place of execution preceded by a *titulus* (πίναξ), a board, plank or placard upon which the motive for the execution was written. Suetonius records the execution of a slave ordered by Caligula, who commanded that the slave's hand be first cut off and that he then be led about among the guests preceded by a *titulus* giving the reason for the punishment: *praecedente titulo qui causam poenae indicaret per coetus epulantium circumduceretur*[100]. The same writer also gives an account of Domitian's ordering a *pater familias* thrown to the dogs in the arena for having spoken impiously: *cum hoc titulo 'impie locutus parmularius'*[101]. In his account of the persecution of the Lyonnais Christians, Eusebius notes that Attalus "was led round the amphitheatre and a placard was carried before him on which was written in Latin 'This is Attalus the Christian'"[102]. In Christian iconography the most celebrated *titulus* of all is, of course, that which surmounted the Cross of Calvary: 'Jesus of Nazareth King of the Jews' (I.N.R.I.)[103]. One could very well assume that the placard which Paul bore or which preceded him to his place of death on the via Ostiense made reference to his being condemned under the laws of majesty and possibly to his alleged hostility to the Emperor.

E) There was a whole range of different modes of capital punishment in the State's repressive arsenal:

---

98 Tacitus, *Ann.* 3,51 (*trans.* J. Jackson, *Loeb*, 1962).
99 Cf. *Martyrium Pauli* 3.
100 Suetonius, *Caligula* 32.
101 Suetonius, *Domitian* 10.
102 Eusebius, *HE.* 5,1.44 (*trans.* K. Lake, *Loeb*, 1959).
103 Jn. 19,19-22. St. John notes that the inscription on the *titulus* was in three languages: Hebrew, Greek and Latin. Cf. Mt. 27,37; Mk. 15,26; Lk. 23,38. Certain variants of St. Luke's Gospel also mention that the inscription was tri-lingual.

"The stages of capital punishments are more or less as follows. The extreme penalty (*summum supplicium*) is held to be condemnation to the gallows (*ad furcam damnatio*). There is also burning alive; this, however, though deservedly included in the term 'extreme penalty', is yet regarded as following after the first, because this class of punishment was devised at a later time. Also there is beheading (*capitis amputatio*). Then, the next punishment after death is sentencing to the mines; after that, deportation to an island".[104]

In his account of the massacre of the Roman Christians in 64 A.D., Tacitus notes that three types of capital punishment were meted out to them: being thrown to the beasts, being crucified or being burnt at the stake[105]. Ignatius of Antioch also mentions these three punishments (πῦρ, σταυρὸς, θηρίων) in his *Epistle to the Romans*[106]. One reads in the *Shepherd of Hermas*: "Flagellation, prison, great afflictions, crucifixion, the beasts, the victims of the early persecutions endured all these for the sake of this Name"[107]. Justin Martyr mentions crucifixion, chains, fire, beasts and other tortures[108]. Decapitation figures nowhere in this sad catalogue of cruel punishments; the Christian victims of these tortures were evidently peregrines, *humiliores*, bereft of any of the protection enjoyed by a Roman citizen.

In his letter to Trajan, Pliny wrote that he had ordered the execution of those Christians who had refused to abjure *perseverantes duci iussi*[109]. This is execution by the sword, the chastisement of Roman citizens convicted of treasonable activities against the State or Emperor. Indeed Pliny explicitly states in his letter that he remanded the Roman citizens who figured amongst the Christians appearing in his court to Trajan for judgement. In his account of the anti-Christian pogrom at Lyons, Eusebius notes that the governor of Gallia Lugdunensis examined the Lyonnais Christians and "beheaded all who appeared to possess Roman citizenship, and sent the rest to the beasts[110]. Further on in the *Historia Ecclesiastica*, Eusebius wrote that decapitation was the penalty prescribed by "an ancient law obtained among them (ἀρχαίου παρ' αὐτοῖς νόμου)" for those Christians who would not renounce their beliefs[111]. This brief legal notice occurs in Eusebius' account of the trial of Apollonius before the Praetorian Prefect Perennius[112]:

"But the martyr, beloved of God, when the judge earnestly begged and prayed him to defend himself before the senate, made before everyone a most learned defence of the faith

---

104 Callistratus (in) *Digesta* 48,19.28.
105 Tacitus, *Ann.* 15,44.
106 Ignatius of Antioch, *Ep. Rom.* 5.
107 *Shepherd of Hermas*, Visio 3,2.
108 Justin Martyr, *Dialogus cum Tryphone* 10.
109 Pliny, *Ep.* 10,96.
110 Eusebius, *HE.* 5,1.47 (*trans.* K. Lake, *Loeb*, 1959).
111 Eusebius, *HE.* 5,21.4 (*trans.* K. Lake, *Loeb*, 1959).
112 Perennius was Praetorian Prefect from 183 to 185 or 186.

for which he was a martyr, and was consecrated by beheading as if by decree of the senate; for an ancient law obtained among them that there should be no other issue for the case of those who once appeared before the court and did not change their opinion".[113]

The sword was a powerful image and had a strong effect upon the psyche of the ancients. The Apostle Paul himself wrote: "For he [the ruler] is God's servant for your good. But if you be wrong, be afraid, for he does not bear the sword in vain (οὐ γὰρ εἰκῇ τὴν μάχαιραν φορεῖ); he is the servant of God to execute his wrath on the wrongdoer"[114]. Luke reports that the Apostle James was slain by the sword[115]. In the Book of Revelation we read that those who had not worshipped the beast or its image had been beheaded[116]. In the *Acta Pauli*, the Apostle himself escapes an ignoble death *ad bestias* in both Ephesus and Philippi, finally to be slain in Rome by the sword. The sword then was the ultimate symbol of power: "le vengeur des lois et l'instrument du supplice", as de Gaiffier has so appropriately phrased it[117]. Yet even the great and invincible power of the sword was overcome by divine intervention: those who, in the Book of Revelation, had been beheaded, would come to life again and reign with Christ[118]. In the *Martyrium Pauli*, the sword had indeed ended Paul's terrestrial life, yet he was immediately resurrected, praying with Titus and Luke at his own tomb and appearing to Nero, the man who had ordered his slaying[119].

The earliest extant references connecting Paul's death to the penalty of decapitation occur in the *Martyrium Pauli*, the final segment of the *Acta Pauli* (c. 160 A.D.) and in Tertullian's *de Praescriptione Haereticorum* 36,1—3 (c. 200 A.D.). There are no rival claims which would witness to the Apostle's having been slain in another way. Tradition uniformly cites decapitation as the mode of Paul's martyrdom[120].

---

113 Eusebius, *HE.* 5,21 (*trans.* K. Lake, *Loeb*, 1959).
114 Rom. 13,4. The expression φορέω μάχαιραν means to bear the sword, to have the power of life and death. The secular background to the Greek idiom used by Paul lies in the magistrate's *ius gladii*.
115 Acts 12,2.
116 Rev. 20,4.
117 B. de Gaiffier, "La mort par le glaive dans les Passions des Martyrs", *RECHERCHES D'HAGIOGRAPHIE LATINE*, Brussels, 1971, pg. 70, note 2.
118 Rev. 20,4.
119 *Mart. Pauli* 6 & 7.
120 Later Christian writers thought of decapitation as a more benevolent or honourable mode of execution. Cf. the *Martyrium S. Apollonii* 45, where the judge declares decapitation to be a *kind* sentence. So too Lactantius, writing of the persecution under Emperor Galerius (ruled 305-311 A.D.): "There were no mild punishments with him — no sending of people to islands, prisons or mines; instead, the fire, the cross and the wild beasts were in prompt and daily use. (...) In capital cases, execution by the sword was granted to very few as a

F) The actual execution was carried out by a *speculator*[121]. This person was "one of the *principales* or headquarters' staff of a legionary commander or provincial governor whose duties included the carrying out of executions"[122]. The term, transliterated into Greek, occurs once in the New Testament at Mk.. 6,27 where it is a σπεκουλάτωρ who decapitates John the Baptist: "And immediately the king sent a soldier of the guard and gave orders to bring his head. He went and beheaded him in the prison".

G) The condemned's clothing and personal effects became State property after his execution. The jurist Ulpianus cites a rescript by Hadrian that the sum of money acquired by the sale of the condemned's *pannicularia* (clothing and other personal effects at the time of his death), were to be kept by the authorities for extraordinary expenses. These expenses typically included providing officials with writing materials, rewarding brave soldiers and gifts to visiting barbarian dignitaries. The proceeds from the sale of the *pannicularia* were not to go to either the *speculator* or his assistants nor were they to be kept for the examining magistrate's own private use[123].

VI. Regulation and Disposition of the Condemned's Corpse

Paul was a Roman citizen and as such enjoyed the right every Roman citizen had to a proper burial. In this matter his rights were safeguarded under the *ius sepulcri*.

VI,1. The *ius sepulcri*

Legally speaking the term *sepulcrum* was defined in Roman Law as a grave or burial site *ubi corpus ossaue hominis condita sunt* [124]. A sepulchre was *familiare* when its owner designated it in his will as the burial place for himself and for the members of his household. It was *hereditarium* when destined only for the testator and his direct heirs[125]. Relatives and friends of an executed

---

benefit, because their merits had earned them a good death" (Lactantius, *de Mort. Pers.* 22; trans. J.L. Creed, Clarendon Press, Oxford, 1984). Cf. *Digesta* 48,19.28.
121 Cf. *Mart. Pauli* 5.
122 *LS*⁹. pg. 1626.
123 *Digesta* 48,20.6.
124 *Digesta* 11,7.2.
125 Cf. A. Berger, *Encyclopedic Dictionary of Roman Law*, Philadelphia, 1953, pg. 533.

person could usually obtain his mortal remains from the authorities without much legal difficulty. In the *Duties of Proconsul*, Ulpianus wrote:

> "The bodies of those who suffer capital punishment are not to be refused to their relatives; and the deified Augustus writes in the tenth book of his *de Vita Sua* that he also had observed this custom. Today, however, the bodies of those who are executed are buried in the same manner as if this had been sought and granted. But sometimes it is not allowed, particularly with the bodies of those condemned for treason (*et nonnumquam non permittitur maxime maiestatis causa damnatorum*)"[126]

All four Gospels record how Joseph of Arimathaea made an official request to the Roman Prefect Pontius Pilate to have Jesus' Body given over to him[127]. Both Matthew and Mark report that John the Baptist's disciples recovered their master's body after his decapitation[128]. Luke records in the *Acts of the Apostles* that "devout men buried Stephen and made great lamentation over him"[129]. Eusebius states that the bodies of the Christian martyrs of Lyons were not rendered to the Christian community of that city, but rather that great violence was done to the corpses:

> "Their conduct thus varied, but in our circle great grief obtained, because we could not bury the bodies in the earth, for night did not avail us for this, nor did money persuade nor entreaty shame, but in every way they watched, as though they would make some great gain, that the bodies should not obtain burial".[130]

After six days what was left of the bodies was burned and the ashes dumped into the Rhône River so that, as Eusebius says, "not even a relic of them might still appear upon the earth"[131]. It is related in the *Martyrium S. Polycarpi* that the Jews of Smyrna tried to prevent the civil authorities from giving up Polycarp's body to the Christian community. The Christians, however, after much effort and great delay were able to gather up the ashes of the holy martyr and bury them amidst prayer and song[132].

Insofar as the Apostle Paul is concerned, he would have been led out of Rome for his execution and then buried nearby in an existing sepulchre. The site of Paul's martyrdom and burial has from very early times been identified with a place along the via Ostiense where the major basilica of St. Paul's without the Walls (San Paolo fuori le mura) now stands. A much later tradition

---

126 *Digesta* 48,24.1. The jurist Paulus wrote that "the bodies of executed persons are to be granted to any who seek them for burial" (*Digesta* 48,24.3.)
127 Mt. 27,57-60; Mk. 15,43-45; Lk. 23,50-53; Jn. 19,38.
128 Mt. 14,12; Mk. 6,29.
129 Acts 8,2.
130 Eusebius, *HE.* 5,1.61 (*trans.* K. Lake, *Loeb*, 1959).
131 Eusebius, *HE.* 5,1.62 (*trans.* K. Lake, *Loeb*, 1959).
132 *Martyrium S. Polycarpi* 17-18.

originating in Byzantine circles in Rome in the 6th Century did indeed locate the place of the Apostle's execution as being at the site of the present-day Abbey of the Three Fountains (Abbazia delle tre fontane) near the via Laurentina. Then, runs the legend, the Apostle's body was brought to the via Ostiense sepulchre for burial. This tale is totally legendary born of a desire to enhance the prestige of the Abbey of the Three Fountains. We should note too, that the 6th Century Byzantine chronicler, John Malalas, reports a tradition that Peter and Paul remained *unburied* after their martyrdoms: "The Basileus Nero", writes John Malalas, "ordered that the bodies of the Holy Apostles not be handed over for burial, but remain unburied (ἀλλα' ἄταφα μεῖναι)"[133]. John Malalas is, to be sure, an oftentimes uncritical compiler, but he had access to important sources no longer extant. The tradition to which he witnesses is then older than the 6th Century. It is, however, extremely unlikely that the body of Paul, a Roman citizen, remained unburied. That would have constituted not only a singular aggravation of the sentence against the Apostle, but also a violation of the *ius sepulcri*.

VI,2. Violatio Sepulcri

The sepulchre became a *locus religiosus* when the owner (or the *familiares* or *heredes*) had been buried therein[134]. It was the presence in fact of the mortal remains which made it *religiosus*[135]. Once a burial place had become a *locus religiosus*, the State assumed its protection and watched over it lest it in any way be profaned[136]. The keeping of the *loca religiosa* was the duty of the several *pontifices*; with the introduction of the Principate, the Emperor, as *pontifex maximus*, came to assume a particular responsibility in this area[137]. The Emperors strove to strongly enforce the rules against tomb spoliation and to punish those who did despoil them. This can be seen from the text of the famous Διάταγμα Καίσαρος, a rescript engraved on marble which came to light in Nazareth and which is conserved in the old Froehner Collection in Paris:

> "It is my pleasure that sepulchres and tombs, which have been erected as solemn memorials of ancestors or children or relatives, shall remain undisturbed in perpetuity. If it be shown that anyone has either destroyed them or otherwise thrown out the bodies which have been

---

133 John Malalas, *Chronographia* 10.
134 *Digesta* 11,7.2.
135 *Digesta* 1,8.6; 11,7.2. Cf. P. Testini, *Le catacombe e gli antichi cimiteri cristiani in Roma*, Bologna, 1966, pg. 39.
136 P. Testini, *op.cit.*, pg. 39-40.
137 F. Cumont, "Un réscrit impérial sur la violation de sépulture", *REV.HIST.*, Vol. 163; 1930, pg. 247-248.

buried there or removed them with malicious intent to another place, thus committing a crime (ἀδικίᾳ) against those buried there, or removed the headstones or other stones, I command that against such persons the same sentence be passed in respect of solemn memorials of men as is laid down in respect of the gods. Much rather must one pay respect to those who are buried. Let no one disturb them on any account. Otherwise it is my will that capital sentence be passed upon such persons for the crime of tomb spoliation (τυμ βωρυχίας)".[138]

The overall legal evidence clearly demonstrates imperial concern and solicitude in protecting the principle of the perpetual inviolability of sepulchres. True from time to time in very exceptional circumstances and under strict legal supervision, a body could be exhumed and transported elsewhere, but such cases were rare. Removing a body from its tomb was clearly an ἀδικία as the imperial rescript shows in so limpid a manner. We should recall that used in this context the Greek term ἀδικία not only encompassed *impietas* but also *iniuria*, that is to say that tomb spoliation was deemed to be an intentionally malicious and criminal injury done to the dead, akin to a *sacrilegium* against the gods[139]. So grievous was this crime of *violatio sepulcri* that those convicted of it could very well receive a capital sentence.

In view of the prevailing legislation and ethos in the matter of tomb spoliation, it is quite probable that the mortal remains of the Apostle Paul, once laid to rest in the sepulchre along the via Ostiense, remained there undisturbed by either the Roman Christian community or the Roman authorities. The famous legend that Paul's body was translated by Christians in the year 258 A.D. — in the midst of the Valerianic persecution — from the via Ostiense site to the Catacombs on the via Appia is thus rather implausible, lacking as it does any serious juridical or historical support.

VII. Paul's Martyrdom and its Relationship to the Christian Persecution of 64 A.D.

Until the persecution which followed the great fire of 64 A.D., whatever legal difficulties the Christian community at Rome might have had with the vested authorities did not spring from the fact that its members professed Christianity as their religion. Christianity's identity was " ... either not clear to the Roman authorities, or if it was they had nothing against Christianity and Chris-

---

138 This translation of the Greek is given in F.F. Bruce, "Christianity under Claudius", *BULL.J.R.LIB.*, Vol. 44; 1961-1962, pg. 319. F. Cumont, *op.cit.*, pg. 245-247, has argued quite plausibly that this imperial rescript dates from the early years of Octavian's reign.
139 F. Cumont, *op.cit.*, p. 250-251.

tians"¹⁴⁰. Indeed in this very earliest period in the history of the Roman Church, the civil authorities considered Jesus' disciples to be a part of organized Judaism. Thus, as they legally sheltered under the Jewish name, the Roman Christians had shared in all the legal advantages and protection afforded official Judaism and like all Jews they were exempted from the obligation to sacrifice to the Emperor¹⁴¹. Yet the Neronian persecution was directed exclusively against the Christians of Rome and no other group. Therefore at some point before the great fire of 64 A.D., the Roman authorities had come to understand quite unmistakably that the Christian community was indeed quite distinct from official Judaism and factually separated from it both theologically and structurally. From the legal point of view this would make Christianity an unauthorized religion, functioning illicitly. Something, some striking public event or adversarial publicity, had brought the mascent Church to the attention of the authorities and had caused her to run afoul of the magistrates.

Tacitus' famous account in the *Annals* of the massacre of the Roman Christians — an account wherein the writer's animosity toward the Christian community is uninhibitedly displayed — furnishes at least a few indications as to the relationship between Nero, the Roman people and the Christians at that most trying hour¹⁴². Tacitus notes that the Christians were condemned not for firing the city, the charge on which Nero strove to inculpate them, but for their alleged anti-social tendencies: *haud perinde in crimine incendii, quam odio humani generis*. The expression *odium humani generis* (cf. Greek μισανθρωπία) would imply abandonment of one's political and religious duties toward the State and a willful separation from — and attitude of exclusiveness toward — the rest of society. On a Roman citizen's part, such deportment would be deemed totally unacceptable not only to a court of law but to society at large as well. Suetonius records, in fact, the killings of the Christians in the section devoted to Nero's *good* deeds in his book on that Emperor's life ¹⁴³. In the very same passage Suetonius states that the Christians were condemned for their *superstitio* which he qualifies as new and evil: *afflicti suppliciis Christiani genus hominum superstitionis novae ac maleficae*. Even though he is a

---

140 P. Keresztes, "The imperial Roman Government and the Christian Church I", *ANRW*. II,23,1; pg. 247. A half century later, Pliny is still in doubt as to whether to punish the Christians who appeared in his court for the sole profession of their religion (that is on an *accusatio nominis*) or for *flagitia*, criminal and immoral acts allegedly associated with the practice of Christianity (Pliny, *Ep*.. 10,96).
141 D.L. Jones, *op.cit.*, pg. 1028.
142 Tacitus, *Ann.* 15,44.
143 Suetonius, *Nero* 16.

later witness, Minucius Felix comes right to the point as to why the Christians were so hated: *deos despuunt rident sacra*[144].

Paul's arrival in Rome in 60 A.D. as an appellant to Caesar's court was a very significant event in the life of the early Roman Church. Some three years earlier, Paul had written to the Roman community and had outlined the purpose of the visit he was proposing to make:

> "For I long to see you, that I may impart to you some spiritual gift to strengthen you, that is, that we may be mutually encouraged by each other's faith, both yours and mine. I want you to know, brethren, that I have often intended to come to you (but thus far have been prevented), in order that I may reap some harvest among you as well as among the rest of the Gentiles. I am under obligation both to Greeks and to barbarians, both to the wise and to the foolish: so I am eager to preach the Gospel to you also who are in Rome".[145]

Paul's arrival in Rome, his lengthy stay there and the mission he conducted had a considerable impact on the Roman Christian community and on the relationship between the nascent Church and official Judaism. The doctrine he taught at Rome, indeed his whole theology, could only have widened the considerable gap between the Church and the synagogue, and in fact made the differences irreconcilable. Paul gave to Roman Christianity a sharper and clearer identity, one that was *Christian* and not Judeo-Christian. He made the Roman community more aware of its specificity and of its uniqueness. He made Roman Christians conscious of the fact that they were part of the Israel of faith, which in God's plan for mankind's salvation, had by-passed the old Israel of flesh. The existence at Rome of a second monotheistic faith rooted in Old Testament teachings and prophecies and claiming to be a descendent of Abraham by faith provoked a very violent reaction on the part of the synagogal authorities. This was all the more the case as both the Church and synagogue were competing for the same group of proselytes and God-fearers who together formed their pool of converts as it were. Luke records the Jewish leaders' rejection of Paul's teachings in Rome in the last chapter of Acts[146]; this rejection engendered feelings of rivalry, jealousy and hate which were to be Paul's undoing. Paul's dispute with the Jewish leadership probably caused dissensions within the Jewish community at Rome. Luke alludes to these

---

144 Minucius Felix, *Octavius* 8,3-4. A.N. Sherwin-White suggests that during the 2nd Century the principal grounds for official legal action taken against the Christians was their perceived *contumacia*. Their obstinacy in refusing homage to the pagan gods coupled with their stubborn refusal to participate in the usual forms of Emperor-worship caused them to acquire a reputation as dangerous dissidents. Such *contumacia* could only beget persecution against the Christian community and martyrdom for some of its members. (A.N. Sherwin-White, "Early Persecutions ...", *op.cit.*, pg. 210-211 and *The Letters of Pliny, op.cit.*, pg. 787).
145 Rom. 1,11-15.
146 Cf. Acts 28,17-28.

internal dissensions in his account [147]. At the same time the struggle between Paul and his Jewish adversaries could only have enormously increased tensions with the Roman Christian community itself between the Judeo-Christians and the Gentile party. All of this religious quarrelling could hardly have been kept a secret for long nor could any resultant violence be hidden from the public view. Undoubtedly the Roman authorities were soon made aware by the Jewish leadership of the presence of a new religious grouping and of its controversial leader: a man with a long record of court appearances in the provinces and who was presently in Rome as a result of an appeal to the imperial tribunal:

> "There can be little doubt that, seeing the activities and the great success of Paul and other leaders of the Church in Rome, such as Peter, the Synagogue, moved by jealousy and envy, enlightened ... Nero and the imperial government about a sect waiting for the coming of the Kingdom of God". [148]

Paul's missionary activity seems to have been crowned by considerable success in Rome; a success strongly implied in the positive note on which Luke ends his account[149]. Writing some thirty years after the Neronian persecution, St. Clement says that an immense crowd (πολὺ πλῆθος) suffered in that persecution[150]. Tacitus uses the expression *multitudo ingens* to describe the number of Christians put to death by Nero's order [151]. A successful programme of evangelization would have had the effect of drawing the new converts away not only from the worship of the old gods[152], but also from the imperial cult. The abandonment of the national religion was an act of disloyalty which all the Julio-Claudian Emperors had long striven to counter through their legislative and juridical powers. Those persuading men to do so could only be considered as mounting a dangerous challenge to the ideological underpinning of the whole constitutionally unstable régime. Paul's arrest in Rome, his final trial and his condemnation by the imperial court would have meant that the foremost member of the Gentile Christian Church at Rome had been found guilty and put to death on a charge of *crimen maiestatis*. If the leader, a Roman citizen, were a renegade to his *patria* and an enemy of the Emperor, what of the

---

147 Acts 28,24: "And some were convinced by what he said, while others disbelieved"; Acts 28,25: "So as they disagreed among themselves, they departed ...". The addition in Acts 28,29 repeats this information: "And when he had said these words, the Jews departed, holding much dispute among themselves".
148 P. Keresztes, "Nero, the Christians and the Jews in Tacitus and Clement of Rome", *LATOMUS*, Vol. 43; 1984, pg. 411.
149 Acts 28, 30-31.
150 Clement of Rome,· *Ep.Cor.* 6,1.
151 Tacitus, *Ann.* 15,44.
152 Cf. Acts 19,27.

group he led? The entire Pauline community at Rome would have become known to the imperial authorities as being a group of dangerous dissenters:

> "There did not need to be a general edict against them, for it was accepted that a man must be subject to some law, and if he was not subject to Jewish law, then he must be subject to that of his own city. If not, he was suspect as an enemy of the gods and thus of the community in which he lived. In such circumstances, denunciation to the authorities by personal enemies, including orthodox Jews, was always a danger for the Christian. Once denounced, and persisting in his outlook, he was at the mercy of the magistrate's *coercitio*".[153]

Paul's re-arrest, trial, condemnation and martyrdom are more likely than not to have occurred before the great fire of 64 A.D. We should like to suggest that the Apostle left Caesarea as an appellant prisoner in the Autumn of 59 A.D., wintered in Malta (59—60) and arrived in Rome in 60. He then spent a *biennium* in that city while awaiting his appeal to be heard by the imperial court. The most likely result of that process was that the Apostle was released from his house imprisonment at the end of the *biennium* in 62, not because he had been found innocent, but because his accusers had not arrived from Jerusalem to pursue the case. A short period of liberty would then have ensued, possibly with a brief journey to Spain. Returning to Rome, the Apostle was arrested on a charge of *maiestas*, tried, condemned and martyred in about late 63 or early 64 A.D. Patristic tradition has, by and large, placed the date of Paul's martyrdom in Nero's last regnal year, 68 A.D. This is, however, a late tradition with no seeming historical basis. The choice of this date is clearly theological, designed to put Paul's martyrdom in a close relationship to the *coup d'état* which overthrew Nero: that ruler's fall from power and subsequent death being considered as divine punishment for his ordering the killing of the two Apostles Peter and Paul.

Paul's trial — that of a Roman citizen, of lesser social rank to be sure, but still a Roman citizen accused of a crime of majesty against his sovereign — could only have had the effect of focussing the attention of the Roman police and magistrates onto the Christian community of which he was the foremost evangelist. Paul was not condemned for being a Christian (for the *nomen*), but his trial and condemnation went a long way in establishing a juridical procedure to be used against the Christians at Rome itself[154]. Paul's trial sensitized the imperial court and the Roman *magistratura* to the real existence and specific identity of a Christian community outside the pale of official

---

153 W.H.C. Frend, *op.cit.*, pg. 169.
154 Cf. Th. Mommsen, "Der Religionsfrevel nach römischem Recht", *GESAMMELTE SCHRIFTEN III*, Berlin, 1907, pg. 395.

Judaism and so enjoying none of its protection. Paul's trial and condemnation to death for treasonable activities would go a very very long way indeed in explaining how in a short period of time the Roman Christians went from being an unknown, innocuous group of no social or political importance whatever to being the scapegoats for a fire which burned down a goodly part of the most important city in the world.

Chapter Two
Paul's Legal Situation at the Close of Acts

I. Acts 16—28: Luke's Narration of Paul's Judicial History

Luke's account of Paul's legal history is not without its ironies. On the one hand, the Evangelist provides a detailed and legally realistic account of Paul's judicial history from the time of his appearance before the ruling Duumvirs in the Roman colony of Philippi till his arrival in Rome as an appellant prisoner a decade later. By contrast, after having brought Paul to Rome and recorded that he lived there a *biennium* while awaiting his appeal to be heard, and after having purposely created an ambience of high drama and expectation, Luke abruptly terminates his narrative saying nothing further of Paul's subsequent life, possible travels, his trial, condemnation or martyrdom. It is clear that Luke's intent was to close his two-volume work *ad Theophilum* on a literary and eschatological, rather than on a juridical or historical note [1]. Nonetheless, the fact that Luke had specific apologetic goals and precise literary aims for Acts does not mean that the value of that scripture is diminished or rendered untrustworthy as radical New Testament critics delight in saying. The final verses in Acts allow one to clearly situate Paul's legal status at the very moment in which he was entering the final period of his life, (starting with his arrival in Rome) about which so little is certain. Moreover the testimony in Acts is pertinent to any attempt at reconstructing the indictment lodged against Paul at his final trial in Rome. Acts was written subsequent to the Apostle's condemnation and martyrdom and its account of Paul's earlier legal history points to the type of charges which he would have had to have confronted at his trial before the imperial tribunal. These charges in fact could only have been very similar to the ones Luke details in his recounting of Paul's earlier court appearances. The catalogue of accusations made against Paul in the provincial

---

1 C.J. Hemer writes that Acts 28,30-31, "... is an intended conclusion, and implies a larger knowledge, tantalizing the reader with the unspecified end of the two-year term". (C.J. Hemer, *The Book of Acts in the Setting of Hellenistic History*, Tübingen, 1989, pg. 349).

courts of law is a veritable prefiguration of the charges composing the indictment formulated against Paul in Rome on which he was eventually condemned.

Paul's legal history essentially starts in the Roman colony of Philippi. There the Apostle was accused before the ruling Duumvirs of disturbing the city and of advocating "customs which it is not lawful for us Romans to accept or practise"[2]. The accusation then was of disturbing public order within the territory of a Roman colony by the preaching of Jesus Christ. That preaching had the effect of unsettling the local religious scene in that it was inducing the Philippians, for the most part Roman citizens, to abandon the worship of the colony's tutelary gods and especially the cult of Rome and Augustus. In Ephesus the same sort of thing transpired. Luke notes that the riot came about when the townspeople concluded that the cult of Artemis was seriously threatened by Paul's preaching. Luke's rendition of Demetrius the Silversmith's speech is revealing:

> "And you see and hear that not only at Ephesus but almost throughout all Asia this Paul has persuaded and turned away (μετέστησεν) a considerable company of people, saying that gods made with hands are not gods. And there is danger not only that this trade of ours may come into disrepute but also that the temple of the great goddess Artemis may count for nothing, and that she may even be deposed from her magnificence, she whom all Asia and the world worship"[3]

The Gospel's proclamation was here as elsewhere a threat to the vested political and religious interests of the city.

In Thessalonica, the Jews accused Paul of even greater offences. Here the charge of disturbing public order re-appears, but accompanied by the deadly accusation that Paul and his followers were "all acting against the decrees of Caesar, saying that there is another king, Jesus"[4]. Thus Paul was not only accused of attacks on the officially recognized Jewish community and of disturbing the life of that Greek free city, but squarely of sedition. Paul's foes were depicting his proclamation of another king and another kingdom as a direct challenge to the authority and majesty of the Emperor[5].

In Corinth, the local Jewish authorities instituted formal legal proceedings against the Apostle charging him before the Proconsul Gallio with " ...

---

[2] Acts 16,21.

[3] Acts 19,26-27. The Greek verb μεθίστημι which Luke uses here is quite stark implying as it does a complete alteration in belief or behaviour; thus, to turn away from, to change from, to cease from doing something, to go over to another party or group.

[4] Acts 17,7.

[5] Cf. the charge lodged against Jesus in Jn. 19,12: "every one who makes himself a king sets himself against Caesar".

persuading men to worship God contrary to the law"[6]. Thus in this passage, Luke introduced yet another legal factor into his account of Paul's judicial history. The Apostle's adversaries were essentially saying that his preaching was aimed at founding a religious group outside of — and indeed hostile to — official Judaism. By combating Mosaic Law, which was the fundamental and organic statute of organized Judaism, and by proclaiming that Jesus of Nazareth, a man whom the Sanhedrin had condemned to death after a formal trial, was indeed the Messiah, Paul had decidedly put himself and his followers outside Judaism. The message of the Corinthian Jews to the Proconsul was clear enough: the Christians should not be considered by Roman authority to be a part of the Jewish name. Consequently the Christians could no longer enjoy the privileges, rights and exemption from Emperor-worship which Judaism enjoyed. They were no longer part of this '*religio licita*'[7], but an unrecognized and therefore illicit group.

The same mixture of religious and political charges occurs in Tertullus' plea against Paul in the procuratorial court at Caesarea. There, in addition to being accused of profaning the Temple of Jerusalem, a capital offence under Jewish law, the Apostle was charged with being a pest, agitator and "ringleader of the sect of the Nazarenes"[8]. Once again Luke stresses the Jewish insistence that the Christians were a sect (αἵρεσις) outside official Judaism and as such enjoying no legal recognition within the Roman juridico-political system. Paul's Jewish adversaries were making a forceful attempt to brand nascent Pauline Christianity as a particularly subversive form of political messianism. In this schema of things, the very existence of Pauline Christianity was not only a direct defiance of the established Jewish religious hierarchy, which was recognized as a *bona fide* interlocutor by Rome, but a clear challenge to Roman authority as well, especially to that of the Emperor with his many and variegated divine-like attributes and titles. The Christian acclamation that Jesus was King, Lord and Saviour constituted a diminution of the dignity and majesty of the Emperor himself, in whose cult such titles as *dominus* and *soter* appeared with great frequency. Luke is careful in his apologetics to refute all political charges against Paul; in his defence before Felix, the Apostle terms Christianity a *Way* (ὁδός) a term having much more neutral legal implications than *Sect* (αἵρεσις). In general Paul's apologetic discourse in Acts is characterized by its mainstream Pharisaic flavour and by its political innocuousness, as seen in his remarks to the Procurator Festus: "Neither against the law of the Jews, nor

---

6 Acts 18,13.
7 The expression is Tertullian's: *sub umbraculo insignissimae religionis, certe licitae* (*Apol.* 21).
8 Acts 24,5-6.

against the temple, nor against Caesar have I offended at all" (Acts 25,8). It was vital for Luke's apologetic purposes to exculpate Paul from all charges of anti-Roman political activity in order that the Pauline communities left behind by the martyred Apostle should not have to suffer any further harm.

The defining moment in Paul's legal history was his appeal to Caesar[9], which was made at the moment in which the Procurator Festus, having found Paul innocent of sedition, proposed surrendering him to the Sanhedrin's jurisdiction for trial on the charge of profaning the Temple[10]. Paul's appeal blocked that extradition process and placed him in a quite altered juridical situation. As a Roman citizen, Paul had the right to invoke the judicial protection of the Emperor (who held, as we have seen, the *tribunicia potestas*) against an arbitrary decision of a lower magistrate. His case would henceforth be reserved for the decision of the Emperor (*a cognitionibus Augusti*). In Rome only the *political charges* previously lodged against Paul would be examined anew, not the doctrinal controversy or religious accusations formulated by his Jewish foes, matters hardly cognizable by the imperial tribunal functioning as a court of appeals.

Luke endeavoured in his narrative to show that the Roman magistrates before whom Paul appeared did not consider him guilty of any charge that might be subsumed in the category of *crimen maiestatis*; nor did they seem to know of any specific enactment banning or impeding the practice of Christianity. In Acts, Luke presents the Roman officials handling Paul's case as generally favourable to the nascent Christian community, never spontaneously intervening in its affairs or in those of its leaders unless a cognizable judicial charge was submitted to them by the community's legal adversaries. Throughout his narrative, Luke tried hard to stress the nascent Church's political loyalty to the Principate precisely by stressing the fact that Paul and his followers had never been deemed by the examining magistrates to have violated existing Roman statutes. Yet Luke's lenitive writing does not always succeed in obscuring how conflictual Paul's relationship to the Roman State really was. The Apostle's preaching of the Kingship of Jesus, of His exclusive sovereignty, of salvation in His name alone, ran counter to the very tenets of Emperor-worship which formed one of the most important ideological bases of the Principate. Paul's evangelism induced men to cease worship of the old gods and drew them away from the cult of *Roma* and of the divine-like rulers; and this was a direct challenge to the majesty of the Emperor and the authority of the State.

---

9 Acts 25,11.
10 Acts 24,10. That Paul could only expect a death sentence from the Sanhedrin is clear from the response of the Jewish populace which Luke relates in Acts 22,22: "Away with such a fellow from the earth! For he ought not to live".

II. Luke's Omission of Paul's Martyrdom

Luke's silence in Acts as to Paul's last days in Rome and to his martyrdom is, of course, disappointing to the modern reader and at first glance might seem perplexing behaviour on the part of an author who had oftentimes provided such dramatic depictions of much less significant events[11]. But Luke's silence should not really surprise one. The Evangelist had formulated a clear and delimited literary plan for Acts in order to attain his theological and political aims. His omitting any account of Paul's martyrdom was quite consistent with those goals and by no means signifies that Acts is an incomplete book[12]. Luke knew, of course,

> "... that Paul died as a martyr, and he knows also that it will add to the effectiveness of his adulatory picture if he can introduce the shadows of martyrdom as they fall, not too darkly, across his hero's path, and can also indicate that Paul was aware of what was to happen. This in fact is what he does; and we may probably see here the reason why Acts stops where it does. An account of the martyrdom itself, especially if at the time Paul was deserted by his friends and the victim of some kind of treachery, would not enhance the record of Paul's devotion and might detract from the sense of confidence, victory and unity that permeates the book".[13]

By the time Luke composed Acts, Paul had already been martyred. The Evangelist in fact alludes to Paul's death in his account of the Apostle's speech to the Ephesian presbyters at Miletus[14]. Paul's condemnation and violent death made it necessary for Luke to present to the early Pauline communities, now bereft of their founder, a clear image of who Paul was and a historical understanding of his life, work and doctrine[15]. Luke presents Paul's doctrine in a way which would enable the newly-founded Churches to increase their awareness of their own specific identity as Gentile Christian, as well as to provide them with a solid foundation on which they could affirm their set of beliefs and mode of worship against any philosophic, political or juridical gainsayers. In his account of the Apostle's sermon to the Roman Jewish leaders in the final chapter of Acts, Luke reiterates for the last time the essential theme of his apologetic programme: the resurrected Jesus is indeed the Messiah, the Hope of Israel. As official Judaism had rejected this truth, despite the witness of Moses and the prophets, it would be the Gentiles who would listen to and receive the message of Salvation[16]. Having fully elaborated his apologetic

---

11 Cf. F.F. Bruce, "St. Paul in Rome I", *BULL.J.R.LIBR*; Vol. 46; 1963-1964, pg. 343.
12 H. Conzelmann, *Die Apostelgeschichte*, Tübingen, 1963, pg. 150.
13 C.K. Barrett, "Pauline Controversies in the post-Pauline Period", *NTS*. Vol. 20; 1974, p. 240.
14 Acts 20,17-38.
15 Cf. M. Hengel, *Acts and the History of earliest Christianity*, London, 1979, pg. 38.
16 Acts 28,28; cf. Acts 13,46 and 18,6.

programme, Luke did not need to say anything further about Paul in Acts. He had brought the Apostle of the Nations from Jerusalem to Rome and had fulfilled all his projected objectives. Acts was never intended to be a trial brief or a piece of martyrdom literature. Luke's essentially Roman audience already knew the details of Paul's last days and how and in what circumstances the Apostle had perished. They would not need to have these events recounted to them.

Luke also had a precise political programme in Acts. Throughout his two volume work, Luke had "carefully, consistently and consciously presented an *apologia pro imperio* to his church"[17]. The Evangelist's pro-Roman stance is especially evident in his account of Paul's legal encounters with the Roman magistrates. He specifically exculpated the Roman Procurators, Felix and Festus, from procedural malfeasance in Paul's case. He neutralized all that was negative in their views on Paul's case; indeed he took great pains to emphasize the positive in their involvement in Paul's legal history. Luke highlighted Paul's appeal to Caesar, portraying it as a strong expression of the confidence which the Apostle, a Roman citizen, had in the basic justice and equity of the Roman legal system in general and in the Emperor's own personal administration of justice in particular. In the last chapter of Acts, Luke stressed the very lenient form of custody in which Paul was detained and how the Apostle was able to pursue the all important mission to Rome without legal let or hindrance.

Luke therefore not only presented a strong case for Paul's innocence of the charges laid against him, but also stressed to his readers that Rome did not view nascent Christianity as an illicit or subversive movement, intrinsically hostile to the State and its ruler and actively bent on subverting or overthrowing the Principate. He constantly represents the Christians as loyal and apolitical subjects of the Emperor and their communities as politically unthreatening (*apologia pro ecclesia*). Luke, just as constantly, directs his reader's attention to the Roman authorities' benevolence towards the Church and to the political stability and peace which the Principate provided and which allowed the Christian mission to progress with such rapid strides (*apologia pro imperio*)[18].

Luke's political aims and juridical objectives in Acts were meant to demonstrate first and foremost that the Apostle Paul was innocent of all charges which might have fallen under the heading of *crimen laesae maiestatis*. Luke wished to demonstrate that the continued existence of the Pauline

---

17 P.W. Walaskay, '*And so we came to Rome*': *the political Perspective of St. Luke*, Cambridge, 1983, pg. 64.

18 P.W. Walaskay notes: "Throughout Luke-Acts, the Evangelist has done his best to modify his sources in order to sculpt the virtues of the empire in high relief" (Walaskay, *op.cit.*, pg. 25).

communities did not threaten the State nor did it diminish the Emperor's power and authority. He also had to simultaneously convince the Church that despite the bloody events under Nero, the imperial authorities were basically benign in their attitude to Christianity[19]. In relating Paul's legal history, Luke was aiming less at giving a full biography of the Apostle or a detailed account of the trial proceedings than at achieving toleration and recognition by the Roman State of the nascent Christian communities[20]. It was therefore essential for Luke to conciliate Church and State as much as possible by guarding the Church from embracing an *ideology of martyrdom*[21].

III. Acts 28: Luke's Account of Paul's Two-Year Roman Captivity

Luke's description of Paul's life in Rome is very succinct. The Evangelist's main interest in the final chapter of Acts was to relate Paul's sermon to the Roman Jewish leaders, their rejection of it and his final and definitive turn to the Gentiles. The information which Luke provides about Paul's personal and legal status extends over a mere three verses (Acts 28,16 and then Acts 28,30—31). From a compositional point of view these verses frame Paul's two speeches to the Roman Jewish leaders. In the first of the two

---

19 The benignancy of Roman judges and other officialdom is a consistent theme of later Christian martyrological literature. So Musurillo: "Yet in the Christian *acta* and *passiones* the Roman officials are for the most part fairly portrayed — save in the *Letter from the Churches of Lyons and Vienne* and in the *Martyrdom of Polycarp*. They beg the martyrs to take time for reflection; ... they are ready to grant a stay of execution; ... they beg the martyrs to consider their youth; ... they are portrayed as interested in the doctrines of Christianity ... . Thus there is little of the caricature of the Roman official of the sort we often find in the *Acta Alexandrinorum*; nor do the martyrs assail or verbally abuse their judges or executioners. It is a different sort of ἀρετή that is being held up before the eyes of posterity". (H. Musurillo, *THE ACTS OF THE CHRISTIAN MARTYRS*, Oxford, 1972, introduction, pg. lv.
20 Cf. M. Hengel, *op.cit.*, pg. 60: "Luke's relatively positive attitude towards the Roman State is not only governed by the fact that as a forerunner of the apologists he wants to achieve public toleration and recognition by the Roman authorities of the new religion as it represents the true Judaism and thus deserves to share its special status ... rather, he is well aware that the Church will come up against further and increasingly more severe persecutions".
21 Cf. R. Maddox: " ... Luke's purpose in deliberately suppressing the theme of martyrdom, except in the special case of Stephen ... was to disparage a tendency, perhaps already making its appearance, to glamorize a martyr's death, as was to happen in the second century in Ignatius (especially in his *Epistle to the Romans*) and in the *Martyrdom of Polycarp*. The Christian's business is not to play the hero, but to bear his witness in humility" (R. Maddox, *The Purpose of Luke-Acts*, Göttingen, 1982, pg. 81.

speeches (Acts 28,17—20), Luke has Paul recapitulate his legal history; in the second (Acts 28,23—28), Luke records Paul's proclamation of the Gospel and the Jewish rejection of it. Despite their brevity, the three verses are laden with juridical language and allusions; as such they cast a precious light on the Apostle's legal situation in Rome during his first captivity and on his future prospects.

III,1. Acts 28,16: Paul in *custodia militaris*

> "And when we came to Rome, Paul was allowed to stay by himself, with the soldier that guarded him". (ὅτε δὲ εἰσήλθομεν εἰς Ῥώμην, ἐπετράπη τῷ Παύλῳ μένειν καθ' ἑαυτὸν σὺν τῷ φυλάσσοντι αὐτὸν στρατιώτῃ).

The Western tradition of Acts amplifies the B-text by providing two additional pieces of information. First it names the official to whose custody Paul was remanded and secondly it stresses that Paul had his own lodging outside the praetorian barracks:

> And when we came to Rome, the centurion delivered the prisoners to the Stratopedarch, but Paul was allowed to stay by himself outside the barracks, with the soldier that guarded him".

The textual expansions are three in number:

a) ὁ ἑκατοντάρχης παρέδωκεν τοὺς δεσμίους τῷ στρατοπεδάρχῳ
b) τῷ δὲ Παύλῳ ἐπετράπη
c) ἔξω τῆς παρεμβολῆς[22].

A) Rome: the new centre of Paul's missionary work

With just a few words Luke marks Paul's arrival in Rome. The great city will be Paul's final missionary station, the base of operations for his Apostolic ministry till the end of his life, the scene of his last trial and of his martyrdom. Paul's entrance into Rome was a deeply significant event. It marked the culminating point of his life and work and it shifted the centre of Pauline Christianity from the Hellenistic East to the Empire's capital:

> "From the beginnings of Christianity, it was easy to see that the future of the new religion would be decided in the Empire's capital, that meeting place of all races and the centre from

---

[22] The addition, "the centurion delivered the prisoners to the Stratopedarch" is found in δ 614[byz], g p vg[codd] syp syh* sa eth tepl prov. The addition "outside the *Castrum*" occurs in δ 614 1611 2147 g p vg[codd] syh* prov Ambst. The Vg. reads: *cum autem venissemus Romam, permissum est Paulo manere sibimet cum custodiente se milite*.

which all doctrines spread. Only the genius of Rome could impart that seal of universality which the new religion needed to assure its diffusion and which it would acquire by shedding the Jewish particularism inherited from its origins. The Apostle to the Nations understood this very well ... "[23].

Paul's appeal to Caesar had furnished the great and providential leap which brought the Apostle to the Empire's centre. But it is clear that Paul himself very much desired to go to Rome to preach the Gospel of Salvation. In the first chapter of his *Epistle to the Romans*, the Apostle wrote: "For God is my witness, whom I serve with my spirit in the gospel of his Son, that without ceasing I mention you always in my prayers, asking that somehow by God's will I may now at last succeed in coming to you"[24]. Later in the chapter he told his readers why he wanted to come: "I am under obligation both to Greeks and to barbarians, both to the wise and to the foolish: so I am eager to preach the gospel to you also who are at Rome"[25]:

> The Apostle saw in Rome not only an immense missionary field with many souls to be won to the Lord ... but especially he recognized Rome as being a centre of world importance whose conversion would give a specific turn to successive Christian missionary endeavours ... "[26]

Paul's arrival in Rome was a defining moment in his Apostolic ministry, ushering in, as it did, the ultimate and most crucial phase of his long and arduous mission: that of preaching the Gospel of Christ in the greatest city of the ancient world. St. John Chrysostom, in one of his most beautifully spiritual works, *de Laudibus Pauli*, has put it best: "It was not an inconsequential struggle which was proposed to Paul, but the conversion of the city of Rome"[27]. Paul was to die a martyr in that struggle. If Jerusalem were the Alpha of Paul's apostolate, then surely Rome was its Omega[28].

B) "The centurion delivered the prisoners to the Stratopedarch"

The B-text of Acts 28,16 indicates that Paul was allowed to stay by himself in his own lodgings outside the *Castrum*, but it does not indicate who gave this authorization. The later Western expansion filled in this gap by specifically naming the Stratopedarch. The title Stratopedarch was used to designate a

---

23 J.B. Frey, "Les communautés juives à Rome aux premiers temps de l'Eglise", *RSR*, Tome 20; 1930, pg. 269-270.
24 Rom. 1,9-10.
25 Rom. 1,14-15.
26 P. Brezzi, "La funzione storica di Roma nel pensiero di San Paolo", *STUDI PAOLINI*, Rome, 1969, pg. 21.
27 John Chrysostom, *de Laudibus Pauli*, Panegyric 7,9.
28 P. Brezzi, *op.cit.*, pg. 14.

military commander, the commandant of a camp or a camp prefect (i.e. quartermaster-general)[29]. The title appears as the equivalent of the Latin *praefectus castrorum* in some bilingual inscriptions[30]. The related word στρατόπεδον designated the *Castra praetoriana* [31]. Although a number of scholars have identified the Stratopedarch with the *Princeps peregrinorum*[32] or with the Praetorian Perfect himself[33], A.N. Sherwin-White suggests identifying the Stratopedarch with the *Princeps castrorum*, a subordinate of the Praetorian Prefect. As the *Princeps castrorum* was the chief administrator of the *officium* of the Praetorian Guard, Sherwin-White's proposal seems to be the most plausible identification:

> "This post happens to be known at Rome only from the Trajanic period onward, but it corresponded in duties and standing to the like-named officer in the legionary army, the *princeps praetorii legionis*, the head of the organizational command of a legion. This necessary post is testified, in the legions, from the time of Claudius onwards, and there is

---

29 Josephus, *BJ.* 2,531. In *BJ.* 6,238, the Stratopedarch is the 'prefect of all the forces', a quartermaster-general with control over all the camps. Cf. Dionysius Halicarnassensis 10,36.6 where Stratopedarch refers to the post of *primipilus* in a legion that had lost its commander in battle.
30 *CIL.* 3,13648: *Sex. Vibio Gallo ... praef Kastror leg XIII gem.*; also *CIL.* 3,14187 (4,5); *P. Oxy.* 2760 (year 179/180 A.D.). H.J. Mason notes: "In the period before 250 A.D., it is most easily understood as the version of *praefectus castrorum* ... although there is a traditional crux in the reading and interpretation of Acts 28,16" (H.J. Mason, *Greek Terms for Roman Institutions*, Toronto, 1974, pg. 13.).
31 *LS*[9]. pg. 1653. Dio Cassius relates that after Caligula's assassination, the soldiers hailed Claudius as Emperor and conducted him to the στρατοπέδον (Dio Cassius 60,1.) Cf. the verb στρατοπεδαρχέω meaning *praefectus esse castrorum* (H.J. Mason, *op.cit.*, pg. 87).
32 P.K. Baillie Reynolds writes that quite possibly the *Castra peregrinorum* "was established partly as a place of detention for persons from the provinces awaiting trial". He believes that it is a "virtual certainty" that the office of *Princeps peregrinorum* as well as the *Castra peregrinorum* were in existence as early as Nero's reign. (P.K. Baillie Reynolds, "The Troops quartered in the Castra Peregrinorum", *JRS*, Vol. 13, 1923, pg. 185-186.) G. Ricciotti is nearer the mark, however, when he expresses grave doubts that the *Castra peregrinorum* existed as early as Nero's reign (G. Ricciotti, *Gli Atti degli Apostoli*, Rome, 2nd. Ed., 1951, pg. 423).
33 Cf. H. Conzelmann, *op.cit.*, pg. 149. A. Wikenhauser, *DIE APOSTELGESCHICHTE*, Regensburg, 4th Edition, 1961, pg. 286. The word *Stratopedarch* is in the singular and this led Wikenhauser to conclude that Paul was handed over to Afranius Burrus, Prefect from 51 to 62 A.D., for following Burrus' death, Nero named two men, Faenius Rufus and the notorious Caius Ofonius Tigellinus, as joint commanders of the Guard (Tacitus, *Ann.* 14,51). Faenius was arrested later on and died in the purge following the discovery of the Pisonian conspiracy (65 A.D.) (Tacitus, *Ann.* 15,68). That the Praetorian Prefect received prisoners is plain from Pliny, *Ep.* 10,57 in which Trajan answers Pliny's query about a prisoner who failed to lodge an appeal within the allotted *biennium* saying "*vinctus mitti ad praefectos praetorii mei debet*".

no reason to suppose that the *princeps castrorum* of the Praetorian Guard was a later creation. This official is the personage most likely to be in executive control of prisoners awaiting trial at Rome in the Julio-Claudian period"[34]

C) "but Paul was allowed to stay by himself ... with the soldier that guarded him"

All the major manuscript traditions concur that Paul was not imprisoned in the barracks but allowed his own lodgings. The Western text adds the conjunctive particle δέ emphasizing thereby that the Stratopedarch made a distinction between Paul and his fellow-prisoners. They were presumably incarcerated within the *Castrum*, while the Apostle was singled out for special treatment by being placed under house arrest. In other words he was not placed under the régime of *carcer*, but under that of *custodia militaris*. He was therefore able to live in his own dwelling, receive regular visits from friends and associates and conduct his own business. He was, nonetheless, still a prisoner (*reus in custodia*)[35], closely guarded by a soldier[36] and strictly forbidden to leave Rome[37].

Custodia militaris was a creation of the Principate[38]. Under this type of custody, the prisoner was to be constantly guarded by one or more soldiers —

---

34 A.N. Sherwin-White, *Roman Society and Roman Law in the New Testament*, op.cit., pg. 110. Cf. *P.Lond.* 196,5.
35 In Acts 28,17, Paul describes himself as a δέσμιος, the one bound, i.e. a prisoner or captive. Cf. Acts 23,18; 25,14. In Phlm. 1 and 9 the Apostle terms himself "a prisoner for Jesus Christ". The term also occurs in Eph. 3,1; 4,1. Cf. Josephus *Ant.* 13,203 (Jonathan, prisoner of Tryphon) and Ant. 17,145 (Antipater, prisoner of Herod); *P. Oxy.* 580. Paul was bound by the ἅλυσις, a chain for wrists. When he was arrested by the Tribune Lysias, Luke notes that he was immediately "bound with two chains" (δεθῆναι ἁλύσεσι δυσί) (Acts 21,33). In Eph. 6,20, Paul uses the term "ambassador in chains". In 2 Tim. 1,16, it is noted that Onesiphorus succoured the Apostle during his last Roman imprisonment, "he was not ashamed of my chains". In Acts 12,6, it was Peter who was bound with two chains to soldiers on either side of him. Ignatius of Antioch talks of his being chained to "ten leopards", i.e. a detachment of guards (*Ep.Rom.* 5,1).
36 Possibly a *frumentarius*; cf. P.K. Baillie Reynolds, *op.cit.*, pg. 186.
37 Cf. Edict II of the Edicts of Augutus from Cyrene (7-6 B.C.). Here Aulus Stlaccius Maximus was accused of removing from public places statues among which there was one inscribed with the name of Augustus. The charge was clearly one of *maiestas*. The accused was forbidden to leave Rome by the Emperor pending the investigation into his case. In this case confinement at Rome was a simple administrative measure destined to facilitate the inquiry. (Cf. de Visscher, *op.cit.*, pg. 85, note 2). Claudius subsequently made this type of confinement into a particular form of *relegatio* by which the accused was not banished from, but rather confined to, Rome without loss of citizenship or confiscation of property. Cf. Suetonius, *Claud.* 23.
38 Tacitus, *Ann.* 3,22. Cf. H.F. Hitzig, "Custodia", *RE.* Vol 4,2; 1901, col. 1898.

the normal rule was two[39] — while awaiting trial. The soldiers' duty was to assure that the prisoner appeared before the judge (*exhibitio reorum*) at whatever moment his case came up for examination. If through dereliction of duty, the prisoner had succeeded in escaping, then the surveillants themselves were liable to rather heavy penalties, including corporal punishment and demotion[40]. Those surveillants who had been bribed into allowing the detainee to escape were liable to capital punishment[41]. In view of this, charge over prisoners was not usually confided to raw recruits or other inexperienced soldiers[42].

Custodia militaris was a more lenient type of custody than the rule of *carcer*[43]. The prisoner had some margin of maneuver in choosing his dwelling and could attend to his business or other affairs (*rei suae superesse*) although he remained at all times under guard[44]. Paul had much more privacy under this type of custody than he would have had under the rule of *carcer* and could thus preach, receive visitors, direct the course of his mission through his disciples and perhaps to work at his trade[45]. Luke stressed the lenient conditions under which Paul was held in order to demonstrate for a final time that the Roman authorities did not consider their prisoner to be guilty of any sort of treason which would have led them to have placed the Apostle under a more rigorous type of custody. As such Luke's account clearly implies that there had been a favourable legal conclusion to Paul's appeal to Caesar or at the very least that the worst had been avoided.

D) "outside the barracks"

The Western expansion specifies that Paul's dwelling was outside the Praetorian barracks. There is unfortunately no further evidence which would allow a more specific identification as to where those lodgings actually were.

A certain number of scholars have concluded that Paul's lodgings could only have been located in close proximity to the barracks. So G. Ricciotti: "The house rented by St. Paul was in the immediate neighbourhood of the *Castra*

---

39 *Digesta* 48,3.14.
40 *Digesta* 48,3.12.
41 *Digesta* 48,3.14.
42 *Digesta* 48,3.14.
43 Cf. *Codex Iustinianus* 10,19.2.1: *aperta et libera et in usum hominum instituta*; cf. *Codex Theodosianus* 11,7.3.
44 *Digesta* 4,6.10.
45 H.J. Cadbury, *op.cit.*, pg. 321. Cf. Josephus' account of the conditions of Agrippa's imprisonment in Rome and how they were subsequently altered (*Ant.* 18,203-204; 18,235).

praetoriana from which the Praetorians who alternated in guarding him came"[46]. H. Leclercq, in his magisterial article on St. Paul in the *DACL* even went so far as to assert that Paul's house was doubtlessly within the perimeter of the *Castra praetoriana*[47]. At first glance this theory would seem to be the most reasonable approach to the question. It goes without saying that guarding Paul would have been immensely facilitated by his living in the vicinity of the barracks. On the other hand, no ancient tradition confirms this thesis in any way. While admittedly local traditions, even those venerable with age, can at times be faulty guides, yet the total absence of any tradition associating Paul with a site around the barracks is eloquent, showing as it does that the early Church never thought of Paul as having lived in that area. Moreover, the Praetorian guards were scarcely confined to barracks; they could carry out their duties in all parts of the city. It was not necessary for Paul to live near the barracks to be well guarded by them.

An old tradition associates Paul's lodging with the site in central Rome on which the beautiful, although largely unknown, Rococo church of San Paolo alla Regola now stands. A body of evidence, which we should emphasize is all of a circumstantial nature, tends to support the hypothesis that this is indeed the location of Paul's dwelling.

First of all the Church is located on the via San Paolo alla Regola, an old street running parallel to the Corso Vittorio Emmanuele to its North and perpendicular to the via Arenula to its East from which it is separated by a modern building belonging to the Ministry of Justice. This area is thought to be the place where tanners plied their trade, as it is close by the Tiber. If Paul worked at tentmaking in Rome as he did in Corinth[48], then this section of Rome would have been a suitable one for him to have inhabited, in any case a more suitable location than around the barracks which are eccentric to the city.

A second piece of evidence comes from the late 2nd Century *Martyrium Pauli* which states that Paul rented a grange (*horreum*) in which he taught all those who came to him[49]. Excavations adjacent to the Church, conducted when the Ministry of Justice building was constructed, uncovered ruins believed to be *horrea*. In the same passage, the *Martyrium Pauli* locates Paul's *horreum* outside the City (*extra Urbem*). At the time the *Martyrium Pauli* was composed the expression *extra Urbem* would have meant outside the old Servian Walls. While the Church is in the geographical centre of Rome; still it is outside the Servian Walls.

---

46 G. Ricciotti, *op.cit.*, pg. 426.
47 H. Leclercq, "Paul (Saint)", *DACL*. Vol. 13,2; 1938, col. 2648.
48 Acts 18,3.
49 *Mart. Pauli I.*

Another piece of evidence is that historically San Paolo alla Regola was the only Church within the Aurelian Walls to have been dedicated solely to St. Paul. It also is unique in having within its precincts a *sacellum* bearing the significant titling of *Divi Pauli Apostoli Hospitium et Schola* [50].

Once again we must emphasize the fact that the evidence supporting the theory that San Paolo alla Regola stands on the site of Paul's house is merely circumstantial and not conclusive. Nonetheless the case in its favour is certainly less flawed than that of rival claims, one of which places his house on the site of the present day Church of Santa Maria in via Lata, located on the Corso (*via Flaminia*) in the heart of the city.

III,2. Acts 28,30—31: Paul exercises his ministry at Rome *sine prohibitione*

> "And he lived there two whole years at his own expense, and welcomed all who came to him, preaching the kingdom of God and teaching about the Lord Jesus Christ quite openly and unhindered".

It is with this account of the two-year period Paul spent in Rome awaiting his appeal to be heard that Luke closes Acts. Luke's final verses, while very brief indeed, are nonetheless a precious witness to Paul's sojourn in Rome. They are replete with clear judicial allusions and inferences. The sum total of these indicate that Paul not only was able to continue his Apostolic ministry without there being any crippling legal prohibitions placed on his activities by the custodial authorities, but also that he was eventually released from captivity at the end of the appeals process.

A) "And he lived there two whole years" (ἐνέμεινεν δὲ διετίαν ὅλην)

This little phrase offers two pieces of chronological information. First the verb ἐμμένω is in the Aorist tense meaning that the sojourn being described has ended. Secondly διετία (*biennium*) indicates a two-year period. Luke insists on

---

50 The present *sacellum*, or School of St. Paul, is a small rectangular chapel located to the right of the choir of the main church and partly below present street level. The chapel is very austerely furnished. Above the altar which flanks the shorter wall of the rectangle is a modern mosaic of Paul standing chained to the wall with his Roman guard reclining behind him and looking up at him with awe. On the opposite, rear wall are two modern inscriptions. One has the text of Acts 28,30, the other states that this was where Paul lodged during his first Roman captivity. In the apse of the main Church there are three large paintings by Luigi Garzi, a sadly neglected 17th Century Roman religious painter, depicting Paul's conversion, his preaching the Gospel and a rare portrayal of his decapitation.

the fact that the period was two *complete* years by qualifying the noun with the adjective ὅλος (*totus*)[51]. The mention of a *biennium* is more than a simple chronological indication of the length of Paul's first captivity in Rome. There existed in Roman juridical use fixed time limits of varying length, by the end of which accusers were obliged to appear in the court of appeals to renew the charges they had lodged against the accused in a lower court. Philo mentions just such a two-year period in his account of Lampo's trial[52]. Pliny also mentions a *biennium* when talking about another case[53]. There is an extant edict, the *Edictum de temporibus accusationum*[54], which sets specific time limits which both accuser and accused had to respect in appellate cases heard by the imperial tribunal. The maximum delays accorded both parties to appear in capital cases were 9 months for parties living in Italy and a year and a half for those outside Italy. The edict's date is uncertain, but one as early as the 1st Century is not to be excluded.

B) "at his own expense" (ἐν ἰδίῳ μισθώματι)

The principal meaning of this word is "price agreed on in hiring" or "contract price"[55]. It can also designate the contract itself and much less frequently "rent"[56]. The Vg. translates this verse as *mansit autem biennio toto in suo conducto*. The noun *conductum* can mean a lease or contract, but also a rented residence or lodging[57]. It is clear that the Vg. understanding of the passage is that the Apostle lived in his own hired house. The controversy over whether the Greek means wages or hired lodgings obscures the real message Luke is conveying to his readers. The use of the word μίσθωμα is first and foremost *juridical*. Paul is not being held under the rule of *carcer*, but under the more lenient *custodia militaris*. The conclusion which Luke wishes his readers to draw is that if the Apostle is in this type of custody it is because the Roman authorities deemed him no threat to the public order or common weal, nor was his missionary work considered seditious in nature:

---

51 Cf. Josephus, *Ant.* 2,74; *P. Ryl.* 169,16; *P. Oxy.* 707,24.
52 Philo, *in Flaccum* 16,128-129.
53 Pliny, *Ep.* 10,56.
54 *BGU.* 2,628.
55 *LS9*, pg. 1137. In Herodotus 2,180, the term designates the costs of finishing the temple of Delphi.
56 *IG.* 12(7),55.15. Cf. *P. Oxy.* 707,24 where the word means a specific rent as set forth in a lease.
57 Cf. Cicero, *pro Cluentio* 175; Seneca, *de Beneficiis* 7,5.3. The *conductor* was one who rented a house, that is the lessee.

"The language of paying rent μίσθωμα is itself civil, but points to a certain status granted to a prisoner appealing against a criminal charge".[58]

C) "'and welcomed all those who came to him, preaching the kingdom of God and teaching about the Lord Jesus Christ"

The terms of his custody allowed the Apostle not only the opportunity of renting his own lodgings and of earning wages, but more importantly of continuing his Apostolic ministry. Luke uses three verbs in this passage to summarize Paul's missionary programme in Rome:

1. ἀποδέχομαι — to welcome someone, to receive favourably. The Christian welcome is extended to all (πάντας). Luke wishes to express the idea of universality even though it is clear from his own account that the Pauline mission in Rome was mainly directed towards the Gentiles[59].

2. κηρύσσω — to announce, make known, proclaim; here to proclaim the Kingdom of God. Paul is ever faithful to his calling as herald of the Good News; in these his latter years, herald in the Latin West.

3. διδάσκω — to teach; here about the Lord Jesus Christ. But as we have seen, teaching that there was another King was a very dangerous thing to do.

D) "quite openly" (μετὰ πάσης παρρησίας)

The basic meaning of the word παρρησία is outspokenness, freely speaking, a frankness of speech which "conceals nothing and passes over nothing"[60]. The word occurs over 30 times in the New Testament; nearly half of these occurrences are in the Johannine literature. The term is used a mere five times in Acts and occurs not at all in Luke's Gospel.

The term has two rather distinct meanings in the New Testament[61]. Firstly it expresses the idea of openness, that is openness to the public before whom a speech or deed takes place. The stress is on speaking in public or publicly, making something known openly. In Jn. 7,4, Jesus' brothers say to Him: "For no man works in secret (ἐν κρυπτῷ) if he seeks to be known openly (ἐν παρρησίᾳ). If you do these things show yourself to the world". The same idea

---

58 D.L. Mealand, "The Close of Acts and its Hellenistic Greek Vocabulary", *NTS*. Vol. 36; 1990, pg. 586.

59 J. Dupont notes that the adjective "stresses the inclusion of the Gentiles, but this inclusion does not entail any exclusion" (J. Dupont, "La Conclusion des Actes et son rapport à l'ensemble de l'ouvrage de Luc", (in) *Les Actes des Apôtres: Tradition, Rédaction, Théologie*, Louvain, 1979, pg. 377.

60 Arndt and Gingrich, pg. 635.

61 P. Joüon, "Divers sens de 'Parresia' dans le Nouveau Testament", *RSR*, Vol. 30; 1940, pg. 239.

is present in Jn. 18,20: where Jesus says: "I have spoken openly to the world; I have always taught in synagogues and in the temple, where all Jews come together, I have said nothing secretly". What Luke wishes to underline when he uses this term at the end of Acts is that Paul's ministry in Rome was public and not secret, he was allowed by the custodial authorities to conduct his ministry openly; he was not forced to go into clandestinity to carry out his missionary programme. The term παρρησία here then has an apologetic nuance about it.

It also has a definite juridical shade of meaning as well. The word παρρησία also denotes an outspokenness, a confidence (cf. Latin *fiducia*), a bold and free speaking, a freedom of speech (*liberior sermo, libertas*). In the *Republic*, Plato noted that liberty, freedom of speech and freedom of action were the privileges of a democratic society[62]. For Euripides, Athens was glorious because its sons were free with unfettered tongues[63]. Freedom of speech was a privilege enjoyed by the Athenians, a privilege inherent in their citizenship in the *polis*; the characteristic which distinguished the free Athenian citizen from the slave who had no political rights at all[64]. So Euripides writes:

"Of Athens daughters may my mother be,
That by my mother may free speech be mine.
The alien who entereth a burg (πόλιν)
of pure blood, burgher though he be in name,
hath not free speech; he bears a bondsman's tongue".[65]

It is clear that the concept of παρρησία as a political and juridical prerogative of a free citizen was firmly established in Greek constitutional practice long before New Testament times.

The term παρρησία retained this juridical and political sense in Paul's time as well. For Philo, παρρησία was reserved for the virtuous and righteous whose life's work serves the common good of all mankind:

"But let those whose actions serve the common weal use freedom of speech (παρρησία) and walk in daylight through the midst of the market-place, ready to converse with crowded gatherings, to let the clear sunlight shine upon their own life and through the two most royal senses, sight and hearing, to render good service to the assembled groups ..."[66]

In Acts, Luke uses the term παρρησία in a kerygmatic and didactic, as well as juridical, context. It is an essential characteristic of Christian Apostleship

---

[62] Plato, *Respublica* 557 B; cf. Polybius 2,38.6.
[63] Euripides, *Hippolytus* 422.
[64] Cf. Leviticus 26,13 (*LXX*).
[65] Euripides, *Ion* 671-675 (*trans.* A.D. Way, *Loeb*, 1958). In *Phoenissae* 390-391, Euripides noted that the worst sting of exile was the lack of freedom of speech.
[66] Philo, *de Spec. Legibus* 1,321 (*trans.* F.H. Colson, *Loeb*, 1958).

and Christian mission; indeed the term is often used with a verb denoting speaking such as εἰπεῖν or λαλεῖν[67]. The παρρησία is a gift of the Holy Spirit[68] and allows the disciple to make his confession of faith that Jesus is the Messiah and Saviour of the world[69]. This proclamation is not only made before ordinary listeners, but also directed to the political and judicial authorities; e.g. Peter and John before the Sanhedrin[70], Paul before King Agrippa [71]. In Ephesians, Paul writes that it is in Christ that we have confidence, through faith in Him we have access to God[72]. It is precisely this *fiducia* which enables the Christian to appear before his judges and testify without flinching even when threatened with the death penalty[73].

By using the term παρρησία when describing Paul's first captivity in Rome, Luke stressed first of all how Paul's Roman citizenship gained for him crucial juridical and political rights *vis-à-vis* the authorities. He underlined the consideration Paul was held in by the authorities and the benevolence they showed the Apostle. Finally Luke strongly implied that Paul was released from captivity at the end of the *biennium* and completely recovered his freedom of movement.

E) "unhindered" (ἀκωλύτως)

This is the only time the word ἀκωλύτως appears in the New Testament. Luke closes his two-volume work with this term which E. Delebecque, in his monumental study of the textual tradition of Acts, quite appropriately describes as a "beautiful Platonic adverb ... so rich in meaning"[74]. It is indeed a word rich in nuance for in closing his account of Paul's sojourn in Rome with the term ἀκωλύτως, Luke has quite purposefully chosen to end on both a theological and juridical note:

> "The text ends on a note of *unhindered freedom* just as a medical treatise of Plutarch ends with the thought of the unhindered exercise of virtue. Here however it is not virtue which

---

67 Cf. Acts 2,29: "I may speak to you confidently"; Acts 4,29: "to speak thy word with all boldness"; Acts 4,31: "spoke the word of God with boldness".
68 Acts 4,31.
69 H. Schlier points out that the presupposition of παρρησία is 'righteousness'. It is the righteous man who has it, not the impious (H. Schlier, "*Parresia*", *ThWb.* Vol. 5; 1967, pg. 876).
70 Acts 4,13.
71 Acts 26,26.
72 Eph. 3,12.
73 H. Schlier notes that παρρησία is the courage of openness or candour: "This candour opposes all those who would limit the right to reveal the truth or hamper the unveiling of the truth, especially the *tyrannos*" (H. Schlier, *op.cit.*, pg. 873).
74 E. Delebecque, *Les deux Actes des Apôtres*, Paris, 1986, pg. 159.

is in mind, but the message of God's reign. It is this proclamation which goes on unstopped. The Greeks acknowledged that Fate or Destiny or the gods act without let or hindrance. Here the author of Acts directs the attention of his readers to the proclamation of God's reign and teaching about the Lord Jesus as something which is unchecked, unstopped, unhindered".[75]

The term ἀκωλύτως appears frequently in legal documents in the sense of 'without let' or 'without hindrance' (*sine prohibitione*) [76]. Once again Luke stressed the lenient custody under which Paul was held, a custody which allowed the Apostle to preach freely, without constraint, save that of house arrest. By allowing the Apostle to preach freely, were not the authorities in fact demonstrating that they did not consider his ministry as a seditious activity, his proclamation of Jesus as a crime of majesty or his leadership of a Christian community as treasonable? This was just the apologetic message Luke was striving to convey to his readers: Paul was innocent of any crime of majesty against the Emperor or treason against the State. Indeed in Luke's view there was no overriding reason why the Roman State and Christian Church could not co-exist in peace.

IV. The Witness of The Captivity Epistles I

The four Captivity Epistles, Colossians, Philemon, Ephesians and Philippians, which Paul wrote in Rome while awaiting his appeal to the imperial court to be heard, are, chronologically speaking, the last of the genuine Pauline Epistles. All four Epistles are distinctly Pauline in their theology, Christology, in their sacramental and liturgical witness and in their general thought and purport. A freshness and newness characterize them. How marvellous this is, all the more so when one considers that they came from the pen of an aged man under house arrest! In writing these letters, Paul was addressing himself to a new Christian generation and to the changing circumstances of the Church and its mission. Despite his status as an appellant prisoner, Paul was still very much in control of his Apostolate. In this the Captivity Epistles are quite concordant with Luke's witness in Acts.

The Captivity Epistles do not supply us with a tremendous quantity of evidence relating to Paul's juridical situation or his future prospects. Yet they contain enough references, as brief as they may be, to cast a little light on Paul's first Roman captivity.

---

75 D.D. Mealand, *op.cit.*, pg. 596.
76 Cf. *P. Oxy.* 502,29-31; *P. Lips.* 26,11; *BGU.* 3,917.14. Cf. Josephus, *Ant.* 16,41 where the author relates the plea made by Nicholas of Damascus to Marcus Agrippa that the Jews of Ionia be allowed to preserve and practice their ancestral religion "without hindrance".

IV,1. The *Epistle to the Colossians*

Paul's epistle to the Church at Colossae, as brief and succinct as it is, yet so rich in its Christology and profound in its meditation of the mystery of Salvation, contains some of the Apostle's own reflections on his personal situation:

A) Paul, nearing the end of his life and work, assimilates his sufferings to Christ's:

> "Now I rejoice in my sufferings (παθήμασιν) for your sake, and in my flesh I complete what is lacking in Christ's afflictions (ἀνταναπληρῶ τὰ ὑστερήματα τῶν θλίψεων τοῦ Χριστοῦ ἐν τῇ σαρκί μου) for the sake of his body, that is the church".[77]

1. τὸ πάθημα — suffering, affliction, that which is suffered. Paul used the term to describe Christ's sufferings in 2 Cor. 1,5. Cf. the related work παθητός — *destined* to suffer, which Luke employed in reference to Christ in Acts 26,23. In Lk. 22,15 and 24,26 the verb πάσχω takes on the meaning of suffering death.

2. ἀνταναπληρόω — to complete, to fill up. This is the only occurrence of this word in the NT. It does not appear at all in the *Septuaginta* and rarely figures in the Greek writers.

3. τὸ ὑστέρημα — shortcoming, deficiency, need. U. Wilckens, after noting that Col. 1,24 is "difficult and much contested", writes:

> "As Epaphroditus in Phil. 2,30 fills up the ὑστέρημα of the church in his own person as their envoy, so Paul as an Apostle of Christ represents the exalted Kurios to the Church. But the lack which he fills up herein consists in the θλίψεις τοῦ Χριστοῦ which the Apostle takes upon himself in his sufferings (παθήματα) in his physical, earthly life. Christ Himself, whom he has to proclaim (v. 23,25—27), is now in Heaven (vv. 15—20) as the Head of His body, the Church (v. 18). As such He has overcome His sufferings. His place on earth, the place of His sufferings, is now taken by the Apostle, who is honoured to be able to suffer for the Church as the body of Christ"[78]

4. ἡ θλῖψις — properly speaking, this noun signifies a pressure, compression or squeezing. In metaphorical usage it denotes an affliction, or an anguish of heart or mind (so 2 Cor. 2,4: "I wrote you out of much affliction and anguish of heart"), trial, tribulation or distressing circumstances. Cf. Mt. 24,9: "Then they will deliver you up to tribulation, and put you to death".

In Colossians, Paul understands his Apostolic ministry as essentially to "make the Word of God fully known"[79], that is "the mystery hidden for ages

---

77 Col. 1,24.
78 U. Wilckens, "hysteros, ktl.", *ThWb*. Vol. 8; 1972; pg. 599-600.
79 Col. 1,25.

and generations, but now made manifest to his saints"[80]. In fulfilling that ministry, he was destined to share Christ's tribulations and to endure persecution and death because Christ also endured them in His ministry[81]. That Paul's part is to share in these tribulations is neither unique to him nor is it surprising, for affliction is the normal Christian condition in this sinful world until the return of Christ at the end of time. Paul's existence as a Christian believer and especially his particular ministry of Apostle inexorably lead him to suffer persecution and violent death as Christ did. This is the very essence of the Apostle's mystical union with his Lord. Sufferings and martyrdom do not, however, frighten the Apostle; rather he rejoiced in them. As John Chrysostom put it so poetically:

> "Thus he willingly embraced these sufferings and his chains were to him an ornament more glorious than the diadem which crowned Nero's head".[82]

Paul's sufferings were for the sake of the Church, the body of Christ on earth[83]. He is the model of perseverance and of faithfulness till the end. His attitude toward suffering, persecution and death are guides for succeeding generations of Christians. The importance of Col. 1,24 lies in the explanation, both personal and theological, which Paul gives to the Church about the real meaning and significance of his present tribulations and coming martyrdom.

B) It is clear from the *Epistle to the Colossians* that Paul is a prisoner. In his exhortation in Chapter 4, the Apostle bids the faithful at Colossae to "pray for us also that God may open to us a door for the word, on account of which I am in prison (δι' ὃ καὶ δέδεμαι)"[84]. When mentioning Aristarchus, Paul calls him "my fellow-prisoner (ὁ συναιχμάλωτος)"[85]. In the closing verse of the Epistle, which Paul says he wrote with his own hand, he asks the Colossians to remember "my fetters (τῶν δεσμῶν)"[86].

1. ὁ συναιχμάλωτος — In Rom. 16,7, Paul asks the Romans to greet Andronicus and Junias, "my kinsmen and my fellow-prisoners". In Phlm. 23, it is Epaphras who is Paul's fellow-prisoner and who sends his greetings. Here it is Aristarchus, "my fellow-prisoner", who transmits his greetings. The word

---

80 Col. 1,26.
81 Cf. 1 Thess. 3,3.
82 John Chrysostom, *de Laudibus Pauli*, Homily 2 (*PG.* 50, col. 480).
83 Cf. 2 Cor. 1,5-6; Rom. 5,3.
84 Col. 4,3.
85 Col. 4,10.
86 Col. 4,18.

συναιχμάλωτος occurs only thrice in the NT, all in the Pauline Epistle in the context of extending greetings.

The term itself is of military origin. The verb αἰχμάζω means to throw a spear; αἰχμαλωτίζω — to take prisoner; αἰχμάλωτος is the captive or prisoner (taken by the spear). The συν-prefix, of course, adjoins the idea of fellowship to the root verb; thus συναιχμαλωτίζω — to take captive along with; συναιχμάλωτος — a fellow-captive. The word συναιχμάλωτος, however, is quite rare even in the classical Greek writers[87].

Paul's use of the term here is not to be taken literally, for it does not express a formal judicial co-detention. Rather the Apostle employed the word in a figurative sense as a synonym to σύνδουλος ἐν κυρίῳ[88]. Had he wished to express the idea that Aristarchus was under house arrest in Rome along with him, the Apostle would have used other compounds such as συνδέσμιος or συνδεσμώτης, all the more so as he had already used the term δέσμιος to indicate his legal status[89] and not the word αἰχμάλωτος[90]. Despite the relatively mild conditions of his custody, Paul was a prisoner at Rome and this fact was very much on his mind when he wrote the Epistle.

2. Paul's partners in labour in Rome: The *Epistle to the Colossians* closes with the Apostle's transmitting personal messages and greetings. Many of his closest and dearest συνεργοί were in Rome with him at that time and shared in those greetings.

First and foremost was Timothy, "our brother", co-sender of the Epistle [91], Paul's most cherished disciple[92]. Tychicus, the "beloved brother", "faithful minister", and "fellow servant in the Lord"[93] has been sent by Paul along with Onesimus, a Colossian, "the faithful and beloved brother"[94], to deliver the Epistle to its destination; they are additionally charged with telling the

---

87 Cf. Ps-Lucian, *Asinus* 27, where the term unambiguously designates the person sharing captivity.
88 G. Kittel, "aixmalatos, ktl.", *ThWb*. Vol. 1; 1964; pg. 197. Kittel notes in the same passage that the συν- compound words " ... are not applied to all fellow-workers, but have a special emphasis which singles out individuals".
89 Cf. Eph. 3,1; 4,1; Phlm. 1; Phlm. 9.
90 The noun αἰχμάλωτος occurs only in Lk. 4,18 where the Evangelist quotes Is. 61,1. The verb αἰχμαλωτίζω occurs 4 times in the NT. In Rom. 7,23: "captive to the law of sin", in 2 Cor. 10,5 there is the same type of metaphorical usage: "and take every thought captive to obey Christ". Luke uses the verb in its true sense of taking prisoners of war when he relates Jesus' prophecy of Jerusalem's destruction (Lk. 21,24).
91 Col. 1,1.
92 Cf. Phil. 2,19-24; Acts 16,1-3; 1 Cor. 4,17; 10,10-11; 1 Thess. 3,2-6.
93 Cf. Acts 20,4.
94 Col. 4,9.

Colossians "of everything that has taken place here"[95]. Aristarchus[96], Mark[97] and Jesus Justus[98] are also mentioned; these were the only Jews in Paul's inner circle in Rome. Paul terms them his "fellow workers for the kingdom of God" and says that "they have been a comfort to me"[99]. Mark appears here with Paul in Rome; Paul mentions him again in the *Epistle to Philemon* as being in Rome[100] and he is also named as being with Peter in that city in 1 Pet. 5.13. Paul transmits the greetings of Epaphras[101]. This disciple, a Colossian himself, was the man who evangelized Colossae[102] as well as Laodicaea and Hierapolis[103]. Luke, "the beloved physician", faithful companion of Paul's joys and sorrows, is mentioned next along with Demas, the only man in the list about whom Paul says nothing at all except to assure the Colossians of his greetings[104]. Paul's uncharacteristically cold treatment of Demas strongly suggests a deterioration in their relations, a theme which is expanded upon in the Pastoral Epistles[105].

Paul then was surrounded by a substantial group of co-workers and through them was able to direct a mission having a wide geographical scope. The *Epistle to the Colossians* conveys the idea that the Apostle's custody was quite lenient. He was able to receive his friends, exhort, teach, send letters to the Churches and supervise the missionary activity of his fellow servants in the Lord.

IV,2. The *Epistle to Philemon*

This stirring appeal written to Philemon on behalf of Paul's child in God, Onesimus, also contains information about the Apostle's imprisonment. The notice which Paul gives about his situation in Rome is similar to that given the Colossians, except here the Apostle expressed the hope of visiting Philemon after his release: "At the same time, prepare a guest room for me, for I am hoping through your prayers to be granted to you"[106]. This is a fairly strong

---

95 Col. 4,9.
96 Cf. Acts 19,28; 20,6.
97 Cf. Acts 12,12; 12,25; 13,13; 15,37-38.
98 Otherwise unknown in the NT.
99 Col. 4,10-11.
100 Phlm. 24.
101 Col. 4,13.
102 Col. 1,7.
103 Col. 4,13.
104 Col. 4,14.
105 2 Tim. 4,10 relates Demas' desertion of Paul during the latter's second Roman captivity.
106 Phlm. 22.

indication that Paul planned another trip to the East. Does this mean that the Apostle had abandoned his earlier idea of evangelizing Spain? There is no evidence that Paul had decided to substitute a journey to the East, where he had completed his mission, for his intended journey to Spain, a new missionary field. It is more likely that the Apostle, being an energetic man and indefatigable in the pursuit of his Apostolate, would have wished to have undertaken both journeys. In any case, the Epistle suggests that Paul was expecting release once his appeal had been heard.

A) Paul makes multiple references to his imprisonment in the *Epistle to Philemon*. He calls himself a "prisoner (δέσμιος) for Christ Jesus" on two occasions[107]. He states that he became Onesimus' spiritual father "in my imprisonment (ἐν τοῖς δεσμοῖς)"[108]. Paul strongly desired to keep Onesimus with him in Rome "in order that he might serve me on your behalf during my imprisonment for the Gospel (ἐν τοῖς δεσμοῖς τοῦ εὐαγγελίου)"[109]. Nonetheless the Apostle decided to send the slave back to his lawful master. From the legal point of view, the last thing that it behooved an appellant prisoner to do was to keep a fugitive slave with him as this act would make him guilty of a serious infraction of the law.

B) Like Colossians, the *Epistle to Philemon* conveys the idea that Paul's conditions of custody were mild. First as he himself notes, he was able to write to Philemon with his own hand[110]. Secondly he mentions a group of fellow workers around him in Rome who were helping in the missionary work. The list is shorter than that figuring in Colossians and terser in its description of the people mentioned, but all those cited in Philemon also figure in Colossians. This is a strong indication that both Epistles were written about the same time and in the same conditions. Once again the beloved Timothy figures as the principal co-worker and he joins the Apostle in sending the letter to Philemon[111]. Epaphras, "my fellow prisoner in Christ Jesus (ὁ συναιχμάλωτός μου ἐν Χριστῷ Ἰησοῦ)"[112], is with the Apostle as are four fellow workers (συνεργοί): Mark, Aristarchus, Demas and Luke[113].

---

107 Phlm. 1; Phlm. 9.
108 Phlm. 10.
109 Phlm. 13.
110 Phlm. 19.
111 Phlm. 1.
112 Phlm. 23.
113 Phlm. 24.

IV,3. The *Epistle to the Ephesians*

This great Epistle is Paul's ultimate meditation on the mystery of God's plan of Salvation, hidden for generations, realized in Christ Jesus, revealed to the Apostles, lived in the Church, the body of Christ. In this Epistle, the aged Paul, nearing the end of his life, addresses the critical situation in which the Church finds itself at the end of the Apostolic period. Ephesians is Paul's final exhortation to and blessing on the universal Church. It is a powerful celebration of Divine Grace and the Apostle's belief in redemption in Christ alone. It is a formulation in a few chapters of Paul's profoundest thoughts on the mystery of the union of Christ and His Church, whose members — the baptized — are to build up this terrestrial body of Christ in unity and love until the fullness of time[114].

"To the Ephesians" is surely a misnomer for this Epistle. Paul does not seem to know the addressees of the Epistle[115] which would exclude the Ephesian Church as the true recipient of the letter. It would seem more reasonable in fact to identify this letter with the *Epistle to the Laodicaeans* which Paul mentions that he wrote in Col. 4,16. But in fact, the Epistle was not really addressed to one local community whatever its original destination may have been. Ephesians is an Epistle-circular which addresses not the doctrinal or ecclesiological problems of a particular congregation, but rather formulates responses to the real spiritual and practical needs of the universal Church at the very moment in which the Apostles themselves were passing from the scene.

A) Although Ephesians contains much less information about Paul's imprisonment and future prospects than Colossians, the little description it does provide indicates that it was written at the same time and in the same conditions as Colossians and Philemon. Paul refers to his status as prisoner three times in this letter. In Eph. 4,1, the Apostle calls himself a "prisoner for the Lord (ὁ δέσμος ἐν κυρίῳ)". In Eph. 3,1 he is even more specific: "I, Paul, a prisoner for Christ Jesus on behalf of you Gentiles (ὁ δέσμιος τοῦ Χριστοῦ Ἰησοῦ ὑπὲρ ὑμῶν τῶν ἐθνῶν)". Finally in Eph. 6,19—20, the Apostle asks the prayers and supplications of his readers "that utterance may be given me in opening my mouth boldly (ἐν παρρησίᾳ) to proclaim the mystery of the Gospel, for which I am an ambassador in chains (ὑπὲρ οὗ πρεσβεύω ἐν ἁλύσει); that I may declare it boldly (παρρησιάσωμαι), as I ought to speak".

---

114 Eph. 1,9-10.
115 Eph. 1,15.

1) ἐν παρρησίᾳ/παρρησιάσωμαι — The similitude of Paul's language here to the closing verses of Acts is clear and significant. Despite his status as a prisoner Paul has the freedom to proclaim the Gospel *cum fiducia* without let or hindrance.

2) ὑπὲρ οὗ πρεσβεύω ἐν ἁλύσει — (cf. Vg. = *pro quo legatione fungor in catena*).

a) πρεσβεύω — to be an elder or ambassador, to perform the duties of an ambassador (πρέσβυς). Paul had previously used the term when describing his functions in 2 Cor. 5,20: "So we are ambassadors for Christ, God making His appeal through us. We beseech you on behalf of Christ, be reconciled to God".

The word contains the nuance of a superior place in a hierarchical order, i.e. to rank before, to put first in rank, to take precedence, to rule over; cf. the special usage at Rome: "to act as *legatus* [116]. Although chained to his guards (an ironical place for a πρέσβυς to be, at least in the human order of things!), Paul is still carrying out his Apostolate. In fact being in chains did not lessen the Apostle's role or rank: he is still head of his community and directing its mission not only in Rome, but in the Christian *oikoumené* as well.

b) ἡ ἅλυσις — Paul is chained with the ἅλυσις (hand chain) to the attending Praetorian guards in conformity with the conditions of *custodia militaris*.

B) Except for Tychicus, no other disciple is mentioned in the Epistle. Paul is not transmitting greetings to a specific local Christian community so it is not altogether surprising that a list of his co-workers is missing from the concluding chapter of Ephesians. Tychicus' mission is the same as in Colossians and Philemon. This "beloved brother" and "faithful minister in the Lord" is being sent to the recipients to tell them "how I am and what I am doing"[117]. In fact in the next verse Paul specifically defines Tychicus' mission: "I have sent him to you for this very purpose, that you may know how we are, and that he may encourage your hearts"[118].

V. The Witness of the Captivity Epistles II:
The Epistle to the Philippians

Numerous scholars have dismissed the traditional teaching that the Apostle Paul composed Philippians while awaiting trial in Rome. In their view

---
116 *LS*⁹. pg. 1462.
117 Eph. 6,21.
118 Eph. 6,22.

Philippians has many more affinities to Galatians and to 1 and 2 Corinthians than it does to the other Captivity Epistles. Therefore they would assign the date of the Epistle's composition to Paul's imprisonment in Caesarea or to an even earlier, unknown imprisonment in Ephesus.

Perceived thematic similitudes do not necessarily provide as cogent an argument against a Roman origin for the letter *ad Philippenses* as some exegetes would like, for, as P.T. O'Brien has recently reminded us, "parallel ideas, phrases and vocabulary are spread throughout Paul's letters"[119]. Moreover one has to keep in mind the sad temptation of tendentiousness on the part of some exegetes, a tendentiousness born largely of modern polemical motives and concerns and which has as its goal, in the case at hand, to diminish the importance of the role which Rome played in Paul's ministry. The fact of the matter is that the personal and legal situation which the Apostle himself describes as being his in the *Epistle to the Philippians* can only reasonably be dated to his two-year stay in Rome. The Epistle's own internal evidence does in quite an unmistakeable way confirm Tradition here: that Paul did indeed compose Philippians while a prisoner in Rome. Moreover Philippians provides some clear indications that it may very well have been the *last* of the Captivity Epistles, chronologically speaking, written, not at the outset, but at the end of the two-year captivity, that is about the year 62 A.D.

V,1. *In omni Praetorio*

In Philippians, as in the other Captivity Epistles, Paul emphasizes that he is a prisoner. But he is perhaps even more emphatic about his status in this respect in Philippians than in the other Captivity Epistles: in a few verses in Chapter I of the Epistle, Paul repeats four times that he is "in imprisonment". Doubtlessly the length of his detention coupled with its approaching legal conclusion caused the fact of his imprisonment to weigh more heavily on his mind than hitherto and consequently appear in a more emphatic way in the Epistle:

A) *Phil. 1,7*: "It is right for me to feel thus about you all, because I hold you in my heart, for you are all partakers with me of grace, both in my imprisonment (ἐν τε τοῖς δεσμοῖς μου) and in the defense and confirmation of the Gospel (καὶ ἐν τῇ ἀπολογίᾳ καὶ βεβαιώσει τοῦ εὐαγγελίου)."

---

119 P.T. O'Brien, *The Epistle to the Philippians*, Grand Rapids (Michigan), 1991, pg. 23.

The verse's syntax is clear. The grace (χάρις) refers equally to the chains and to the defence/confirmation. The Philippians share in both imprisonment and in evangelical labour, as, on the one hand they were alleviating Paul in his imprisonment while at the same time carrying out their own mission of evangelization and teaching. They are thus truly partakers with him of the Divine grace, the grace manifested in both Paul's chains and in his apostolic labour.

1. ἐν τε τοῖς δεσμοῖς μου
Here Paul reiterates his situation at Rome. He is a prisoner awaiting the pleasure of the imperial tribunal.

2. ἐν τῇ ἀπολογίᾳ καὶ βεβαιώσει τοῦ εὐαγγελίου
Both nouns have a double meaning in this verse. Paul had the freedom to preach and teach the Gospel to any and all who would come to him. But the ἀπολογία τοῦ εὐαγγελίου was also his plea in court, the legal *defensio* against the charges laid before the judge by his accusers. If Paul could successfully defend the Gospel in the imperial tribunal in Rome, then the Gospel itself would be confirmed in the eyes of society by a favourable decision of the court.

B) *Phil. 1,12—14*: 'I want you to know, brethren, that what has happened to me has really served to advance the Gospel, so that it has become known throughout the whole Praetorian Guard and to all the rest, that my imprisonment is for Christ; (ὥστε τοὺς δεσμούς μου φανεροὺς ἐν Χριστῷ γενέσθαι ἐν ὅλῳ τῷ πραιτωρίῳ καὶ τοῖς λοιποῖς πᾶσιν)".

1. ἐν ὅλῳ τῷ πραιτωρίῳ (Vg. = *in omni praetorio*)
The word πραιτώριον, a transliteration of the Latin *praetorium*, has several shades of meaning. It originally designated the place in the camp where the General had his tent; by extension it came to designate the house and tribunal of the Praetor. The term was also used to describe the official residence of a provincial Governor. Cicero used the word in just that sense in the *Verrines*, when he noted that Verres had taken up official residence *in domo praetorio quae regis Hieronis fuit*[120]. In like manner the term appears in the Gospel accounts of our Lord's Passion: Jesus' case was heard by the Prefect, Pontius Pilate, in the Jerusalem Praetorium[121]. In Acts, Luke reports that after his arrest in Jerusalem, Paul was transferred to the jurisdiction of Felix, Procurator of Judaea, whose seat was in Caesarea. Felix ordered the Apostle to be held in

---

120 Cicero, *Verr*. II,v.31.80.
121 Mt. 27,27; Mk. 15,16; Jn. 18,28; 18,33; 19,9.

Herod's Praetorium while awaiting the arrival of his accusers from Jerusalem to come and press their case in the procuratorial court [122].

In Rome, the term designated both the Praetorian Guard and sometimes its barracks[123] as well as the imperial bodyguard[124]. As we have seen, Paul had been led to the Praetorium on arriving in Rome and had been found innocuous enough to be placed in *custodia militaris* instead of being incarcerated in the barracks' dungeons. He was thus well known in the Praetorium as was the reason for his imprisonment. The word Praetorium as used in Phil. 1,13 refers to the imperial authorities in overall charge of Paul's case and more specifically to the custodians (*Praetoriani*) mandated to keep him under guard until his case could be heard.

Paul did not state that he had actually converted any of his guards as later legends were wont to state. He limited himself to saying that it had become φανερός (= clear, conspicuous, well-known, manifest) that he was imprisoned ἐν Χριστῷ. Paul's affirmation was not only theological, i.e. that he was sharing in Christ's sufferings, but eminently juridical as well. Paul's preaching (the defence of the Gospel) and his teaching about Jesus Christ (the confirmation of the Gospel) had not given rise to any fears in the Praetorium that he was engaged in a seditious activity or that through this preaching and teaching he was consciously and intentionally demeaning the Emperor's majesty. The verse strongly implies just the contrary: that there was a respect for and an interest in Paul's ministry on the part of the Praetorians. Paul's captivity then had not hindered the spread of the Good News at Rome; rather it had greatly aided his evangelical labours. Paul could thus write in Phil. 1,12 without any exaggeration: "what has happened to me (τὰ κατ' ἐμέ) has really served to advance the Gospel". While, from a purely linguistic point of view, the idiom τὰ κατ' ἐμέ is a general one for expressing how someone is or what his circumstances are, Paul is specifically alluding here to his appeal to Caesar, that great providential leap which brought him to Rome and into direct contact with the Praetorium and Caesar's household [125]. Paul's defence of the Gospel before the Empire's supreme judicial instance could only have had the effect of making the Gospel better known and causing its progress or furtherance (i.e. ἡ προκοπή τοῦ εὐαγγέλιου):

---

122 Acts 23,35. The Praetorium to which Luke was referring in that passage was the palace built by Herod the Great in Caesarea for his own use and subsequently taken over by the Governors of Judaea to be used as their official residence.

123 Cf. *OGIS*. 707.

124 Cf. Bo Reicke, "Caesarea, Rome and the Captivity Epistles", (in) *APOSTOLIC HISTORY AND THE GOSPEL*, Exeter, 1970, pg. 283.

125 Cf. Col. 4,7 where Paul uses this same expression when talking about his legal situation. Cf. Eph. 6,21. Luke also uses it when talking about Paul's case in Acts 25,14.

"Here the expression has to do with the result of Paul's circumstances, while the perfect tense ἐλήλυθεν draws attention to the continuing effects and how the matter now stands, that is, 'has redounded, has served' to advance the Gospel. For Paul this goal overrides all else; personal inconveniences, sufferings, and imprisonment serve this end".[126]

2. Καὶ τοῖς λοιποῖς πᾶσιν

Not only were the Praetorians favourably impressed by Paul's defence and confirmation of the Gospel, but also those beyond the Praetorium, that is the members of the divided Christian community at Rome and especially the part of that community which was receiving Paul's message with joy: "and most of the brethren (καὶ τοὺς πλείονας τῶν ἀδελφῶν) have been made confident in the Lord because of my imprisonment and are much more bold to speak the word of God without fear (ἀφόβως τὸν λόγον τοῦ Θεοῦ λαλεῖν)"[127].

a) καὶ τοὺς πλείονας τῶν ἀδελφῶν — the majority, the greater number, the more in quantity, the greater part.

While Paul seems to have rallied the majority of the Roman Christian community to his side and to have instilled in them renewed confidence, it is clear that the community was badly divided. Paul had not succeeded in rallying the totality of the brethren. The Judeo-Christians remained estranged from Paul and this was most dangerous to the Apostle.

b) ἀφόβως τὸν λόγον τοῦ Θεοῦ λαλεῖν (ἀφόβως — fearlessly, intrepidly, boldly). Paul's use of this adverb here recalls Luke's expression μετὰ πάσης παρρησίας in Acts 28,31.

The dangers alluded to here do not come from the civil authorities whom both Paul and Luke described as benevolent toward the Pauline mission. The hostility originated with the synagogal leadership who had rejected Paul's message at the beginning of his two-year stay in Rome and from the Judeo-Christians influenced by that leadership. Yet Paul's very presence in Rome, his continuing Apostolic labours and the kind treatment he received on the part of Roman officialdom had stimulated the Gentile Christians to go out and preach the Word of God *sine timore*. No longer were these brethren— the majority according to Paul — intimidated by the risk of imprisonment or by the unrelenting hostility of the Judeo-Christians. Rather, they were encouraged to imitate the Apostle in his work and to partake of his ministry.

---

126 P.T. O'Brien, *op.cit.*, pg. 91.
127 Phil. 1,14.

3. ὥστε τοὺς δεσμούς μου φανεροὺς ἐν Χριστῷ γενέσθαι

Paul reveals here the veritable dimension of his imprisonment which is its intimate connexion with Christ; that is the Apostle shares in a profound way in Christ's sufferings. Paul's fearless preaching of Christ had led to his arrest in Jerusalem in the first place and to all the subsequent legal proceedings which had finally culminated in his appeal to Caesar and consequent arrival in Rome. Now in the Empire's capital he was preaching and affirming the Gospel to all who would listen despite his chains. But these very chains had, in fact, been transformed from the shameful bonds which normally fetter a malefactor into something glorious in that Christ was also made manifest in them.

C) *Phil. 1,15-17*: "Some indeed preach Christ from envy and rivalry, but others from good will. The latter do it out of love, knowing that I am put here for the defence of the Gospel; the former proclaim Christ out of partisanship, not sincerely but thinking to afflict me in my imprisonment".

This passage with vigorously polemical language and antithetical verbal structure is a poignant evocation of the divided state of Roman Christianity. These verses are clearly linked to the preceding ones in that here Paul describes the "majority" that he mentioned in Phil. 1,14. These brethren were his supporters, members of the Pauline party; those who preach Christ "from good-will" (δι' εὐδοκίαν) and "out of love" (ἐξ' ἀγάπης) for the Apostle "knowing that I am put here for the defence of the Gospel". Sharply contrasting with this segment of the Church are "some" (τινὲς) who are preaching Christ "from envy and rivalry (διὰ φθόνον καὶ ἔριν). Their proclamation of Christ was insincere because it was made not from love, but "out of partisanship" (ἐξ' ἐριθείας); their goal, says Paul, was "to afflict me in my imprisonment". Paul's condemnation of his adversaries within the Roman Church is unequivocal.

1. διὰ φθόνον καὶ ἔριν

a) ὁ φθόνος — (Vg. = *invidia*) is a very strong word signifying a deep spite, ill-will or malice, especially "envy or jealousy of the good fortune of others"[128]. Cf. the adjective φθονόλετρος — enviously destructive.

The noun occurs nine times in the N.T. where it describes utter vileness and baseness. It figures prominently in Paul's list of vices in Rom. 1,29 and his list of the "works of the flesh" in Gal. 5.21. For Paul to apply such a word to full members of the Roman Church reveals both the depths of their antagonism toward him and his ministry as well as the amplitude of his condemnation of them.

---

128 *LS*[9], pg. 1930.

b) ἡ ἔρις — strife, quarrel, discord, contention, rivalry (Vg. = *contentio*). Cf. the goddess Eris who excited men to war.

This noun also occurs nine times in the N.T., seven times in the Pauline corpus and twice in the Pastorals. It too figures in Paul's list of evils in Rom. 1,29 and is regularly connected to the word ζῆλος as in Rom. 13,13 and 1 Cor. 3,3.

More than just a grievous internecine polemic is involved here. Clement of Rome, writing only thirty years after Paul's martyrdom, clearly places the blame for the Apostle's death on the feelings of rivalry and envy his foes had for him: "By reason of rivalry and envy (διὰ ζῆλον καὶ φθόνον) the greatest and most righteous pillars [of the Church, i.e. Peter and Paul] were persecuted and put to death"[129]. The minority members of the Roman Christian community were much more than bitter theological foes of the Apostle. They were also very dangerous *legal* adversaries as well, capable of any base behaviour including stirring up the authorities against Paul.

2. ἐξ ἐριθείας

ἡ ἐριθεία — The origin of this word lies in the political lexicon of the Greek city-state where it meant canvassing for public office or intriguing for the same office[130]. In the N.T. the term designated a selfish and factious ambition[131]; intriguing, partisan squabbling or a strong party spirit[132].

Paul's foes here are clearly the Judeo-Christians who had formerly been the dominant (albeit not exclusive) element in the nascent Roman Church, but who now found themselves threatened by Paul's presence in Rome as well as by his successful mission to the Gentiles, which had left the Judeo-Christians a disgruntled and antagonistic minority in the overall community. The Judeo-Christians had a deep personal antipathy to Paul and their actions were motivated by a visceral invidiousness and contentiousness which had led them not only to impugn Paul's person, but also his Apostolate. Paul responded vigorously: his chains had not impeded the furtherance of the Gospel. Moreover he rejoiced that his foes too were preaching Christ even if their motives were selfish and insincere. What mattered to the Apostle was the Gospel's spread, to which aim all personal feelings and partisan squabbles were subordinated.

The success of Paul's mission in Rome, which had made the Gentile Christians the predominant grouping within the Roman Church, had had the

---

129 Clement of Rome, *Ep.Cor.* 5,2.
130 Cf. Aristotle, *Politica* 1302 b 4 (election intrigues); 1303 a 14 (election contests).
131 James 3,14; 3,16.
132 Rom. 2,8; 2 Cor. 12,20; Gal. 5,20; Phil. 2,3.

effect of exacerbating the already-strained personal relations between members of the two groups as well as deepening the theological cleavages dividing the Roman Church. Ironically these were the very divisions which Paul had tried to address in his *Epistle to the Romans*. Paul's stay in Rome had not conciliated the Judeo-Christians, ever under the influence of the synagogal authorities; rather it had augmented the malice aimed at him. Paul had acquired some very vindictive enemies in Rome with whom he was forced to contend and whose untoward actions would eventually pose a very grave danger to his life.

V,2. The Saints of Caesar's household

The *Epistle to the Philippians* does not conclude with an extended list of greetings. Paul mentions only two of his disciples by name, Timothy and Epaphroditus, and he mentions them in the body of the Epistle and not at its conclusion.

Timothy is with Paul at the moment of the Epistle's composition; but the Apostle hopes to dispatch him to Philippi "just as soon as I see how it will go with me"[133]. The τὰ περὶ ἐμέ obviously refers to the legal proceedings at Rome in which Paul was engaged. The verse would imply that a decision was expected on Paul's appeal in the very near future. Timothy in fact was being kept in Rome until Paul's case was disposed of[134], at which time he would be sent to Philippi.

As in Phlm. 22, Paul expresses his intention of visiting the Epistle's recipients, a visit that would take place in the wake of Timothy's. But here the language is much stronger. In Phlm. 22, Paul had expressed the *hope* of making the journey: "At the same time, prepare a guest room for me, for I am hoping (ἐλπίζω) through your prayers to be granted to you". In Phil. 2,24 the Apostle is quite *persuaded* that he would be making the journey: "and I trust (πέποιθα) in the Lord that shortly (ταχέως) I myself shall come also".

A) πέποιθα — I trust, I am assured, I felt sure of, I am convinced. Here Paul is using the ancient middle Perfect, πέποιθα, an intransitive signification, to exhibit a present meaning[135], that is that he is strongly convinced, quite certain

---

133 Phil. 2,23.
134 Although the verse does not say so explicitly, it is not impossible that Timothy was himself involved in some way in the legal proceedings and was obliged to remain in Rome until the court decided the appeal.
135 Moulton, *Prolegomena*, pg. 147. Cf. Zerwick, *GB.*, pg. 96, sect. 285: The Perfect indicates "not the past action as such, but the present 'state of affairs' resulting from the past action".

in fact, that he will be able to come and visit the Philippian brethren whom he loves so dearly. Paul is optimistic about the outcome of his appeal to Caesar, fully expecting release and not condemnation.

B) ταχέως— quickly, speedily, soon, shortly. Paul expects the court's decision in the immediate future. The use of this adverb is a clear indication that Paul is nearing the end of his two-year period of house arrest.

The second disciple whom Paul specifically names is Epaphroditus, who is mentioned twice in the NT: here and at Phil. 4,18. The Apostle describes Epaphroditus as "my brother and fellow worker and fellow soldier, and your messenger and minister to my need (τῆς χρείας μου)"[136].

A) The terms "brother", "fellow worker" and "fellow soldier" express the high esteem Paul had for Epaphroditus. The last term, συστρατιώτης, which Paul applied only to Epaphroditus and to Archippus[137], is especially significant in that it implies shared sufferings, tribulations and persecutions and quite possibly shared confinement[138].

B) τῆς χρείας μου
ἡ χρεία— need, necessity[139].
The personal want to which Paul refers here, was almost certainly pecuniary. Paul would quite probably have had a pressing need for a monetary gift this late into his two-year captivity. His personal expenses must have been quite high and court costs, especially in appellate cases, were very elevated.

The *salutationes* which conclude the *Epistle to the Philippians* were particularly brief, but they do contain a unique reference: "Greet every saint in Christ Jesus. The brethren (ἀδελφοί) who are with me greet you. All the saints (ἅγιοι) greet you, especially those of Caesar's household (μάλιστα δὲ οἱ ἐκ τῆς Καίσαρος οἰκίας)"[140].

A) ἀδελφοί/ ἅγιοι — Paul distinguishes between "brethren" and "saints", conferring on each of the two words a particular nuance. The ἀδελφοί were the Apostle's immediate circle of co-workers and companions; in this passage

---

136 Phil. 2,25.
137 Phlm. 2.
138 Phil. 2,27.
139 Cf. Rom. 12,13: "Contribute to the needs of the saints, practice hospitality"; Acts 20,33-34: "I coveted no one's silver or gold or apparel. You yourselves know that these hands ministered to my necessities, and to those who were with me.
140 Phil. 4,21-22.

ἀδελφοί becomes synonymous with συνεργοί. The ἅγιοι refer to all God's people, to every baptized member of the Church. The inclusive nature of this usage is emphasized by the adjective "all": i.e. *all* the saints of the Roman Church salute *all* the saints of the Philippian Church.

B) μάλιστα δὲ οἱ ἐκ τῆς Καίσαρος οἰκίας (Vg. = *maxime autem qui de Caesaris domo sunt*)

1. μάλιστα — The superlative of μάλα vastly strengthens the word or phrase it modifies, hence the meaning "especially", "most of all", "above all".

Paul has kept the greetings succinct, general and anonymous, but he does quite emphatically single out the Christian members of the imperial household for especial mention.

2. οἱ ἐκ τῆς Καίσαρος οἰκίας — The expression Καίσαρος οἰκίας refers here to the imperial household at Rome[141]. It is a collective term designating primarily the imperial servants and not the members of the Emperor's family, relationships or immediate retinue (i.e. the *Neronis familiares*). The Christian members of the imperial household whom Paul mentions in the Epistle were slaves and freedmen belonging to the humblest ranks of the household's hierarchy[142]. They were full, baptized members of the Roman Christian community, who had most likely been converted by Paul and who were now ministering to him during his detention. As such Paul cherished them and made this especial note of them in his otherwise anonymous *salutationes* to the Philippian Church.

The verse clearly indicates that Christianity had spread among certain retainers of the imperial household itself. This Pauline penetration, although involving only those at the bottom of the palace's hierarchy and being much circumscribed in scope, was deeply significant. The presence of Christian converts among the palace retainers could not have been kept a secret. Thus it would have come to the attention of higher ranking functionaries that a new, exclusively monotheistic religion was making inroads amongst the palace staff. As this previously unknown religion was drawing men away from the worship of the traditional gods and from the cult of the Emperor, and as its leader was in Rome under house arrest, the progress of the new faith could not have been too favourably seen by these officials.

A very perilous coalescence of hostile elements was slowly forming around Paul as his two-year captivity drew to its end. The unrelenting malevolence of the Roman Jewish leaders, the deep antagonism of the Judeo-Christians and the

---

141 The expression can also be used of the imperial servants outside Rome, in the rest of Italy or in the overseas provinces. Cf. Philo, *in Flaccum* 35.
142 Cf. Arndt & Gingrich, pg. 560.

probably less than favourable view the palace officials were increasingly wont to take had immeasurably increased the perils confronting Paul in Rome. Little wonder it is then that the aged Apostle expressed in this same Epistle his desire to depart and be with Christ.

V,3. "My desire is to depart and be with Christ, for this is far better"

At this crucial moment in his life and ministry when an unfavourable decision by the appeals court would mean his death, Paul serenely addresses his future, proclaiming his unswerving fidelity to Christ, his readiness to continue his Apostolic ministry or contrariwise to die for the Master's sake. Paul is hardpressed to choose, but finally, an elderly man with much Apostolic labour behind him, he expresses a wish to depart this world for eternal life with Christ. Phil. 1,19—23 then is a revealing, intimate look at how Paul approached the subject of his own martyrdom:

> "For I know that through your prayers and the help of the Spirit of Jesus Christ this will turn out for my deliverance, as it is my eager expectation and hope that I shall not be at all ashamed, but that with full courage now as always Christ will be honoured in my body, whether by life or by death. For to me to live is Christ and to die is gain. If it is to be life in the flesh, that means fruitful labour for me. Yet which I shall choose I cannot tell. I am hard pressed between the two. My desire is to depart and be with Christ, for that is far better (τὴν ἐπιθυμίαν ἔχων εἰς τὸ ἀναλῦσαι καὶ σὺν Χριστῷ εἶναι, πολλῷ γὰρ μᾶλλον κρεῖσσον)".

A) τὴν ἐπιθυμίαν ἔχων
ἡ ἐπιθυμία —expresses a very strong or even violent desire, having one's heart set upon something (be it good or evil), a strong yearning for, a great longing. Cf. Lk. 22,15: "And He said to them, 'I have earnestly desired to eat this passover with you before I suffer;' ... ". Paul uses the present participle ἔχων and the definite article τὴν with ἐπιθυμίαν to formulate a very strong expression of desire (cf. Vg. *desiderium habens*)[143].

Paul's sights are on his life in and with Christ in the fullness of the Kingdom. Yet the Apostle is not actively *seeking* martyrdom. While his own longing is to be with Christ (σὺν Χριστῷ εἶναι), he is nonetheless ready to continue his earthly ministry, that "life in the flesh" (τὸ ζῆν ἐν σαρκί) which means "fruitful labour for me". The Apostle's attitude was much in contrast to that of Ignatius of Antioch for example, who glorified in his approaching martyrdom and who

---

[143] Cf. Josephus, *contra Apionem* 1,255: ἔσχε τὴν ἐπιθυμίαν. In 1 Thess. 2,17, the Apostle uses the expression ἐν πολλῇ ἐπιθυμίᾳ.

therefore strongly rejected any attempts on the part of his co-religionists to save his life: ἐπιτρέψατέ μοι μιμητὴν εἶναι πάθους Χριστοῦ τοῦ Θεοῦ μου exclaims the blesséd Ignatius in his *Epistle to the Romans*[144]. There are no affinities between Paul's approach to martyrdom and that of many of the later martyrs who sought martyrdom by conscious design.

B) εἰς τὸ ἀναλῦσαι καὶ σὺν Χριστῷ εἶναι

ἀναλύω — The basic meaning of this verb is to loose, untie, dissolve; it can also mean to depart or go away. Here Paul uses it as an euphemism for 'dying' (i.e. to depart from this life)[145]. The noun ἡ ἀνάλυσις appears with this same sense of departure from life in 2 Tim. 4,6: "For I am already on the point of being sacrificed; the time of my departure has come".

The preposition εἰς introduces the two infinitives which are the objects of Paul's ἐπιθυμία: that is to depart this life and to be with Christ. There is no sadness at the thought of departing this life as Paul's fondest wish for closer union with Christ would thereby be fulfilled. Paul's mortal remains might very well be placed into the tomb, but he himself, assured of his identity and his personality, would be in a perfect and blessed fellowship with Christ.

C) πολλῷ γὰρ μᾶλλον κρεῖσσον

κρείσσων (κρείττων) is the comparative of κρατύς, but also frequently appears as the comparative of ἀγαθός. The word means better, more advantageous, superior, more preferable. In the verse here, the comparative is much strengthened by μᾶλλον and both words by πολλῷ.

The Apostle is as emphatic here as grammar and syntax allow. For him it is much better to be with Christ than to preach Him on earth; more excellent to be in His presence in Heaven than to rejoice in Him in a house in Rome. Yet the heaping up of comparatives and superlatives does not mask a central fact: Paul would fain walk with Christ in the Kingdom, but does not for an instant shirk his duty as an Apostle. Moreover his Apostolic and pastoral concerns lie ever with the Churches he has founded:

> "But to remain in the flesh is more necessary on your account. Convinced of this, I know that I shall remain and continue with you all, for your progress and joy in the faith, so that in me you may have ample cause to glory in Christ Jesus, because of my coming to you again".[146]

Far from seeking martyrdom, Paul rejoices at the prospect of his continuing service to the Churches and to their well-being. The Apostle is optimistic as to

---

144 Ignatius of Antioch, *Ep.Rom.* 6.
145 Cf. Diogenes Oenoandensis, *Fragmenta* 2,II,11-12.
146 Phil. 1,24-26.

his likely release from detention for he even projects a visit to the Philippian congregation.

V,4. "That I may share His sufferings, becoming like Him in His death"

Finally Paul identifies and assimilates his own sufferings with Christ's Passion:

> "For his sake I have suffered the loss of all things, and count them as refuse, in order that I may gain Christ and be found in him, not having a righteousness of my own, based on law, but that which is through faith in Christ, the righteousness from God that depends on faith; that I may know him and the power of his resurrection, and may share his sufferings, becoming like him in his death (καὶ κοινωνίαν παθημάτων αὐτοῦ συμμορφιζόμενος τῷ θανάτῳ αὐτοῦ), that if possible I may attain the resurrection from the dead".[147]

A) καὶ κοινωνίαν παθημάτων

τό πάθημα — in general, suffering, misfortune, affliction, that which is endured. Paul used it in just this sense in Col. 1,24: "Now I rejoice in my sufferings for your sake, ... " and in Rom. 8,18: "I consider that the sufferings of this present time are not worth comparing with the glory that is to be revealed to us". The sufferings about which Paul was talking in these passages were the sufferings which all Christians endure; it is through these very sufferings that they enter the Kingdom. In Hebr. 2,10, the term is used to designate Christ's sufferings. In 2 Cor. 1,5, Paul writes: "For as we share abundantly in Christ's sufferings (ὅτι καθὼς περισσεύει τὰ παθήματα τοῦ Χριστοῦ εἰς ἡμᾶς) so through Christ we share abundantly in comfort too". Paul used the verb περισσεύω = to abound in; that is to say that as Christ's cup of suffering overflows and the believer shares abundantly in it and suffers with Him, so too through Christ, comfort and consolation overflow in which the believer, here also, greatly abounds.

The language in Phil. 3,8—11 is much stronger than in 2 Cor. 1,5. It is the language of an old man reflecting on his approaching death and meditating on its real significance. Here the Apostle express the desire to obtain a complete knowledge of Christ's sufferings which can only be attained by a full κοινωνία, i.e. sharing, participation, fellowship in them, by this intimate and symbiotic communion with the suffering Lord and Saviour: "The suffering Christian stands in close relation to the suffering Christ. He suffers as Christ did, or for Christ's sake, or in mystic unity with Christ"[148].

---

147 Phil. 3,8-11.
148 Arndt & Gingrich, pg. 607.

B) συμμορφιζόμενος τῷ θανάτῳ αὐτοῦ

This little participial phrase is primordial in understanding how Paul viewed the question of martyrdom. Here Paul delved into the deepest mystery of Christ's Passion, its true meaning for the Christian disciple and for himself at this crucial moment in his life. This little section of the letter *ad Philippenses* is the epitome of the Apostle's Passion mysticism, a deeply spiritual and profoundly beautiful part of the Pauline corpus.

1. συμμορφίζω — The Active voice means to grant or confer the same form (ἡ μορφή) on, to invest with the same form. The verb appears neither in the *Septuaginta* nor in the classical writers and only here in the N.T., leading P.T. O'Brien to suggest that it was "probably coined by Paul"[149]. Like most ζω — verbs, it is derived from a more primitive verb in ω — pure, in this case συμμορφόω which has the same meaning (outside the N.T.)[150].

2. συμμορφίζομαι — In the Passive voice, the verb means to be conformed to, to take on the same form as[151]. In this phrase Paul uses the Present Passive Participle συμμορφιζόμενος.

3. The cognate word σύμμορφος = of the same shape or form as, appears twice in the N.T. in Rom. 8,29 = "to be conformed to the image of his Son"; and in Phil. 3,21 = "who will change our own lowly body to be like his glorious body".

The phrase συμμορφιζόμενος τῷ θανάτῳ αὐτοῦ explains the true dimension of the παθήματα immediately preceding it. Paul has consciously chosen to participate in the sufferings of Christ, to attain full communion with the Master. The Apostle's use of the Passive Participle shows that he understood this conscious choice to identify himself with Christ's sufferings must inexorably lead to his being conformed to Christ's death:

> "The words in συν — point everywhere to fashioning in accordance with the Christ event. (...) This fashioning is the redemption of the body and glorification. It is thus the end of the process which begins with calling and justification. United with Christ, man acquires a share in what Christ is and is thus made like Him, so that God's purpose as Creator attains its goal".[152]

The Apostle has suffered the "loss of all things", that he may know the Lord and the "power of his resurrection". The sharing in the παθήματα τοῦ Χριστοῦ

---

149 P.T. O'Brien, *op.cit.*, pg. 408.
150 Cf. W. Grundmann, 'Syn-', *ThWb.*, Vol. 7, 1971, pg. 787, note 99.
151 Arndt & Gingrich, pg. 786.
152 W. Grundmann, *op.cit.*, pg. 788.

is an on-going, dynamic process, but one that is not as yet complete. Full κοινωνία has not been attained in that Paul has not yet been "conformed to His death". The Present Participle here has a quite marked nuance of the Future tense[153]. There is a clear temporal progression from the παθήματα to the θάνατος, from Paul's own present state of sufferings, which he identifies with those of Christ, to his future death as a martyr in Rome, assimilated in its turn to Christ's own violent death in Jerusalem.

---

153 Cf. Zerwick, *GB.*, pg. 93, sect. 278: "The *present* very often stands for the future, apparently owing to the influence of Aramaic, which readily uses the (present) participle especially for the proximate future ... ". In Sect. 284 (pg. 96), Zerwick adds: "The question may be raised, whether the present participle may not at times stand for the future one indicating the end in view, in which case the present participle would itself take on a possible final sense".

Chapter Three
Paul in Rome: The Final Period

I. Paul's Two Roman Captivities

As we have seen, Luke's objective in Acts was to present a double political apology: *pro ecclesia* and *pro impero* and not to give a complete account of Paul's encounter with the imperial tribunal. Nonetheless the Apostle had lodged an appeal at Caesarea for Nero's judicial protection and had been transported to Rome as an appellant prisoner to wait for his case to be heard. A legal mechanism had been put into motion and Paul's appeal would have to be disposed of in one way or another.

Luke does provide a significant clue as to what happened to the appeal in his account of the Jewish leaders' response to Paul's recapitulation of his legal history: "And they said to him, 'We received no letters from Judea about you, and none of the brethren coming here has reported or spoken any evil about you'"[1]. The wording of this verse is significant in that it points to a decision by the Sanhedrin not to send a delegation to Rome to pursue the case against the Apostle before the imperial tribunal. Luke's use of the double negative, "*no* letters", "*none* of the brethren" (οὔτε ... οὔτε) was more than a compositional device; it in fact emphasized the Sanhedrin's withdrawal from the case. It would have been unthinkable for the Sanhedrin to have pursued the case against Paul without solliciting the active help of the Roman Jewish community which enjoyed marked influence in the imperial court. Thus the Jewish leaders' professed ignorance of the case points to an intentional silence on the Sanhedrin's part.

Indeed the legal procedure was blocked in Paul's case until the Sanhedrin as the *accusator* (*delator*) brought forth anew (*obiectat*) the accusation against the Apostle. The accuser not only had to draw up and sign a *libellus accusationis* against the defendant, but also provide convincing evidence to support the charge (*probare crimen*). Therefore further legal action depended on the Sanhedrin's active pursuance of the case, within a given framework of time.

---

1 Acts 28.21.

Already a century earlier, Cicero had formulated the legal principle that a defendant, who had not been formally accused, could not be condemned[2]. At the outset of the Principate, Augustus promulgated the *Lex Iulia publicorum iudiciorum* confirming this principle. In Paul's particular case, this would mean that after having waited a legally specified period of time (here a *biennium*) for his accusers to appear and make their charges, the Apostle would have to be released due to the failure of his legal foes to formally pursue the case in court[3].

Luke only dwells briefly on the legal default of Paul's adversaries. His main interest in this final segment of Acts is, of course, to relate Paul's sermon to the Jewish leaders, their rejection of the Gospel and Paul's turn to the Gentiles. Yet the text of Acts itself furnishes some hints as to the reasons which might have motivated the Sanhedrin's default. In his account of Paul's appearance before that body, Luke notes the division and dissension between the Sadducees and Pharisees over the doctrinal issues Paul had raised. The Evangelist also stresses the considerably less hostile attitude the Pharisees entertained toward Paul[4].

These divisions may have in some unknown way hindered the Sanhedrin from continuing the case. After all Paul was out of Palestine and no longer a threat there. A more likely possibility lies, however, in Paul's status as a Roman citizen and in the outcome of his previous court appearances. Luke relates that both Festus and Agrippa had expressed the opinion that there was

---

2 Cicero, *pro Sexto Roscio* 20,55.36.
3 Cf. *Digesta* 38,14.8: "But we hold that a person who has preferred charges and who has wound up his case, bringing it to the point of obtaining a verdict, has brought an accusation. But if he has stopped at an earlier stage, he has not made an accusation, and we observe this rule. But if he has given up when an appeal has been lodged, he will be indulgently regarded as not having carried through his accusation". The *Edictum de temporibus accusationum* (*BGU* 628), as mentioned earlier, deals with the problem of how to avoid delay in the arrival of the two parties in cases heard by the *Princeps*. If neither party appeared within the given limits, the case was dropped from the court roster. In the event of an imperial amnesty, a case could be removed from the court lists and the charge annulled (*absolutio*). An accuser could withdraw a charge before trial, but such a withdrawal required the court's permission. Unjustified withdrawal of a charge left the accuser himself liable to the charge of *tergiversatio*. Finally the Latin legal term of *eremodicium* should be noted. This was the failure to appear to take part in a case by the end of the appointed time (*Cod. Iust.* 3,1; 13.3); the judgement given against either party for default of appearance (*Digesta* 4,4.7.12). Thus the term pertains to an undefended action in which one party does not appear and judgement consequently goes against him due to default of appearance. Cf. the Greek term φυγοδικέω, to shirk or avoid a trial; to desert the court (*P. Thead.* 15,19). Finally it should be noted that the *S.C. Turpillianum* was passed in 61 A.D. to combat the absent accuser (cf. *Digesta* 48,19.5).
4 Acts 23,6-10.

no compelling evidence to support a charge of sedition against Paul[5]. In their view the Apostle was innocent of all political charges laid against him and should normally have gone free[6]. In view of the legal antecedents in the case, the Sanhedrin would have had even less chance of obtaining a conviction in the imperial tribunal on the same political charge using the same irrelevant theological evidence to support it than it had had in the lower procuratorial courts[7].

In Paul's case, the Roman system of justice and customary legal use would have disfavoured the Sanhedrin in its role of accuser. That body, a non-Roman legal entity, had but a weak case to present against Paul, a Roman citizen, whom it was charging with a capital offence:

> "To bring a capital charge was both dangerous and difficult, dangerous because the *calumnia* process enabled the wrongly accused to turn the tables on his accusers, difficult because of the practical limitations on the frequency of capital charges".[8]

The likeliest conclusion that can be drawn is that the Sanhedrin did not re-formulate the accusations within the allotted period of time and that Paul's case was consequently dropped from the court lists[9]. Yet this conclusion was far from affording the type of legal precedent Luke would have wanted to strengthen his *apologia pro ecclesia*. True, Paul had not been condemned; but neither had he been found innocent and officially cleared by the court of all wrongdoing. This simple fact bore with it considerable danger both to Paul and the Pauline community in the event that adversaries of his apostolic ministry were to take up the same sort of accusation again[10].

---

5 Cf. Acts 23,29 where Lysias, tribune of Jerusalem, also expresses the view that Paul was innocent.
6 Acts 25,25; 26,32.
7 Default of appearance was not an uncommon act on the part of an accuser as Dio Cassius notes: "As the number of law-suits was now beyond all reckoning and those who expected to lose their cases would no longer put in an appearance, he [Claudius, year 46 A.D.] issued a proclamation announcing that he would decide the case against them by a given day even in their absence; and he strictly enforced this rule". (Dio Cassius 60,28, *trans*. E. Cary, *Loeb*, 1961). Suetonius corroborates this in *Claud.* 15.
8 A.N. Sherwin-White, "The early Persecutions and Roman Law again", *op.cit.*, pg. 212.
9 L.P. Pherigo speculates that the Apostle was in fact tried and then exiled: "Another possibility has not, so far as I am aware, received any attention. Paul may have been tried and exiled. The only authority for this is Clement of Rome, who states that Paul suffered seven imprisonments, was exiled (φυγαδευθείς) and stoned (5,6)". (L.P. Pherigo, "Paul's Life after the Close of Acts", *JBL.*, Vol. 70; 1951, pg. 278).
10 The *Lex Acilia repetundarum* of 122 B.C. stipulated that the same case could not be proceeded with twice except if there were a later criminal act of the same sort or any act of collusion or conspiracy. (*Lex Acilia* 56 (in) Salvator Riccobono, ed., *FONTES IURIS ROMANI ANTEIUSTINIANI*, Florence, 1941, Vol. I, pg. 96). Ulpian notes that the same

It is therefore necessary to divide Paul's legal history at Rome into two distinct juridical phases. The first is the appellate phase, begun when the Apostle uttered his cry for help, *appello ad Caesarem*, before the Procurator Festus (Acts 25,11) and ended with his case being dropped from the court lists due to the Sanhedrin's default of appearance (alluded to in Acts 28,21). The second phase concerns Paul's arrest in Rome on a majesty charge. The trial which ensued ended in the Apostle's condemnation and execution:

> "Luke also, who committed the Acts of the Apostles to writing, finished his narrative at this point by the statement that Paul spent two whole years in Rome in freedom, and preached the word of God without hindrance. Tradition has it that after defending himself the Apostle was again sent on the ministry of preaching, and coming a second time to the same city suffered martyrdom under Nero. During this imprisonment he wrote the second Epistle to Timothy, indicating at the same time that his first defence had taken place and that his martyrdom was at hand".[11]

Eusebius concludes in the same passage: "We have said this to show that Paul's martyrdom was not accomplished during the sojourn in Rome which Luke describes"[12]

II. Were Roman Judeo-Christians Responsible for Paul's Death?

II,1. The nascent Roman Church: a divided Community

The beginnings of Christianity at Rome are shrouded in darkness[13]. In his narration of the Pentecost story, Luke noted that there were visitors from Rome, both Jews and proselytes, who witnessed the wondrous descent of the Holy Spirit[14]. In all likelihood Christianity reached Rome in the final period of Tiberius' reign (which extended from 14 to 37 A.D.)[15] through "the agency of

---

accuser would not renew the old charge but admits that it was juridically possible for a third party to come forth and pursue a separate case on the same charge (*Digesta* 48,2.7).

11 Eusebius, *HE.* 2,22.1-2 (*trans.* K. Lake, *Loeb*, 1959).

12 *Ibid*, 2,22.7.

13 J. Beaujeu suggests that the reason Christian origins at Rome are so obscure is due " ... in part to the collective executions of 64 A.D. which could not have left many survivors". (J. Beaujeu, *op.cit.*, pg. 78). Cf. P. Lampe, *Die stadtrömischen Christen in den ersten beiden Jahrhunderten*, Tübingen, 1987, pg. 1.

14 Acts 2,10.

15 Cf. Tertullian, *Apologeticum* 5,2; Eusebius, *HE.* 2,2.6. For further discussion, cf. the interesting article by C. Cecchelli, "Un tentato riconoscimento imperiale del Cristo", *STUDI IN ONORE DI A. CALDERINI E R. PARIBENI*, Milan, 1956, Vol. I, pg. 362.

the Jewish diaspora"[16]. In this earliest period of the Roman Church's long history, the great majority of its members came from Judaism; indeed these people *remained* Jews even after receiving the Gospel. The foundation of the Roman Church then was Judeo-Christian; this is clear from Paul's magnificent letter to the Romans. Yet this pre-Pauline Roman Church was not exclusively Judeo-Christian for Gentiles also adhered to the Christian Gospel[17]. The community's heterogenous ethnic composition set the stage for a double conflict: firstly between the Jewish and Christian communities at Rome and secondly an internal struggle between the Jewish and Gentile wings of the Roman Church:

> "As a whole, the Roman Church had accepted the principle of the Gentile world-mission, but there was a small conservative Jewish-Christian enclave within it which had reservations, feeling that total commitment to the Gentile mission would mean final severance of associations with the Jewish people".[18]

The Church did not at first form a breakaway group from official Roman Judaism, but measures taken against the Roman Jews by Emperor Claudius in the years 41 and 49 A.D. had the lateral effect of severing many of the links binding the nascent Church to the synagogal authorities in the city of Rome:

A) Dio Cassius relates that Claudius, in his first regnal year (41 A.D.), ordered the Roman Jews not to hold regular meetings:

> "As for the Jews ... he did not drive them out, but ordered them, while continuing their traditional mode of life, not to hold meetings".[19]

---

16 H. Solin, "Juden und Syrer im westlichen Teil der römischen Welt", *ANRW.* II, 29.2; 1983, pg. 663.

17 Cf. F.F. Bruce, "Christianity under Claudius", *op.cit.*, pg. 317-318; A.J. Guerra, "Romans: Paul's Purpose and Audience with special Attention to Romans 9-11", *RB.*, Vol. 97; 1990; pg. 221.

18 F.F. Bruce, "'To the Hebrews': a Document of Roman Christianity?", *ANRW.* II, 25.4; 1987; pg. 3519. A.J. Guerra rightly points out that the terms Jewish Christian and Gentile Christian cannot be thought of as designating strictly ethnic-based subgroups: "By 'Jewish Christians', I do not mean merely Christians who are ethnically Jewish, but rather those who have an allegiance to the Law or some aspects thereof, and also to the nation of Israel. This group in Rome undoubtedly included some proselytes to Judaism and God-fearers. Likewise by 'Gentile Christians', I mean Christians who affirm complete liberation from all but certain moral dimensions of the Law. This latter group clearly includes some Jews — ethnically speaking, — Paul not least among them". (A.J. Guerra, *op.cit.*, pg. 220, note 3). Cf. J.E. Taylor, "The Phenomenon of early Jewish-Christianity: Reality or scholarly Invention?", *VC.* 44; 1990; pgs. 314-315.

19 Dio Cassius 60,6.6 (*trans.* E. Cary, *Loeb*, 1961).

The effect of this interdiction may very well have led the Gentile Christians to seek out a new organizational structure in order to escape the restrictions which Claudius ordered for the Jews.

B) Suetonius wrote that

"Since the Jews constantly made disturbances at the instigation of Chrestus, he expelled them from Rome (*Iudaeos impulsore Chresto assidue tumultuantis Roma expulit)*".[20]

Claudius' measure — rather harsh in nature in view of the traditional good relations between the court and the Roman Jews — which he took in 49 A.D.[21], markedly altered the Christian community in that only the Judeo-Christians had to leave Rome, whilst the Gentile Christians continued to live in the city. When the Judeo-Christians finally returned "they encountered a Christian community which was quite something other than the one they had left behind"[22].

Jewish life in Rome had not, of course, been completely interrupted by Claudius' actions as probably not all Roman synagogues were involved in the strife, nor was Judeo-Christianity destroyed as many of the Judeo-Christian expellees did eventually take up residence in Rome again. Nonetheless the Christian community had been rent in twain and this cleavage only widened the more with Paul's arrival in Rome in 60 A.D. The Apostle's preaching his Gospel of freedom from the Law, his presentation of the mystery of the Cross of Christ, the opening to the Gentiles could not have failed to have had a tremendous impact on Roman Christianity and on the uneasy balance between its two wings[23].

Luke records that at both Corinth and Ephesus[24], Paul had publicly broken with the synagogue and had established independent religious communities at other locations (i.e. Titius Justus' house in Corinth and the Hall of Tyrannus in Ephesus). In both these cities, the break had been so sensational that it precipitated a public disturbance necessitating the intervention of the local

---

20 Suetonius, *Claud.* 25 (*trans.* J.C. Rolfe, *Loeb*, 1959).

21 This dating is much disputed; cf. my presentation in the *Trial of St. Paul, op.cit.*, pg. 52-54.

22 H. Solin, *op.cit.*, pg. 664. In the *Hist. adv. Pag.* 7,6.16, Orosius wrote: "Here it cannot at all be discerned whether he ordered the restraining and repression of the Jews who were acting tumultuarily against Christ or if he also wanted to expel the Christians with them as men of kindred religion". Luke mentions this expulsion in Acts 18,2.

23 Cf. Ambrosiaster, *In Epistolam ad Romanos* (prologus) (*PL.* 17; col. 46). A.J. Guerra notes that one of Paul's objectives in Rom. 9-11 was " ... to dispel fear that his presence in Rome may exacerbate conflicts between Christians and Jews as well as between Gentile and Jewish Christians and thus possibly lead to a repeat of repressive imperial measures against these communities in Rome". (A.J. Guerra, *op.cit.*, pg. 224).

24 Acts 18,7; 19,8-10.

Roman authorities to keep the peace. A noisesome separation also took place at Rome. Luke recounts the break between the Roman Jewish leaders and Paul in the concluding chapter of Acts and we know from the last chapter of the *Epistle to the Romans* that house-Churches existed in Rome independently of the urban synagogue structure and religious authority[25].

Separation from the established and legally-recognized Jewish community in a city where that community's leadership had access to the imperial court was an act fraught with great peril for Paul and his co-disciples. The efficacity of Paul's preaching to the world at large led to an increase in Jewish antagonism to the Pauline group and a consequent increase in the dissension within the Roman Church between the Judeo-Christians, strongly influenced by the synagogue, and the Gentiles. All of this agitation would also have led to a growing perception on the part of both the authorities and the general public that these Christians formed a new and as yet unrecognized religion in conflict with its Jewish parent. By the time of the Great Fire of July 64, the Christians had acquired a particular identity — a very bad one at that[26] — which led to their being the sole scapegoats for the fire. Dissensions between the Judeo-Christians and the Pauline group would also have facilitated police penetration of the Christian community during the investigation which followed the fire and would have nurtured a climate of fear and mutual denunciation[27]. Paul's presence in Rome and his preaching the Gospel of freedom from the Law would thus go a long way in explaining how the Christians acquired the negative identity that they bore and how they came to be chosen by Nero to suffer for the firing of Rome.

II,2. The Christians as Paul's Accusers: Cullmann's Theory re-visited

Paul's final court appearance in Rome terminated in his being sentenced to death. The legal proceedings leading to the Apostle's martyrdom unfolded against a background of conflict between Christians and Jews and between

---

25 P.S. Minear writes: "We should remember the great size of the city of Rome and its polyglot population, which included a large Jewish ghetto, a large number of satellite suburbs, and various neighbourhoods which retained their own ethnic and cultural distinctiveness within the metropolitan area. (...) Instead of visualizing a single Christian congregation, therefore, we should constantly reckon with the probability that within the urban area were to be found forms of Christian community which were as diverse, and probably also as alien, as the Churches of Galatia and those of Judaea". (P.S. Minear, *The Obedience of Faith: the Purposes of Paul in the Epistle to the Romans*, Naperville, Illinois, pg. 8).

26 As Luke himself says in Acts 28,22 (to say nothing of Tacitus and Suetonius!).

27 Tacitus, *Ann.* 15,44.

Judeo and Gentile Christians. This bitter strife points, in its turn, to the identity of Paul's accusers, that is to those who set into motion the judicial set of dynamics which culminated in the Apostle's martyrdom.

Professor Oscar Cullmann has formulated a hypothesis wherein he proposes identifying Paul's accusers as fellow members of the Roman Christian community. This theory was presented both in his short, but important article, *Les causes de la mort de Pierre et de Paul d'après le témoignage de Clément Romain* (1930) and his subsequent, classic work, *Saint Pierre: Disciple, Apôtre, Martyr* (1952). Cullmann, noting the silence about the death of the two Apostles which both Luke (Acts 28) and Clement of Rome (*EpCor.* 5) maintained, queries the motives for that silence. After examining the linguistic evidence surrounding Clement's use of the terms 'envy', 'jealousy' and 'discord' (ζῆλος, φθόνος and ἔρις) and related literary evidence, Cullmann forms the following judgement:

> "It would be necessary to conclude that Peter and Paul died *victims of the Christians themselves*. We do not mean of course that they were martyred by their own co-religionists, but that the Roman authorities were called on to intervene against them because of the attitude of certain Roman Christians, the same as Moses had to flee before the King of Egypt due to the jealousy of a 'compatriot'. The jealousy of which Clement speaks is not explained further and we are not able to say exactly in what it consisted. But in any case, it appears to be the jealousy of *Christians* and not that of the Roman authorities which caused the Apostles' death. The Roman Christians had not as yet at that period such power which would have kindled the jealousy of the Roman authorities".[28]

Thus Cullmann views the situation as one in which "there was at Rome a dispute so violent, that this dispute between Christians drew the attention of the Roman authorities, who intervened and put to death the two leaders, Peter and Paul"[29]. Cullmann can then explain the silence of Luke and Clement by their desire "to avoid recalling, in too precise a way, this stain which sullied the history of the Roman Church"[30]. The deliberate silence about the deaths of the two Apostles which Luke and Clement created was so complete and pervasive that in later centuries Christian writers were unaware of the infelicitous facts surrounding the martyrdoms. This, concludes Cullmann, is why one has so few references to the martyrdoms in early Christian literature [31]:

> "Doubtlessly the particularly painful circumstances in which these martyrdoms took place were spoken about as little as possible. The example given by Christians who had caused

---

28 O. Cullmann, "Les causes de la mort de Pierre et de Paul d'après le témoignage de Clément Romain", *RHPR.*, Vol. 10; 1930, pg. 297.
29 *Ibid.* pg. 299.
30 *Ibid.* pg. 300.
31 *Ibid.* pg. 300

the death of other Christians had nothing edifying about it. Thus the abrupt end of the Book of Acts can be explained".[32]

Cullmann's hypothesis, which at first approach seems so attractive, contains a number of flaws both in its reasoning and argumentation, the sum total of which renders it less plausible than one would think in attempting to recover the identity of Paul's accusers:

A) While Luke's treatment of the Roman Christian community in Acts is cursory, it is not hostile. In Acts 28,15, Luke notes that the Roman brethren, having learned that the Apostle had left Puteoli, went out of the city and descended the via Appia as far as the Forum of Appius and the Three Taverns, respectively 43 and 33 miles from Rome, to meet Paul and his party (ἦλθαν εἰς ἀπάντησιν ἡμῖν). F.F. Bruce has quite rightly noted that the term ἀπάντησις was a sort of technical term used to describe the official welcome of a dignitary on the part of a deputation which went out of the city to meet him and escort him thither. "There is", writes Professor Bruce, "thus deep significance in the use of this word to describe the welcome received by Paul from the Roman Church".[33]. Luke notes Paul's response to this greeting in the very same verse: "On seeing them Paul thanked God and took courage". Luke's narration of Paul's arrival in Rome and his warm welcome there reflects harmonious relations between the Roman Christians and the Apostle. Yet relations seemed to have deteriorated rather strikingly between Paul and the Judeo-Christians during his considerable sojourn in Rome, as Paul himself implies in the passage we examined from the *Epistle to the Philippians*. It is significant that the only meeting between Paul and the Roman Christians recorded in Acts occurred *outside* Rome; once inside the city Paul seems to have had no further contact with them. Paul certainly had dangerous enemies within the Roman Christian community. Yet one must take into consideration that Luke's silence was due in the main to his apologetic purpose and literary design for Acts. Luke's attention is concentrated on the Roman Jewish community and their rejection of the Gospel and not on the relationship, spiritual or psychological, between the Apostle and the Roman Christians. For Luke, Paul was the paradigmatic witness to Christ and he gradually lessened and then eliminated the presence of all other messengers as the Acts-narrative unfolded and reached its climax in Rome. The Roman Christians drop out of Luke's account; the Evangelist aimed at portraying Paul as the first man to present the Gospel to the Roman Jewish leadership[34]. Paul did have enemies within the Roman

---

32 O. Cullmann, *Saint Pierre, Disciple, Apôtre, Martyr*; Geneva, 1952, pg. 91-92.
33 F.F. Bruce, *The Acts of Apostles*, Grand Rapids, 1951 (8th printing, 1975), pg. 475.
34 Cf. H. Conzelmann, *op.cit.*, pg. 149 "Luke knew that a community already existed in Rome, but he wanted to portray Paul as the pioneer of Christianity".

community, Luke's silence reflects to some extent his embarrassment over their ambiguous stance toward the Apostle, but still one cannot reasonably conclude from Luke's silence that he was deliberately obscuring the fact that Paul's death was to be imputed to a group of Roman Christians alone.

B) Cullmann suggests that when Clement of Rome used the words ζῆλος, φθόνος and ἔρις, he was clearly designating a deadly hatred felt by certain Roman Christians for Paul. It should be noted that from the linguistic point of view, these three words do not necessarily denote 'envy', 'jealousy' or 'discord' as springing *exclusively* from a compatriot or co-religionist; nor do they have an intrinsic implication of internecine conflict. They are general terms for the vices they signify; in this particular case their perpetrators could be equally from without the community as from within it.

C) While Cullmann is correct in stating that the Roman Christians were too weak politically and socially to mount a credible threat to the State or the ruling family and therefore the jealousy and envy which led to the deaths of Peter and Paul were not on the part of the Roman authorities, he is inexplicably silent on the jealousy and envy which the Roman Jewish leadership certainly entertained with regards to Paul and his mission. This jealousy and envy sprang from the very success of the Pauline mission, a success which quite seriously threatened the organized Jewish community, its hierarchy and its vested interests. Cullmann tried to buttress his hypothesis by referring to a sentence of Jesus in Mt. 24,10:

> "And then many will fall away, and betray one another, and hate one another".

Yet surely the preceding verse, Mt. 24,9, is more *à propos* to the case at hand, indicating as it does, that the main threat to the well-being of the Christian community was external to the Church:

> "Then they will deliver you up to tribulation and put you to death; and you will be hated by all nations for my name's sake".

D) The early Christian writers thought of official Judaism as being responsible for the persecutions which the early Church had to endure. The Book of Acts is replete with accounts of Jewish hostility toward the nascent Christian communities in the Hellenistic East. Paul himself arrived in Rome as an appellant prisoner; his appeal having been lodged precisely to escape the iniquitous justice which the Sanhedrin would have meted out to him had he been transferred to its jurisdiction. Later on, Tertullian wrote that all the persecution suffered hitherto by the Christians was prepared in the synagogue:

synagogae Iudaeorum fontes persecutionum [35]. Writing in the mid-3rd Century, the Christian Latin poet Commodian directly accused the Jewish leadership of having fomented the Neronian persecution[36].

E) Although widely disliked by upper-class Romans, the Jews at Rome formed a politically powerful unit. The community was large and influential and its leadership had always maintained good relations with and direct access to the successive Caesars[37]. Insofar as Nero is concerned, Josephus notes that the Emperor's special favourite was the Jewish actor, Aliturus[38]. He also describes Poppaea herself as a God-fearing, Jewish sympathizer (θεοσεβής)[39] and as a person ready to intercede with Nero in favour of the Jews [40]. Although one ought not to exaggerate the Judeophilia of Nero's court — the very same Poppaea also patroned a notorious Jewish enemy, Gessius Florus, last Procurator of Judaea[41] and many of her choices in life would indicate that Josephus' use of the term θεοσεβής was more compositional than literal[42] — it is clear that the Jews wielded considerable influence at court. They had not hesitated in the past in co-operating to the fullest extent with their co-religionists in Palestine and elsewhere in furthering their petitions in Rome[43]. There can be no doubt

---

35 Tertullian, *Scorp.* 10.
36 Commodian, *Carmen Apologeticum* 845-859.
37 Cf. E. Schürer, *The History of the Jewish People in the Age of Jesus Christ*, Revised English Version, Edinburgh, 1986, Vol. III,1; pg. 78; M. Stern, "The Jewish Diaspora", (in) *The Jewish People in the first Century*, Assen, Vol. I, 2nd, printing, 1974, pg. 160ff; H. Solin, *op.cit.*, pg. 654. In Paul's time, there were at least five synagogues functioning in Rome. Unlike the Jewish community in Alexandria and other large Eastern cities, the Roman Jewish community had a decentralized structure and did not form a *politeuma* in the true legal sense of that word. Cf. R. Penna, "Les Juifs à Rome au temps de l'Apotre Paul", *NTS.*, Vol. 28; 1982; pg. 327-331.
38 Josephus, *Vita* 3,13.
39 Josephus, *Vita* 3,16.
40 Cf. Josephus, *Ant.* 20,195. Poppaea was not the only imperial consort who intervened in favour of the Jews. Cf. Josephus, *Ant.* 20,135 (Agrippina and Claudius) and later *P. Oxy.* 1242,26ff (Plotina and Trajan).
41 Josephus, *Ant.* 20,252.
42 Tacitus, *Hist.* 1,22. E.M. Smallwood has argued convincingly against accepting the conclusion that Josephus used the word θεοσεβής as a technical term to indicate that Poppaea was a Jewish sympathizer (E.M. Smallwood, "The alleged Jewish Tendencies of Poppaea Sabina", *JTS.*, Vol. 10; 1959, pg. 333). H. Solin writes: "The picture which the ancient historians have drawn of her show that she had in no way absorbed Jewish moral ideas". (H. Solin, *op.cit.*, pg. 661).
43 Cf. Cicero, *pro Flacco* 28,66.69; Josephus, *Ant.* 17,300; *Vita* 3,13. M. Stern notes that the Roman Jewish community maintained strong national links to other Jews and that "being at the centre of contemporary political life, they also became the lobbyists of the Jews living in other countries" (M. Stern, *op.cit.*, pg. 162).

that the Roman Jews would have done all they could to fight Paul and his disciples here on their own ground in the Empire's capital.

The evidence, scanty though it be, clearly points to the leadership of the Roman synagogues, that is to the very men who stormed out of Paul's lodgings rejecting his Gospel, as the ones who preferred the charge of *crimen laesae maiestatis* against him, the charge on which he was arrested for the final time, tried, condemned and martyred. As the synagogal leaders had considerable influence in court circles, their depicting the Pauline Christians as subversives and their leader as an enemy of the State would not have been an arduous task. Once again, as throughout his career since the Christophany on the road to Damascus, Paul, the former Saul, born "of the people of Israel, of the tribe of Benjamin, a Hebrew born of Hebrews; as to the law a Pharisee"[44], had to face as a consequence of preaching Jesus Christ, "the deadly hatred of the Synagogue"[45].

III. The Pastoral Epistles:
The Beginnings of the Pauline Tradition

III,1. The Image of the martyred Paul as depicted by an early Paulinist: the Pastor

There is a sure and certain relationship between Paul's violent death and the composition of the three Pastoral Epistles. Paul's execution — that is the loss of the great missionary and founder — forced the young Pauline communities to re-think their organization, life, doctrine and *praxis*. The Pastorals vividly set forth the problems faced by the second-generation Pauline Churches. Their author, the Pastor, a sincere Paulinist springing from a genuine Pauline milieu, attempted in his letters to articulate certain doctrinal and ecclesiological responses to these problems; answers which he deemed to be in the straight line of Paul's thinking[46]. The goal of the Pastoral Epistles is quite clearly to

> "seek to offer a Pauline (although in fact deutero-Pauline) infrastructure to the communities shaken by the Apostle's death. We are thus witnessing the pursuance of the Apostle's theological and pastoral work".[47]

---

44 Phil. 3,5.
45 P. Keresztes, "Nero, the Christians and the Jews in Tacitus and Clement of Rome", *op.cit.*, pg. 413.
46 Cf. C.F.D. Moule, "The Problem of the Pastoral Epistles: a re-Appraisal", *BULL.J.R. LIBR.*, Vol. 47; 1964-1965; pg. 433.
47 F. Bovon, "Paul comme document et Paul comme monument", (in) *CHRETIENS EN CONFLIT — L'EPITRE AUX GALATES*, Geneva, 1987, pg. 55.

III. The Pastoral Epistles

Offering a Pauline infrastructure to the communities meant dealing with the person of Paul, the Apostle and Martyr. The Pastorals thus articulate a precise *image* of Paul for the communities. In the face of persecution, imprisonment and martyrdom, the Apostle was a *model* of constancy and of unwavering fidelity to the Master:

> "Paul was not only a model of long-sufferance and endurance in persecution, a sure and certain master who laid out a definite type of orthodox teaching, but also, according to divine will, one whose person must serve henceforth as an example to all believers".[48]

Jesus had joined deed to word and had given Himself as an example to His disciples in all times and in all places. Paul was now following the Master's example; so the Pastor emphasized throughout his three letters that Paul should be followed in his turn. There is thus a continuing process of assimilation of the master by the disciple both in the Father's service and in death. "It is inconceivable," wrote C. Spicq, "that a genuine Apostle would not be ready to follow his Master to martyrdom"[49]. The image which the Pastor wished to convey of Paul in his final days was that of an ever-faithful servant, chained in a dismal Roman dungeon, suffering, abandoned, meditating on Christ's Passion and in turn being totally transformed by the image of the Divine Model as a result of that meditation.

The Pastoral Epistles are texts of Christian witness and it is not always the easiest of tasks to separate the doctrinal (i.e. *apologia, didache*) from the historical. The Pastor was not working with precise court records of Paul's trial and condemnation, but with recollections and this, of course, raises the question of their historical accuracy. Yet it would be far too hasty to conclude that the notices in the Pastorals about Paul's last days are necessarily pure fiction, creations of the Pastor meant to give a pathetic flavour to the letters. The Pastor has, in fact, incorporated genuine Pauline reminiscences into his composition, reminiscences carefully preserved by the Pauline communities. The Pastor may even have had at his disposal material from Paul himself: fragments of letters to Titus or Timothy or other disciples. These fragments as well as the reminiscences would have all been part of a precious tradition on Paul's latter days and would have formed not only a historical nucleus in the midst of the Pastor's three letters ,but also the base on which the later Pauline tradition (and legend) was founded.

The fact that the Pastoral Epistles are pseudonymal does not lessen their value as a witness of the earliest Pauline tradition. They provide a reliable

---

48 C. Spicq, "L'imitation de Jésus-Christ durant les derniers jours de l'Apotre Paul", (in) *MELANGES BIBLIQUES EN HOMMAGE AU R.P. BEDA RIGAUX*, Gembloux (Belgium), 1970; pg. 316.

49 *Ibid*, pg. 317.

testimony to the state of the Church at the dawn of the 2nd Century, to the evolution of its life and to the problems by which it was beset. Indeed the Pastorals provide a cogent response to those problems. In their sundry references to people and places, they demonstrate how far the Pauline mission had extended in the East a third of a century after the Apostle's martyrdom. Finally, for our purpose here, they show to some extent how the Pauline community understood Paul's final days in Rome and his martyrdom:

> "Above all, perhaps, in the Pastorals Paul is represented as the martyr. His death, of course, cannot be described in documents purporting to have been written by his hand, but II Tim. iv brings Paul as close to death as possible: nothing more remains but the crown of righteousness which the Lord will give him".[50]

In the final analysis, the Pastorals mark the beginning of an established Paul-tradition; of a process of fixing Paul as a monument — or better still — as an icon; of giving a firm and definitive form to an image of Paul which was to be transmitted not only to the immediate recipients of the three Epistles, but also to all subsequent generations of Pauline disciples.

III,2. The Theme of Abandonment: "At my first defence ... all deserted me"

The brief notice in 2 Tim. 4,16—17 reflects a legal situation and type of custody quite different from those described in Acts: "At my first defence (ἐν τῇ πρώτῃ μου ἀπολογίᾳ) no one took my part (οὐδείς μοι παρεγένετο); all deserted me (πάντες με ἐγκατέλιπον). May it not be charged against them! But the Lord stood by me (μοι παρέστη) and gave me strength to proclaim the message fully (κήρυγμα πληροφορηθῇ) that all the Gentiles might hear it. So I was rescued from the lion's mouth (ἐρρύσθην ἐκ στόματος λέοντος)".

A) ἐν τῇ πρώτῃ μου ἀπολογίᾳ (Vg. = *In prima mea defensionè*)

The noun ἀπολογία occurs 8 times in the NT[51]. The term signifies a legal

---

50 C.K. Barrett, "Pauline Controversies in the post-Pauline Period", *op.cit.*, pg. 241.
51 Cf. Acts 22,1 where Paul makes his defence before the crowd of rioters in Jerusalem; Acts 25,16 where the term *apologia* is used in its strict legal sense: "I answered them that it was not the custom of the Romans to give up any one before the accused met the accusers face to face, and had the opportunity to make his defence concerning the charge laid against him". In Phil 1,7; 1,17, Paul uses the expression 'defence of the Gospel'. According to 1 Peter 3,15, the Christian must always be ready to make a defence to anyone who calls him to account for his beliefs, especially when hauled into court. The verb ἀπολογέομαι is used in this sense of courtroom defence in Lk. 12,11; 21,14; Acts 24,10; 25,8; 26,1; 26,2; 26,24. Cicero notes

defence[52], "... the plea by which a defendant answers the accusation lodged against him and gives explanations apt to justify his case"[53]. *Apologia* is the legal antonym to 'accusation' (κατηγορία)[54]; it is the judicial moment granted the accused to formally refute before a magistrate *sedens pro tribunali* the charges levelled against him[55] and thereby to establish his innocence [56].

From the earliest times, Roman jurisprudence showed itself concerned with assuring the presence of both parties, accuser and accused, at the trial[57]. The accused had to be allowed to make a personal defence before the judge in order to try to secure his own *salus*[58]. He had the right to confront his accusers face to face (cf. the κατὰ πρόσωπον of Acts 25,16). The Latin legal term *coram* expresses this juridical reality: *arguo aliquem coram* = to accuse someone face to face; *coram defero aliquem* = to accuse someone who is present. A sentence handed down by a court could hardly be termed valid if the accused had not had the opportunity of hearing the accusation from the accuser's own mouth:

> "During the judicial hearing, the two parties were 'before' the magistrate, but also the one 'before' the other. The law required this double confrontation and it judged the latter particularly indispensable in safeguarding the rights of the defence. This was a matter of *aequitas*: if the accused were unable to respond directly to his accuser in the presence of the judge, equity would not be assured".[59]

Dom Dupont adds that if the defendant were not allowed the opportunity of responding directly to his accusers, his case would be *inaudita*, " ... and a sentence of condemnation would go against the *aequitatis ratio*, i.e. it would be 'inequitable' in the true etymological sense of that word"[60]. That is why anonymous denunciations were inadmissible in procedure and could only be rejected by the examining magistrate[61]. Apuleius Madaurensis notes that the order of justice according to ancient custom required the examination of both sides to a case, for the handing down of a hasty sentence was the usage of

---

that the power of truth is so great that it can defend itself against falsehood unaided (*pro Caelio* 63) and castigates the lawlessness of proceedings in which the accused is unable to defend himself (*pro Cluentio* 93).

52 Cf. *BGU.* 531, I,21 (1st C. A.D.); Josephus, *contra Apionem* 2,147.
53 J. Dupont, "Aequitas Romana", *ETUDES SUR LES ACTES DES APOTRES*, Paris, 1967, pg. 536.
54 Cf. Antipho 6,7 who draws a contrast between an unjust accusation and the *apologia* of a just and righteous man.
55 Cf. Hyperides, *pro Euxenippo* 31.
56 Cf. Plato, *Apologia* 28 A; Josephus, *BJ.* 1,621.
57 Cf. *XII Tables* 1,7: "*ambo* (i.e. *actor* and *reus*) *praesentes*".
58 Quintillian 7,2.21.
59 Dupont, "Aequitas Romana", *op.cit.*, pg. 535.
60 *Ibid.*, pg. 546.
61 Pliny, *Ep.* 10,97.

barbaric and cruel tyrants[62]. In the *Verrines*, Cicero had denounced the condemnation of a man with his case unheard (*indicta causa*)[63]. The *Digesta* states that "absent persons should not be condemned; for the argument of justice does not permit of a person's being condemned without his case being heard (*ne quis absens puniatur: et hoc iure utimur, ne absentes damnentur: neque enim inaudita causa quemquam damnari aequitatis ratio patitur*)"[64]. Both Suetonius and Seneca denounced Claudius' abuses in this matter. Suetonius lists the names of high-ranking people Claudius ordered killed on "*crimine incerto, nec defensione ulla data, occidit*"[65]. Seneca is scathing in his denunciation of Claudius' inequities:

> "Come tell me, blessed Claudius, why of all those you killed, both men and women, without a hearing, why you did not hear their side of the case first, before putting them to death? (... *quare quemquam ex his, quos quasque occidisti, antequem de causa cognosceres, antequem audires, damnasti*)? Where do we find that custom? It is not done in heaven"[66].

The Pastor evokes Paul's *first* defence before the imperial tribunal. There could be any number of subsequent sittings of the court before a formal verdict was handed down. The *Apology of Phileas* (*P. Bodmer* 20) provides a good, though later (early 4th C.) judicial example. The text is an excerpt of the official proceedings of the fifth and last hearing which Phileas, Bishop of Thmuis, had before the Prefect of Egypt. In the Greek preamble, the first four hearings are mentioned only cursorily[67]. The first appearance (ἐν μὲν τῇ πρώτῃ ἀπολογίᾳ), was a preliminary interrogation, which took place at Thmuis. This preliminary interrogation was followed by the Bishop's imprisonment in that city and subsequent transfer, chained, to Alexandria to appear before the Prefect. What interested the author of the *Apology of Phileas* was, of course, the accused's defence of Christian doctrine which could be used as a model for the faithful facing persecution. He therefore hurriedly passed over the legal aspects of Phileas' trial. It should be noted however that all the legal proceedings would have been duly recorded in *acta* conserved in the prefectoral archives. Indeed at the beginning of each court session, the official minutes of the last session were read before the proceedings resumed[68].

According to normal Roman procedure, the judge devoted the first hearing (*prima actio*) to information gathering. This would include ascertaining the

---

62 Apuleius Madaurensis, *Meta.* 10,6.
63 Cicero, *Verr.* II,ii,17.43.
64 *Digesta* 48,17.1.
65 Suetonius, *Claud.* 29.
66 Seneca, *Apocolocyntosis* 10; trans. W.H.D. Rouse, *Loeb*, 1919.
67 *P. Bodmer* 20,1.5.
68 V. Martin, ed., *PAPYRUS BODMER XX; APOLOGIE DE PHILEAS*, Cologny-Geneva, 1964, introduction pg. 13.

accused's identity, home province and a preliminary examination of the indictment[69]. If the magistrate felt that more light needed to be shed on the affair, he could pronounce the words *non liquet* or *amplius*, thus making an *actio secunda* necessary[70]. Between sittings, considerable periods of time could elapse. Thus Paul's request for his books and parchments in 2 Tim. 4,13, although likely a detail of the Pastor's own composition, is quite plausible legally speaking. Indeed it might very well reflect an underlying historical reality that a goodly amount of time had passed between the *actio prima* and the *actio secunda* in Paul's case.

B) οὐδείς μοι παρεγένετο (Vg. = *nemo mihi affuit*)

Here the verb παραγίνομαι is used in the sense of to 'stand by', to 'side with', to 'be by the side of', to 'support', to 'come to the aid of'[71].

This abandonment likens Paul's Passion to that of Jesus in that it highlights the image of the lone figure in the grasp of cruel, evil and demonic forces[72]. From the juridical point of view, the lack of a support group at the trial could only have made an unfavourable impression on the court, thus worsening the Apostle's situation. The *actio prima* was normally public and customarily a whole group of people would accompany the accused and stand by his side; their presence was meant to guarantee his innocence, or to put it another way, they acted as a moral surety for the defendant[73].

The tradition contained in this passage is unflattering to the Roman Christian community indicating as it does that Paul received virtually no support from them. Perhaps the abandonment can be partly explained by the very nature of the indictment itself. Paul was charged under the majesty laws, which, as we have seen, were rigorously enforced. It would have been exceedingly dangerous for the Apostle's co-religionists to have shown themselves as his supporters at the trial even if they had been so inclined, which seems not to have been the case[74]. Anyone supporting Paul under the circumstances ran a very serious risk of laying himself open to the charge of

---

69 Cf. Acts 23,34.
70 C. Spicq. *Les Epitres Pastorales*, Paris, 4th Ed., 1969, pg. 818.
71 Cf. Thucydides 3,54.4; Hesiod, *Theogony* 429; Herodotus 3,32.
72 Cf. Mt. 26,56: "Then all the disciples forsook him and fled"; Lk. 22,53: "But this is your hour and the power of darkness".
73 Cf. Cicero, *pro P. Sulla* 2,4; Th. Mommsen, *Römisches Strafrecht, op.cit.*, pg. 377.
74 Cf. Cicero, *pro P. Sulla* 2,6. *Quia in ceteris causis etiam nocentes viri boni si necessarii sunt deserendos esse non putant, in hoc crimine non solum levitatis est culpa verum etiam quaedam contagio sceleris si defendas eum quem obstrictum esse patriae parricidio suspicere.*

participating in (or at least condoning) a crime whose nature was an overt affront to the dignity and authority of the reigning Emperor.

C) πάντες με ἐγκατέλιπον (Vg. = *omnes me dereliquerunt*)

1. ἐγκαταλείπω — to forsake, abandon, desert.
The verb not only expresses the factual abandonment, but also the psychological feeling of loneliness and forsakenness that the Apostle must have endured. The use of πάντες stresses even more the totality of the abandonment.

The verb also appears in 2 Tim. 4,10 where it is used to describe the desertion of Demas, the disciple whose name appears first in the list of Paul's associates. Demas, the companion of Paul's earlier Roman imprisonment, "in love with this present world", perhaps discouraged by Paul's worsening juridical situation and approaching martyrdom, abandoned the Apostle and went to Thessalonica. The Pastor does not consider Demas a foe, either juridically or doctrinally. All he does is merely note his desertion with sadness.

The theme of abandonment also appears in 2 Tim. 1,15: "You are aware that all who are in Asia turned away from me (ἀπεστράφησάν με πάντες οἱ ἐν τῇ 'Ασίᾳ) and among them Phygelus and Hermogenes".

2. ἀποστρέφω — to turn away from, to reject, repulse or desert. The Vg. reads here: *aversi sunt a me omnes*.

This is a deutero-Pauline passage, composed by the Pastor, and probably refers to tensions within the Ephesian Church in his own time rather than in Paul's[75]. Still the mention of difficulties at Ephesus reminds one that the Asian metropolis was the site of some of Paul's earlier judicial troubles and that certain Ephesians were among his worst foes[76].

---

75 Commenting this passage, A.T. Hanson writes: "This must refer to something that happened in Asia and not in Rome. Timothy knows about it, so we must suppose that Paul was arrested in Asia, and at his interrogation in the town where he was arrested his friends, whom he had expected to support him, failed to rally around" (A.T. Hanson, *THE PASTORAL LETTERS,* Cambridge, 1966, pg. 81.). It remains difficult, however, to come to the conclusion on the basis of 2 Tim. 1,15 that Paul was arrested in Ephesus and bound over to Rome and that this arrest occurred between the two Roman captivities. All the text says is that Paul was abandoned by the Asians, not that they were his accusers. It is unlikely that Paul ever visited Ephesus or the province of Asia again after his first Roman captivity (cf. Acts 20,25; 38). The Apostle was arrested in Rome itself.

76 Cf. Acts 19,23ff; 20,17; 21,27; 1 Cor. 15,32; 16,8-9; 2 Cor. 1,8-10.

D) μοι παρέστη

The verb παρίστημι means to come to the aid of someone, to assist, to stand by another person, to support[77]. In this passage it has a strong juridical nuance[78]. Although abandoned by his co-religionists, the Lord's presence beside his faithful servant confirms and guarantees his innocence whatever the verdict of a corrupt court may be[79].

E) κήρυγμα πληροφορηθῇ

Paul was rescued from the mouth of the lion so that he could completely fulfill his Apostolic mission of carrying the Lord's name "before Gentiles and kings and the sons of Israel"[80]. Paul's ultimate and supreme testimony was rendered before the imperial tribunal in Rome. With that testimony, he had fully accomplished his ministry and could now await his reward, the *corona iustitiae*, with full confidence[81]:

> "Paul, unmindful of his own personal case, profited from the prestigious audience which was the imperial tribunal to proclaim the Name of Jesus Christ. His *apologia* as a prisoner was the ultimate dissemination of the *kerygma* which he had been chosen to bring before the Gentiles and kings. He had now fulfilled his calling as *keryx*".[82]

F) ἐρρύσθην ἐκ στόματος λέοντος

This is the proverbial expression indicating great danger. The psalmist in a cry of anguish prays the Lord to "save me from the mouth of the lion"[83]. In 1 Peter 5,8, the devil is depicted as the one who "prowls around like a roaring lion, seeking someone to devour". In Hebr. 11,32-33, the author evokes the names of Gideon, Barak, Samson, Jephtah, David, Samuel and the prophets, men "who through faith conquered kingdoms, enforced justice, received promises, stopped the mouths of lions". The noun lion then was used metaphorically to designate savage persons[84], and, by extension, fierce, cruel and impious rulers

---

77 Cf. Rom. 16,2.
78 In *P.Amh.* 66,40 (year 124 A.D.), the verb is used as a legal term denoting the producing of a witness to testify in someone's behalf.
79 Cf. Jn. 16,32.
80 Acts 9,15.
81 2 Tim. 4,8.
82 C. Spicq, "L'imitation de Jésus-Christ durant les derniers jours de l'Apôtre Paul", *op.cit.*, pg. 319.
83 Ps. 22,21.
84 Aeschylus, *Choephori* 938.

who persecute the righteous[85]. The term lion was also used to designate the Roman Emperor himself. Josephus used it in just this sense when he related Herod Agrippa's reaction to Tiberius' death:

> "the lion is dead".[86]

In the Book of Revelation, the *os leonis* imagery clearly designates Roman authority. Here the Roman imperial power — that which persecutes the saints and blasphemously usurps divine titles — is represented by the beast to whom the dragon gives his power, throne and great authority. This beast is described as being "like a leopard, its feet were like a bear's and its mouth was like a lion's mouth"[87].

In 2 Tim. 4,17, the mouth of the lion clearly refers to the Roman imperial authority, especially to the court hearing the case. Patristic tradition understood the lion to be Nero himself: e.g. Eusebius, in the *Historia Ecclesiastica*:

> "He clearly proves by this that on the first occasion, in order that the preaching which took place through him might be fulfilled, he was delivered from the lion's mouth, apparently referring to Nero thus for his ferocity".[88]

G) Onesiphorus and Luke succour Paul

The Pastor understood Paul to have been quite deserted by the Roman Christian community in his hour of need. This understanding very likely reflected historical reality. Yet in the midst of this bleak account of human frailty and infidelity, the Pastor has chosen to relate two exceptions to this abandonment of the Apostle. Both Onesiphorus and Luke gave comfort to Paul and both these faithful brethren were non-Romans.

1. The Pastor conserves the tradition of a visit by Onesiphorus to Paul in his Roman dungeon.

> "May the Lord grant mercy to the household of Onesiphorus, for he often refreshed me; he was not ashamed of my chains, but when he arrived in Rome he searched for me eagerly and found me".[89]

Onesiphorus is not mentioned elsewhere in the NT[90], although the phrase "household of Onesiphorus" occurs again in the Pastorals at 2 Tim. 4,19. The

---

85 Ps. 7,2; 35,17.
86 Josephus, *Ant.* 18,228.
87 Rev. 13,2.
88 Eusebius, *HE.* 2,22.4 (trans. K. Lake, *Loeb*, 1959).
89 2 Tim. 1,16-17.
90 Onesiphorus does, however, figure in the *Acta Pauli*. In this apocryphal tale, Onesiphorus,

wording in the Epistle strongly implies that Onesiphorus had died — perhaps even before Paul — possibly in the course of his stay in Rome during which he sought out and visited the Apostle.

In view of the general abandonment of the Apostle, Onesiphorus' visit was a strikingly conspicuous event and a tradition which the Pastor was careful to conserve in his account. Indeed the Pastor's choice of words: "not ashamed of my chains", and "searched for me eagerly", could only highlight the desertion of the Roman Christian community in this Paul's direst moment of need.

The contrast could not be greater between Luke's account of the lenient conditions under which Paul was held during his first Roman captivity and the Pastor's evocation of the terribly harsh conditions of the rule of *carcer* under which Paul was detained during the second captivity:

> " ... the Gospel for which I am suffering and wearing fetters, like a criminal (ὡς κακοῦργος)".[91]

The term κακοῦργος denotes the criminal, evildoer or malefactor. It is the person who has committed serious crimes[92], the vilest scoundrel cast into prison[93]; Luke used it to describe the two malefactors crucified alongside Jesus[94]. After his arrest, Paul had been chained and flung into a prison cell[95], guarded by soldiers[96] on detachment who served as prison guards (*carcerarii*)[97] and turnkeys (*clavicularii*)[98]. The material conditions of this type of detention were appallingly bad; it is not hard to imagine how difficult it was for a visitor such as Onesiphorus to find the prisoner he was seeking[99].

2. "Luke alone is with me".[100] The Pastor has conserved a very early tradition which signalled out Luke as an intimate companion of Paul's; one who knew

---

an inhabitant of Iconium, went out of that city onto the royal highway to await Paul and receive him in his house. As Onesiphorus had never met Paul, Titus furnished him with a description of the Apostle, which enabled him to recognize and greet him. The importance of this passage lies less with the appearance of Onesiphorus than with the description of Paul which formed the basis for subsequent Pauline iconography (*Acta Pauli*: Acts of Paul and Thecla 2-3). It was in Onesiphorus' house that Thecla heard Paul for the first time.

91 2 Tim. 2,9.
92 *P. Fay.* 108,11.
93 Josephus, *Ant.* 2,59; *P. Lille* 7,20.
94 Lk. 23,32-33; 23,39.
95 As Ulpian pointed out, prison was for detaining men, not for punishing them; *carcer enim ad continendos homines non ad puniendos haberi debet* (*Digesta* 48,19.8).
96 G. Lopuszanski, "La police romaine et les Chrétiens", *AC.*, Vol. 20; 1951, pg. 38.
97 For the term *carcerarius*, cf. *CIL.* 6,1057.7.4: C. Calpurnius Severus '*karc*'.
98 For the term *clavicularius*, cf. *CIL.* 13,1780: *clavic(ularius) carc(eris) p(ublici) Lug(dunensis)*.
99 For the difficulty of locating someone in Rome, cf. U.E. Paoli, *op.cit.*, pg. 324.
100 2 Tim. 4,11.

his mind very well [101]. The Evangelist had already accompanied the Apostle during his earlier Roman captivity[102]; he seems now to have been the only one of Paul's inner circle still in Rome.

Luke was a most valuable associate serving not only as Paul's travelling companion, but also as his physician[103]. The *Muratorian Canon* mentions Luke's medical role, but also adds that he may have played a legal role as well: *Lucas iste medicus post a(s)censum Xpi. cum eo paulus quasi ut iuris studiosum secundum adsumsisset...*"[104].

III, 3. 2 Tim. 4,6-8: Paul's death as a sacrifice

2 Tim. 4,6-8 forms the dramatic climax to the Pastoral Epistles. In these verses the Pastor presents Paul reflecting, not only on the imminence of his martyrdom, but on its sacrificial aspect as well:

> "For I am already on the point of being sacrificed; the time of my departure has come (ἐγὼ γὰρ ἤδη σπένδομαι καὶ ὁ καιρὸς τῆς ἀναλύσεώς μου ἐφέστηκεν). I have fought the good fight, I have finished the race, I have kept faith (τὸν καλὸν ἀγῶνα ἠγώνισμαι, τὸν δρόμον τετέλεκα, τὴν πίστιν τετήρηκα). Henceforth there is laid up for me the crown of righteousness (λοιπὸν ἀπόκειταί μοι ὁ τῆς δικαιοσύνης στέφανος), which the Lord, the righteous judge (ὁ δίκαιος κριτής), will award to me on that Day, and not only to me but also to all who have loved his appearing".

A) καὶ ὁ καιρὸς τῆς ἀναλύσεώς μου ἐφέστηκεν

ἡ ἀνάλυσις — losing, releasing, dissolving. This is the only occurrence of this noun in the NT.

This word can be used metaphorically in the sense of 'departure from life'[105]; the soul's liberation from the chains in which the body binds it[106]. Plutarch used the noun when reiterating the ancient Greek conception of death as the separation of the body and soul thus allowing one to behold the pure and absolute which is truth[107]. Paul used the cognate verb ἀναλύω in the sense of 'to die', that is to depart this life to have everlasting life with Christ[108].

---

101 Cf. J.C.K. Freeborn, "2 Timothy 4,11: "Only Luke is with me"", *STUDIA EVANGELICA VI*, TU. 112, Berlin, 1973, pg. 120.
102 Phlm. 24.
103 Col. 4,14.
104 *Muratorian Canon* 3-5. For Eusebius' account, cf. *HE*. 2,22.6.
105 Cf. Philo, *in Flaccum* 187: τὴν ἐκ τοῦ βίου τελευταίαν ἀνάλυσιν.
106 Secundus, *Sententiae* 19.
107 Plutarch, *Consolatio ad Apollonium* 13.
108 Phil. 1,23.

III. The Pastoral Epistles

The Pastor understands Paul's death to be the accomplishment of his Apostolic ministry, the final and crowning event in a fruitful life spent in the Lord's service[109].

B) τὸν δρόμον τετέλεκα

1. ὁ δρόμος — the race, the course, the place for running, the race-course. It is used here in the sense of the course of a life/ministry. So Acts 13,25: "and as John was finishing his course ..."; Acts 20,24: "if only I may accomplish my course and the ministry which I received from the Lord Jesus, to testify to the Gospel of the grace of God". Paul himself employed not the noun, but the related verb τρέχω to express the same idea: " ... holding fast the word of life, so that in the day of Christ I may be proud that I did not run (ἔδραμον) in vain"[110]. The same imagery is also used by the author of the *Epistle to the Hebrews*: "... and let us run with perseverance the race that is set before us[111].

2. τελέω — to bring to an end, finish, complete. The Pastor's choice of this verb was intended to liken Paul's death to that of Jesus. The Saviour's earthly ministry reached its perfect and unique fulfillment when He died on the cross. Significantly Jesus' very last word from the cross as reported by St. John, was τετέλεσται — *consummatum est.*[112]

Paul has now completed his earthly ministry; his coming death will totally consummate that ministry and bring it to perfection. The Apostle is at long last, after a life of hard evangelical labour, close to receiving his final reward.

C) ἐγὼ γὰρ ἤδη σπένδομαι

1. ἤδη — already, now, presently, immediately. By his use of this temporal adverb in conjunction with the Present Passive Indicative σπένδομαι, the Pastor stresses that Paul's martyrdom is imminent, that it will take place forthwith. As the hour of his martyrdom is now well nigh (ἤδη), the whole sacrificial aspect, concretized by the use of the verb σπένδω, is presented by the Pastor as being Paul's ultimate and deepest reflexion on the true meaning of his own death.

---

109 A similar usage appears in Clement of Rome (*Ep. Cor.* 44,5): "Blessed are those priests who, having run their course before now, have obtained a fruitful and perfect release from this world, for they have not to fear anyone's depriving them of the place now appointed them".
110 Phil. 2,16.
111 Hebr. 12,1.
112 Jn. 19,30.

2. σπένδω— to pour out a libation, to make a drink offering: " ... before drinking wine a portion was poured on the table, hearth, or altar"[113]. The use of this verb was mainly religious; it very often designated the making of libations to a god. Philo used the verb figuratively: it is the *mind* which is a libation poured out to God[114]. In Phil. 2,17, Paul evokes the possibility (ἀλλὰ εἰ καὶ) that he will make a libation of himself, pouring out his life (σπένδομαι) in the service of Jesus Christ and His Gospel. In the verses at hand, the Pastor goes much farther: Paul is presented in the very act of being sacrificed for the Gospel's sake.

D) τὸν καλὸν ἀγῶνα ἠγώνισμαι

ὁ ἀγών — has a variety of meanings. It can denote a gathering or assembly, a place of contest or the athletic contest itself (*Agon* personified is the divinity of the contest)[115]; in general the noun designates a struggle, fight, battle or conflict, not only a physical but also mental struggle (hence, anxiety). Finally it has a juridical nuance: action at the trial[116] or a speech delivered before a court or a ruler[117]. Paul used it on several occasions in his Epistles; so Phil. 1,29—30:

> "For it has been granted to you that for the sake of Christ, you should not only believe in him but also suffer for his sake, engaged in the same conflict (ἀγῶνα) which you saw and now hear to be mine."

In the Pastorals the stress is on the actual struggle itself and the endurance, perseverance and strength needed for it[118]. This emphasis is amply manifested by the Pastor's juxtaposition of the noun ἀγών with its cognate verb ἀγωνίζομαι. Athletic and military terminology appeared more frequently in Paul's later Epistles; after his death this type of vocabulary became one of the characteristic traits of the Paulinist lexicon[119]. The Pastor's goal was to present Paul as a man who never flagged in his struggle. Timothy and all later Christians were to follow this Apostolic example when confronting doctrinal error, judicial vexations or martyrdom[120].

---

113 *LS*⁹, pg. 1626.
114 Philo. *de Ebrietate* 152.
115 Pausanias 5,26.3.
116 Plato, *Apologia* 24 C.
117 Polybius 9,32.4 (a diplomatic contest).
118 Cf. Clement, *Ep. Cor.* 7,1.
119 V.C. Pfitzner, *Paul and the Agon Motif,* Leiden, 1967, pg. 165.
120 Cf. 1 Tim. 6,12-14.

There is a close connexion between Paul's ἀγών and his martyrdom. Paul's struggle here does not include the actual martyrdom itself, but it is clear that martyrdom is the perfection and accomplishment of the ἀγών. In this passage as well as in James 1,12 and Rev. 2,10, one sees the inception of a Christian martyrdom theology:

> "It is doubtless such passages as these (cf. also Mt. 10,22) which were combined with the already familiar picture of the *Agon* of steadfastness in suffering (e.g. 4 Macc.) to form the language and conception of Christian martyrdom, from the Martyrdom of Polycarp onwards".[121]

E) τὴν πίστιν τετήρηκα

Paul has always taught pure evangelical doctrine as opposed to the erroneous doctrine propagated by the false doctors. The emphasis here, however, is less on doctrinal purity than on loyalty to and fulfillment of the Apostolic ministry. Throughout his entire ministry, Paul belonged exclusively to Christ; his devotion extended over all his previous deeds and now extends to his dying for the Master's sake." His suffering till death", writes V.C. Pfitzner, "is not only the end of his life, but also the final act of his office"[122].

Finally, the Pastor places Paul's martyrdom in an eschatological framework. In the preceding verse, the Pastor summarized Paul's life and work:

— I have fought the good fight,
— I have finished the race,
— I have kept the faith.

One last thing remains and that is God's response to His servant's faith and witness: the awarding of the crown of righteousness.

F) λοιπὸν ἀπόκειταί μοι ὁ τῆς δικαιοσύνης στέφανος

1. ἀπόκειμαί
The primary meaning of this verb, which occurs only four times in the NT, is to 'be stored up', to 'be laid in store for', to 'be reserved to'. Paul used it only once in his Epistles, in Col. 1,5: "the hope laid up for you in Heaven". The impersonal form of the verb used here highlights the certainty that the thing stored up will in fact be accorded the beneficiary[123].

2. ὁ τῆς δικαιοσύνης στέφανος
For the Pastor, the *corona iustitiae* is Paul's adornment and pride, conferred by

---

121 V.C. Pfitzner, *op.cit.*, pg. 185.
122 *Ibid.*, pg. 183.
123 Arndt & Gingrich, pg. 92.

the Righteous Judge himself on His faithful Apostle. It is Paul's symbol of joy, the sign of his certain triumph and the assurance of his immortality. In this burst of eschatological exultation, the Pastor evokes Paul's crowning, viewed as a felicitous gift bestowed on the Apostle after a life of devotion and a martyr's death.

The image of the crown as a symbol of immortality and a visible sign of the eschatological reward of the righteous occurs elsewhere in the later books of the NT[124]. So James 1,12: "Blessed is the man who endures trial, for when he has stood the test he will receive the crown of life (τὸν στέφανον τῆς ζωῆς) which God has promised to those who love him". The expression 'crown of life' is also used in Rev. 2,9—10: "I know your tribulations and your poverty (but you are rich) and the slander of those who say they are Jews and are not, but are a synagogue of Satan. Do not fear what you are about to suffer. Behold, the devil is about to throw some of you into prison, that you may be tested, and for ten days you will have tribulation. Be faithful unto death, and I will give you the crown of life". In 1 Peter 5,4, the expression 'crown of glory' (τῆς δόξης στέφανον)[125], also occurs within an eschatological setting.

G) ὁ δίκαιος κριτής

The crown of righteousness is bestowed on Paul by Christ, termed here the Just Judge. The adjective δίκαιος stressed the righteousness motif of the verse. It is also likely to have been employed with a juridical thought in mind. The Pastor is contrasting Christ, the *iustus iudex*, to the inequitable human judge who condemned Paul to death.

IV. Excursus 1: Paul and The Mamertinum Prison

The ancient Mamertinum Prison at the Forum is presently englobed within the precincts of the Church of San Giuseppe dei Falegnami, forming the two lower levels of that small, though quite beautiful Baroque edifice. The façade of the Mamertinum Prison faces the central Forum and on it is quite conspicuously placed a modern inscription describing the structure as being *la prigione dei SS. Apostoli Pietro e Paolo* (the prison of the Holy Apostles Peter and Paul). This inscription is surmounted by a square stone sculpture depicting the two Apostles behind bars looking out.

---

124 In the *Testament of Levi* 8,2, the expression 'crown of righteousness' is used in a sacerdotal, rather than eschatological sense (Edition: R.H. Charles).
125 Cf. the *Testament of Benjamin* 4,1 (Edition: R.H. Charles).

IV. Excursus 1

The Mamertinum Prison is composed of two superimposed chambers. The upper chamber, a few meters below present street level, contains a number of modern artifacts citing the Mamertinum as the place in which the two Apostles were detained while awaiting martyrdom:

A) a large slab inscribed in Latin affirming this to be historical fact;

B) another stone slab listing the distinguished Christians imprisoned in the Mamertinum until the Peace of the Church. Under Nero's reign appear the names of Peter and Paul, their jailers Processus and Martinianus, whom they were said to have converted and baptized while awaiting execution, and diverse anonymous Roman proto-martyrs;

C) above the small altar a bust of the two Apostles;

D) at the head of the stairs leading down to the lower chamber is an indented stone. Legend has it that Peter's head was pushed against this stone by brutal guards while he was being flung into the lower chamber and that the imprint of his head remained miraculously etched in the stone.

The lower chamber, the *sotterraneo Tulliano*, is a veritable dungeon. Originally this lower floor was a water cistern fed by a spring of water, which still exists, although now welled up. In Antiquity, the lower chamber was entered only by a hole in the floor of the upper chamber. Prisoners cast into the *sotterraneo Tulliano* were either starved to death or subsequently removed and decapitated[126]. The lower chamber contains a column about a meter high to which Peter and Paul were said to have been chained. Nearby to the right of an altar is a small bronze sculpture depicting the Apostles baptizing their two jailers. Before the column, there is a shallow well, still containing fresh water, as we said above. A slab in the *sotterraneo Tulliano* reads as follows:

> "This is the column to which the Holy Apostles Peter and Paul were chained; where they converted the Holy Martyrs Processus and Martinianus, custodians of the prison and 47 others to the faith of Christ, whom they baptized with water from this fountain which had miraculously gushed forth".

Thus the modern visitor encounters these sundry affirmations that the Mamertinum was the prison of Peter and Paul during their last days in Rome. The question remains as to how historical this tradition is (if at all), or to phrase the question in another way, as to when the association of Peter and Paul with the prison entered Holy Tradition.

---

126 G. Lugli., *Itinerario di Roma antica*, Milan, 1970; pg. 219.

The mediaeval martyrologies, e.g. the *Martyrologium of Usuard*, the *Martyrologium of Ado*, and the *Martyrologium of Notker* already knew the tradition. Under the feast day of the 47 martyrs (14 March) the *Martyrologium of Usuard* (c.875 A.D.) has the following notice:

> "Romae, passio sanctorum quadraginta et septem. Hi baptizati sunt a beato Petro apostolo, cum teneretur in custodia Mamertini, cum coapostolo suo Paulo, ubi novem menses detenti sunt; qui omnes sub devotissima fidei confessione, Neroniano gladio consumpti sunt"[127].

The language in Ado (c.865 A.D.)is virtually the same:

> "Romae, passio sanctorum martyrum quadraginta et septem qui baptizati sunt a beato Petro apostolo, cum teneretur idem apostolus in custodia Marmurtini cum coapostolo suo Paulo ubi novem menses detenti sunt, Qui omnes sub devotissima fidei confessione, Neroniano gladio consumpti sunt".[128]

The notice entered the *Martyrologia* through Ado who extracted the information in it from the text of the *Passio Sanctorum Processi et Martiniani Martyrum*[129]. This is a 6th Century work which gives the legend of these two men, identified as the jailers. The outline of the story is as follows: After the death of Simon Magus, Nero remitted Peter and Paul to the custody of Paulinus who had them placed in the Mamertinum where they remained for nine months. Many Christians of Rome came to the prison to be healed or exorcised by the two Apostles. There were many guards, the chiefest of whom were Processus and Martinianus. It is not altogether clear how these old Roman martyrs, already venerated by the Roman Church from the end of the 3rd Century, came to be identified as the two Apostles' jailers. In any case, the two men, having witnessed the miracles performed by Peter and Paul, asked to be baptized. Following their baptism, 47 fellow prisoners also requested Peter to baptize them (episode of the miracle of the baptismal water)[130]. The Eucharist was then celebrated. Thus in this *Passio*, the dismal, dark and dangerous Mamertinum was transformed into a place of Apostolic preaching, conversion, miracle and celebration. After this, Peter and Paul quit the Mamertinum and Paul disappears from the narrative. The *Passio* continues by an evocation of the *quo vadis* episode, the relation of the martyrdoms of Processus and Martinianus and their

---

127 *Martyrologium of Usuard*, 14 March (*PL.* 123, col. 841-842).
128 *Martyrologium of Ado*; 14 March (*PL.* 123; col. 239). The *Martyrologium of Notker* gives a shorter version, but adds the words *in vinculis* to *detenti sunt* (*PL.* 131; col. 1054).
129 For the text of the *Passio SS. Processi et Martiniani Mart.* see B. Mombritius (ed.), Vol. 2; pg. 403-404.
130 Peter's working of the miracle of the spring and the two jailers drinking thereof is one of the three central motifs in early Petrine iconography. Along with representations of the Apostle's arrest and his denial of Christ (depicted by a cock), it forms a part of the *trilogia petrina*, appearing on an important number of ancient Christian sarcophagi.

burial by Lucina on her property near the site of their martyrdom, the via Aurelia. The *Passio SS. Processi et Martiniani Mart.* then is a typical example of a later Christian martyrological literature springing from an already well developed tradition about Peter and Paul in Rome. It is an entirely legendary tale without any historical foundation whatever. U.M. Fasola notes that the development of a Petro-Pauline tradition identifying the Mamertinum as the Apostles' Roman prison and the transformation of that site into a Christian cultic place, pre-dated the writing of the *Passio SS. Processi et Martiniani Mart.*, but even so is not any earlier than the 5th Century[131].

In conclusion, the tradition associating Peter and Paul with the Mamertinum is both late and unhistorical:

A) The story of the baptizing of the two jailers and of the 47 others is a legendary accretion to the Petro-Pauline apocryphal *corpus* already in circulation in Rome. It most likely used as its model Luke's account of the imprisonment of Paul and Silas in Philippi where the two Apostles converted and baptized their jailer[132].

B) Historically, the Mamertinum was a state prison reserved for important prisoners. Those detained there included some of the most famous enemies of Roman power, such as Jugurtha or Vercingetorix. Peter, the fisherman from Galilee and Paul, the tentmaker, were simply not in that category of political prisoner[133]. It is vastly more reasonable to think of Paul as awaiting execution in one of the dungeons of the Praetorian Barracks than in the Mamertinum.

C) It is highly unlikely that Peter and Paul were imprisoned together. The twinning of Peter and Paul is a process which began relatively early in the history of the Roman Church, but it is not the earliest tradition, which had the two Apostles exercising their ministries in Rome and giving final witness at different times. Moreover, it is Peter, rather than Paul, who is associated with the Mamertinum[134]. Peter plays a much larger role in the *Passio SS. Processi et Martiniani Mart.* than Paul, who is clearly a secondary figure. Indeed, in this

---

131 U.M. Fasola, *Pietro e Paolo a Roma: orme sulla roccia*, Rome, 1980; pg. 57.
132 Acts 16,23-34.
133 G. Lugli notes that there existed a building adjacent to the Mamertinum, the *Lautumiae*, a less fearsome place, which was used for the temporary detention of less important prisoners (G. Lugli, *op.cit.*, pg. 219). Cf. S.B. Platner, who writes that the *Lautumiae* were "quarries on the slope of the Capitoline just above the Carcer, which were also used as a prison" (S.B. Platner, *A topographical Dictionary of ancient Rome*, Rome, 1965; pg. 316.
134 In fact the street to the rear of the Marmertinum bears the name of via di San Pietro in Carcere.

respect the *Passio* is very characteristic of later Roman martyrological literature. While Peter's imprisonment deeply impressed the ancient Roman Church, Paul's imprisonment in the city of Rome — although better documented historically — was gradually effaced from the memory of the Roman Church, even as the memory of Peter's imprisonment became ever more vivid[135].

V. Excursus 2: 'Usque ad ultimum terrae': Did Paul Visit Spain between his two Roman Captivities?

V,1. The westward Thrust of Paul's later Ministry

From the time of his arrival as an appellant prisoner till his final imprisonment and martyrdom, Rome was Paul's base. The question which needs to be asked in this context is whether the Apostle ever left the city to conduct a mission in the brief moment of freedom he enjoyed between his two captivities. Did he ever return to the East to visit Philemon or the Philippian Church as he thought of doing?[136] Or more importantly to our purpose here, was the Apostle able to fulfill his goal of going to Spain?

It is unlikely that Paul ever returned to the Hellenistic East. In Rom. 15,19, he wrote " ... I have completed the preaching of the Gospel of Christ from Jerusalem as far round as Illyricum". Neither Jerusalem, seat of the original community, nor the thoroughly Gentile land of Illyricum, already so far to the West (and North) of the Gospel's starting point, constituted a primary field of missionary activity for Paul[137]. The Apostle mentions these geographi-

---

135 U.M. Fasola, *op.cit.*, pg. 57.
136 Phlm. 22; Phil. 2,24.
137 Illyricum marked the north-western boundary of the Pauline mission at the time the Apostle composed his letter to the Roman community. The preposition μέχρι — 'even to', 'as far as', 'all the way up to' (cf. the Latin *usque in*), would indicate that Paul had preached and founded new Churches in Western and Northern Macedonia up to the Illyrian border (Acts 20,2), but does not necessarily imply that he actually crossed that border to preach in Illyricum itself. One would assume that Paul followed the *via Egnatia* into Western Macedonia as he had done earlier in the Eastern part of the province. The reference in Titus 3,12 to Paul's intention of wintering in the Epirote city of Nicopolis — if it has any historical basis at all — should be placed in the context of the mission to Macedonia described in Acts, rather than to any hypothetical journey between the two Roman captivities. Cf. W.M. Ramsay, who argues that Paul really did sojourn in Nicopolis between the two captivities and that it was in Nicopolis that Paul was arrested for the final time and dispatched back to Rome (W.M. Ramsay, "Nicopolis", *HDB.*, Vol. III, pg. 549). M. Dibelius and H. Conzelmann consider the reference to Nicopolis in Titus 3,12 to be merely "a legendary expansion of Paul's travels into the northwestern part of the Balkan peninsula which originated in the context of Rom. 15,19 (*The Pastoral Epistles*, Philadelphia, 1972; pg. 153).

cal *termini* within an essentially eschatological context: Jerusalem and Illyricum not only convey the idea that the triumphal march of the Gospel had been from East to West, but also that the territory located to the *east of Rome* had already been *fully* attained. There is the idea of plenitude, both geographic and cosmic, in Paul's message[138]. Thus in Rm. 15,19, the Apostle used the particular expression πεπληρωκέναι τὸ εὐαγγέλιον τοῦ Χριστοῦ : "I have completed the preaching of the Gospel of Christ". The verb πληρόω means to fill, make full, make complete, to carry through to the end, to pervade with. Paul's use of the Perfect Infinitive indicates that the action has been accomplished: the Apostle preached the Gospel in such a full, replete and effective way that it is now widely known, acknowledged and embraced in the geographical area indicated by the *termini*, Jerusalem and Illyricum:

> "The Gospel has been heard: more could not be expected before the Parousia. Thus Paul is free, or rather, is impelled to break new ground in the fulfillment of the eschatological programme entrusted to him as an Apostle (vs. 23)".[139]

Another reference which provides strong evidence that the Apostle never returned to the East occurs in Acts in the course of Paul's speech at Miletus to the Presbyters of the Church of Ephesus: "And now, behold, I know that all you among whom I have gone about preaching the Kingdom will see my face no more"[140]. To emphasize the fact even more strongly, Luke repeated the reference at the close of the speech: "And they all wept and embraced Paul and kissed him, sorrowing most of all because of the word he had spoken, that they should see his face no more"[141].

Here, then, Luke unambiguously states that Paul's departure from the East was a definitive one. The Evangelist not only recorded a significant turning point in Paul's Apostolic ministry, that he would henceforth concentrate his efforts on evangelizing the Latin West, but also, writing as he did after Paul's martyrdom, the historical fact that Paul had never returned to the East[142].

---

138 Cf. F.J. Leenhardt, *L'Epitre de St. Paul aux Romains*, Geneva, 2nd. Edition, 1981; pg. 208; E. Käsemann, *Commentary on Romans*, English trans., London, 1980; pg. 394.

139 C.K. Barrett, *A Commentary on the Epistle to the Romans*, London, 1962; pg. 276. For R.D. Aus, the full number of the Gentiles (πλήρωμα τῶν ἐθνῶν) of Rom. 11,25, " ... will only be complete when Paul has also brought Christian representatives from *Spain*, the most distant site in the OT vision of the end events, with their gifts to Jerusalem" (R.D. Aus, "Paul's, travel Plans to Spain and the 'full Number of the Gentiles' of Rom. XI,25", *NOVUM TESTAMENTUM*, Vol. 21; 1979; pg. 260-261).

140 Acts 20,25.

141 Acts 20,37-38.

142 "His mind was on Rome and the West", writes D.T. Rowlingson, (in) "The geographical Orientation of Paul's missionary Interests", *JBL.*, Vol. 69; 1950; pg. 344.

V,2. Spain as a missionary Objective

In the pla de Palau, a small square located behind the magnificent Cathedral in the old city of Tarragona, there is a modern statue of St. Paul, sadly obscured by the numerous automobiles parked in front of it. On the statue's pedestal appears the following inscription:

> "Al apostol San Pablo
> en la XIX centenario
> de su venida a Espana
> y de su estancia en
> Tarragona" MCMLXIII

Thus the ancient belief transmitted down through the ages by the Church of Tarragona that the Apostle had come to that city in the year 63 A.D. is still a living tradition[143]. Does this tradition that Paul visited Tarragona have any historical foundation? For Geza Alföldy, not at all:

> "The tradition that the Apostle Paul had already come to Tarragona and converted a part of the population to Christianity can in no way be supported by the evidence... . It is only from the middle of the 3rd Century that Christians are unequivocally documented as being in Tarragona; notably in literary sources. From the 4th Century many epigraphical and archeological sources also exist".[144]

Alföldy's analysis seems rather over sceptical. When Bishop Fructuosus was martyred, along with his Deacons Augurius and Eulogius, in the Valerianic persecution of 258 A.D., he was the spiritual leader of a well-structured Christian community whose establishment considerably pre-dated this fierce persecution[144a]. Indeed Christian graves dating from the 3rd Century, and possibly earlier, have also been discovered in Tarragona, especially in the Western section of the city. The fact that Paul's visit to Tarragona left no archeological traces does not necessary mean that it never took place. Such a conclusion is too hastily drawn. A short mission to Tarragona, especially if that mission had been a failed one, would hardly have left durable archeological traces.

The Catalan historian J.M. Recasens i Comes puts forth another hypothesis. He believes that Paul came to Spain at some point between 61 and 65 A.D., but evangelized the region of Baetica and not Tarragona:

---

143 Other Spanish cities have conserved the tradition that Paul consecrated their first Bishop: e.g. Bishop Rufus of Tortosa (*Dertosa Iulia Augusta*), the Rufus of Mk. 15,21 and Rom. 16,13. For further discussion, cf. E. Dassmann, "Archeologische Spuren frühchristlicher Paulusverehrung", *RQS.*, Vol. 84; 1989; pg. 276.

144 G. Alföldy, "Tarraco", *RE.* Supplementband 15; 1978; col. 641.

144a For mention of the early Spanish Church, cf. Irenaeus, *Adv. Haer.* 1,10.2; Tertullian, *Adv. Iud.* 7.

"... today one is inclined to think that the propagation of Christianity in the peninsula began in Baetica and not in the Tarraconense. This is because the social classes in Baetica were more Romanized and thus more influenced by cultural currents coming from the Eastern and North African provinces; they would thus have been more receptive than the other Hispanic provinces. We also must not forget that the Baetica was the most densely populated province: a circumstance favourable to those who were interested in an efficacious propagation of the new religion".[145]

Recasens i Comes' comments are certainly plausible with regards to the definitive evangelization of Spain in the generations after Paul's death. But they do not explain why Paul, coming from Rome, would bypass a city like Tarragona, which was the very type of Romanized, urban provincial capital that he had so favoured in his various missions in the Hellenistic East[146]. That Paul visited the more distant Baetica region during his Spanish journey cannot be excluded from the realm of the possible, but that he skipped Tarragona does not seem possible[147].

V,3. N.T. Evidence

Nowhere in the NT is there any specific reference to Paul's journey to Spain having been accomplished. Both Acts and the Pastoral Epistles pass Spain over in complete silence. Paul himself only refers to a possible Spanish journey in his letter to the Romans and he does not re-iterate his desire to go there anywhere in the Captivity Epistles. The silence of any NT witness to the journey does not, however, signify that Paul was unable to fulfill his self-proclaimed goal of going to Spain:

A) Luke's theological design for Acts was to bring Paul from Jerusalem to Rome, his final missionary station and the site of his martyrdom. Luke consciously left unmentioned many other early Christian missions conducted both by Paul and the other Apostles when these missions had no precise relationship to — or effect on — his apologetic programme for Acts. The

---

145 J.M. Recasens i Comes, *La Ciutat de Tarragona*, Barcelona, 1966, Vol. I, pg. 150.
146 Tarragona was known as the *Colonia Iulia Urbs Triumphalis Tarraco*. Its busy port benefited from the fertile plain of the Ebro and the city itself was an important centre for a whole network of roads along which all the produce of Northern Spain flowed: "It is likely that its economic development was favoured by the city's political situation, both in that it was the residence of the provincial governor as well as by the presence in Tarragona of the altar of *Roma et Augustus*" (J. Rougé, *Recherches sur l'Organisation du Commerce maritime en Mediterranée sous l'Empire romain*, Paris, 1966, pg. 143).
147 Cf. J. Serra-Vilaró, *Fructuós, Auguri i Eulogi: Màrtirs sants de Tarragona*, Tarragona, 1936; pg. 12-13.

Pastoral Epistles were not from Paul's own pen and they largely treat the ecclesiastical situation in the East in the Pastor's own time. This would negate any need for mentioning a mission to the West. In the Captivity Epistles, Paul was dealing with persons/communities in the East; repeating his desire to go to Spain would be an unnecessary addition to his letters. Finally if the Spanish mission had been less than successful — and we recall in this context that Paul was both aged and ill by this time — then this could in part explain the NT silence on a Spanish mission.

B) A universal mission had been confided to the 12 Apostles by the Risen Lord just before His Ascension: "And you shall be my witnesses in Jerusalem and in all Judaea and Samaria and to the ends of the earth (καὶ ἕως ἐσχάτου τῆς γῆς)"[148]. In Luke, Jesus says that repentance and forgiveness should be preached in His Name "to all nations, beginning from Jerusalem"[149]. The same idea occurs in Mt. 28,19 where Jesus tells his followers to "make disciples of all nations baptizing them in the Name of the Father and of the Son and of the Holy Ghost". The longer conclusion to Mark's Gospel contains an exhortation by Christ to the Eleven to "go into all the world and preach the Gospel to the whole creation"[150]. The shorter conclusion to Mark adds to Mk. 16,8: "And after this, Jesus himself sent out by means of them, from east to west (ἀπὸ ἀνατολῆς καὶ ἄχρι δύσεως) the sacred and imperishable proclamation of eternal salvation. All these *logia* are representative of the early Church's understanding of how God fulfilled His plan for mankind's salvation in the coming, death, resurrection and glorification of His only-begotten Son. This salvation, proclaimed by Paul and the other Apostles and witnessed to in the confessing communities which they had founded, is circumscribed by no ethnic, social, political or geographical barrier. The term, 'ends of the earth', is not a hollow rhetorical device; rather it is a tangible expression of the concept of the universality of salvation, a universality which is both cosmic and geographic.

C) Paul had the special mission of bringing the Gospel to the farthest flung regions of the Roman Empire. This is clear from a sentence in Paul's speech in the synagogue of Pisidian Antioch: "For so the Lord had commanded us, saying 'I have sent you to be a light for the Gentiles, that you may bring salvation to the uttermost parts of the earth'"[151]. Paul himself wrote that he had received grace and Apostleship to bring about the obedience of faith for the

---

148 Acts 1,8.
149 Lk. 24,47.
150 Mk. 16,15.
151 Acts 13,47.

sake of His name "among all nations"[152]. The Apostle's ambition was to preach the Gospel "not where Christ has already been named, lest I build on another man's foundation, but as it is written, 'They shall see who have never been told of him[153]. Paul was not talking about Rome here, but about Spain, the *ultima terra*, where as yet Christ had not been preached. Spain represented the *West*. It was at the extremity of the Western world, forming the Western enclosure of the Mediterranean Sea. It was one of the most Romanized and best integrated provinces in the whole Empire. It was the type of place, with its urban, Latin culture for which Paul had a predilection as a missionary field. The evangelization of Spain, the extension of the Pauline mission to that Western land, would symbolize geographically the universality and fullness of the Kingdom, thus accomplishing the command given by the Lord to all His disciples to go forth and baptize all nations:

> "It is clear that Spain had always been a fixed and explicit element in the Divine Providence's economy of salvation and that an Apostle, conscious of having to preach the Gospel to all creation, could not but have the Iberian peninsula before his eyes".[154]

D) So Paul briefly outlines in his letter to the Romans the contours of his coming mission to the West. First he would visit Rome, which was his primary goal:

> "For God is my witness ... that without ceasing I mention you always in my prayers, asking that somehow by God's will I may now at last succeed in coming to you. For I long to see you, that I may impart to you some spiritual gift to strengthen you, that is, that we may be mutually encouraged by each other's faith, both yours and mine. I want you to know, brethren, that I have often intended to come to you (but thus far have been prevented), in order that I may reap some harvest among you as well as among the rest of the Gentiles. I am under obligation both to Greeks and to barbarians, both to the wise and to the foolish: so I am eager to preach the Gospel to you also who are in Rome".[155]

Paul's future missionary work would concentrate on Rome and Spain to the exclusion of the territory "from Jerusalem as far round as Illyricum", where he had laboured so long and so fruitfully:

> "But now, since I no longer have any room for work in these regions, and since I have longed for many years to come to you, I hope to see you in passing as I go to Spain, and to be sped on my journey (προπεμφθῆναι) there by you, once I have enjoyed your company a little".[156]

---

152 Rom. 1,5.
153 Rom. 15,20-21.
154 C. Spicq, "Saint Paul est venu en Espagne", *HELMANTICA*, (Salamanca), Tomo 15; 1964; pg. 53.
155 Rom. 1,9-15.
156 Rom. 15, 23-24.

A few verses later, Paul once again links his arrival in Rome with the planned journey to Spain:

> "When therefore, I have completed this [the journey to Jerusalem], and have delivered to them what has been raised, I shall go on by way of you to Spain; and I know that when I come to you I shall come in the fulness of the blessing of Christ".[157]

The verb προπέμπω occurs nine times in the NT. It means to accompany, escort a departing traveller, help a traveller on his journey with food, money, companions or guides, furnish the means for travelling[158]. Paul's use of it here is deeply significant. Just as the Church at Antioch had sponsored missions to evangelize the East, so Paul here is asking the Church at Rome to supply him with the means of carrying out a mission to Spain and thereby to begin the evangelization of the Western Mediterranean basin[159].

V,4. Patristic witness to the Spanish Journey

Patristic literature has conserved and transmitted the tradition that Paul did in fact fulfill his objective of going to Spain. The Fathers as a whole understood this to be a historical reality on the basis of the sources which they had at their disposal.

The earliest witness is Clement of Rome who composed his *Epistle to the Corinthians* scarcely three decades after Paul's martyrdom. The Pauline reminiscences contained in Clement's letter are probably first hand; that is to say that Clement was an eyewitness to the events to which he alludes in his composition. Irenaeus of Lyon understood this to be the case when he wrote of Clement's relationship to the Holy Apostles Peter and Paul: "*Clemens ... vidit apostolos ipsos, et contulit cum eis et cum adhuc insonantem praedicationem apostolorum et traditionem ante oculos haberet*"[160]. Moreover,

---

157 Rom. 15, 28-29.
158 Acts 20,38; Acts 21,5; also Acts 15,3; 1 Cor. 16,6; 11; 2 Cor. 1,16; Titus 3,13.
159 P.S. Minear writes: "There were logistic reasons for writing to the Romans in connection with that visit, although Paul is not very explicit about them. Certainly this letter reminds us of Paul's penchant for planning his travels well in advance; he would go from Corinth, by way of Ephesus, to Jerusalem, thence to Rome, and thence to Spain. (...) More important, though less certain, we may suppose that Paul wanted to avoid the catastrophe of having his work in Spain ruined by opposition from the Roman congregations. He had learned how important for missionary activity is a loyal base, a city where various congregations share whole-heartedly in a common enterprise. Nothing more quickly jeopardized the survival of infant churches than strife among supporting churches. (P.S. Minear, *op.cit.*, pg. 2).
160 Irenaeus, *adv. Haer.* 3,3.3.

in view of the temporal proximity between Paul's death and the composition of the *Epistle to the Corinthians*, other Roman Christians were still alive who also had known the Apostles personally and who would have known first hand what they did in their last days and how they died. So Irenaeus wrote that Clement was not alone: "*non solus; adhuc enim multi supererant tunc ab apostolis docti*"[161]. Clement's brief account of Paul's mission and of his death — all too brief, alas — "does not appear", writes A.C. Vega, "to depend on any known author; his reference has the air of being a direct and personal piece of information"[162].

Insofar as Paul's missionary journey to Spain is concerned, Clement says the following: Paul "was a herald both in the East and in the West (κῆρυξ γενόμενος ἔν τε τῇ ἀνατολῇ καὶ ἔν τῇ δύσει)", he "taught righteousness to all the world (ὅλον τὸν κόσμον)" and he "had reached the limits of the West ... (ἐπὶ τὸ τέρμα τῆς δύσεως ἐλθὼν)"[163].

A) ἡ δύσις

This is the *West*, the part of the firmament where the sun sets. It is the antonym of ἀνατολή , the quarter of the sunrise[164]. The word occurs in the Greek writers[165], but only once in the *Septuaginta*, where it denotes the 'setting of the sun'[166]. It does not occur in the NT, except in the variant short ending of Mark's Gospel[167]. Rather the West is expressed in the NT by the related word δυσμή which occurs five times. West and East taken together designate the totality of the world. Jesus used these terms in a precise eschatological setting: "I tell you, many will come from East and West (ἀπὸ ἀνατολῶν καὶ δυσμῶν) and sit at table with Abraham, Isaac and Jacob in the kingdom of Heaven"[168]. So too Clement, when he used the expressions "was a herald both in the East and in the West"

---

161 *Ibid.*
162 A.C. Vega, "La venida de San Pablo a Espana y los varones apostolicos", *BOLETIN DE LA REAL ACADEMIA DE LA HISTORIA*, Madrid, Tomo 154; 1964; pg. 17.
163 Clement of Rome, *Ep.Cor.* 5,6-7 (*trans.* K. Lake, *Loeb*, 1912).
164 Cf. *OGIS. 199.33.*
165 E.g. Thucydides 2,96; Polybius 1,42.5; 5,104.7.
166 *Ps.* 103,19. Philo uses the expressions ἀπ᾽ ἀνατολῆς ἐπὶ δύσιν and ἀπὸ τῶν ἑσπερίων ἐπὶ τὰ ἑῷα to describe the movements and passage of the stars (*de Cherubim* 22). His phrasing suggests not only spherical limits, but the wholeness of the heavens.
167 Mk. 16,8b: "But they reported briefly to Peter and those with him all that they had been told. And after this, Jesus Himself sent out by means of them from East to West (ἀπὸ ἀνατολῆς καὶ ἄρχι δύσεως), the sacred and imperishable proclamation of eternal salvation". The short ending is not of Mark's authorship; its date of composition being the first half of the 2nd Century.
168 Mt. 8,11. Cf. Lk. 13,29. The eschatological setting is also obvious in Mt. 24,27.

and "taught righteousness to all the world", was not merely naming precise geographical limits, but by emphasizing the wholeness of the Petrine and Pauline missions and the plenitude of their proclamation, he was formulating a distinct conception of a Christian world mission.

B) ἐπὶ τὸ τέρμα τῆς δύσεως

τὸ τέρμα—the boundary, the end. Technically the word designated the "goal around which horses and chariots had to turn at races"[169]. Here, however, Clement was not using this term in that specific sense (although both the *Epistle to the Corinthians* and the Pastorals abound in race-course metaphors), but in the sense of an extreme limit or terminus.

The key question then is whether Clement had Spain or Italy in mind. From the Greek point of view, the West, or Western land, *Hesperia*, was Italy. Indeed the term *Hesperia* was the Greek poetical designation for Italy[170]. This word was first absorbed into Latin with just that meaning[171]. Later *Hesperia* came to mean Spain; whether the word designated Italy or Spain was largely determined by a given writer's geographical location and cultural outlook:

A) Ignatius of Antioch used the terms East and West as an Eastern writer would: εἰς δύσιν ἀπὸ ἀνατολῆς refers to Italy and Syria respectively[172].

B) Strabo called Gades and the Pillars of Heracles the ends of the inhabited world (τέρμονας εἶναι τῆς οἰκουμένης)[173].

C) For the Latin poet Lucan, Spain was the uttermost Western point: *extremique orbis Hiberi*[174].

D) For Silius Italicus, Gades was land's end: *terrarum finis Gades*[175].

E) Philostratus notes that after Nero had proclaimed that no one could

---

169 *LS*⁹, pg. 1777.
170 Cf. Dionysius Halicarnensis 1,35.3.
171 Cf. Q. Ennius, *Annalium* 17 (23), which is most likely the earliest extant attestation. Cf. Ovid, *Fasti* 1,498 and Virgil, *Aeneid* 1,530.
172 Ignatius of Antioch, *Ep.Rom.* 2,2.
173 Strabo, *Geo.* 3,5.5.
174 Lucan, *Pharsalia* 7,541.
175 Silius Italicus, *Punica* 17,637.

publicly teach philosophy in Rome, Apollonius directed his steps to the Western parts of the earth: ἐπι τὰ ἑσπέρια τῆς γῆς, that is to Spain[176].

F) In Horace, *Hesperia* designates Italy in *Carminum* 1,28.26 and 3,3.8 and Spain in *Carminum* 1,36.4. It is important to note that Horace added the qualificative *ultimus* to make his meaning clearer: *Hesperia sospes ab ultima* designates Spain[177].

The use of the qualificative, then, would emphasize that the writer had Spain and not Italy in mind when he used the word West. Clement penned his Epistle from Rome. It is ludicrous to maintain that he could have thought of Rome as being the Westernmost terminus of the inhabited world or the uttermost part of the earth. Moreover Clement never conceived of the Westernmost point of Paul's missionary field as being identical to the location of his martyrdom. They were two quite distinct places[178].

Clement's use of so exact a phrase as ἐπι τὸ τέρμα τῆς δύσεως could only mean that he had Spain in mind and that he personally knew of Paul's journey there, or — if for some unknown reason he had no first hand knowledge of it — that there were members of the Roman Church still alive at the time he composed his Epistle who could positively assert and personally vouch as eyewitnesses that Paul had indeed undertaken the journey to Spain. Clement's testimony is a strong attestation to the historical reality of Paul's journey to Spain.

The *Muratorian Canon* is another ancient witness which attests to the factuality of Paul's journey:

" ... Acta aute omniu apostolorum sub uno libro scribta sunt lucas obtime theofile conprindet quia sub praesentia eius singula gerebantur Sicuti et semote passione petri evidenter declarat Sed (et) profectione pauli ab urbes ad spania proficescentis ..."[179].

---

176 Philostratus, *Vita Apollonii* 4,47.
177 In his commentary on the *Aeneid*, the 4th century grammarian, Servius, says: "*Hesperiae duae sunt, una quae Hispania dicitur, altera quae est in Italia. Quae hac ratione discernuntur: aut enim Hesperiam solam dicis et significas Italiam, aut addis 'ultimam' et significas Hispaniam quae in occidentis est fine, ut Horatius qui nunc Hesperia sospes ab ultima*". Servius, *Commentarius in Vergilii Aeneidos* 1, 530.
178 *Contra* G. Lüdemann who insinuates that they were one and the same place (G. Lüdemann, *Das frühe Christentum nach der Traditionen der Apostelgeschichte*, Göttingen, 1987; pg. 275-276).
179 *Muratorian Canon* 34-39. The Latin text is in L.A. Muratori, "Fragmentum acephalum Caii, ut videtur Romani Presbyteri, qui circiter Annum Christi 196 floruit, de Canone sacrarum

"But the Acts of all the Apostles were written in one volume. Luke compiled for 'most excellent Theophilus' what things were done in detail in his presence, as he plainly shows by omitting both the death of Peter and also the departure of Paul from the City, when he departed for Spain".[180]

A) The *Muratorian Canon*, composed at Rome at the end of the 2nd Century[181], that is about the same time as the compilations of the apocryphal *Acts of Peter* and the apocryphal *Acts of Paul*, provides, along with the former work, the most ancient witness which specifically affirms that Paul had left Rome and gone to Spain[182]. The testimony of the *Muratorian Canon* is invaluable, not only because of its ancientry, but also because it, with its indelible Roman character, provides a telling look at early Roman tradition concerning the two Apostles.

B) The text firmly links Luke, who is really the subject of these lines, to Peter and Paul[183]. The *Muratorian Canon* maintains that Luke only recorded in Acts those events which he had personally witnessed. This was the early Roman Church's understanding of why neither the story of Peter's death nor that of Paul's departure for Spain appears in Acts. The implication here is that Luke was well acquainted with these events so critical to the history of the Church of Rome, but that, in accordance with the criteria which he himself had laid down for the composition of Acts, he consciously omitted them.

C) The *Muratorian Canon* juxtaposes the *passio Petri*, not with the *passio Pauli*, as one would have expected and as later tradition so insistently did, but rather with the *profectio Pauli ab Urbes*, a linkage which also occurs in the *Acts of Peter*. For the 2nd Century Church of Rome, Peter's martyrdom and Paul's departure for Spain were in the same category of truths, that is, they were indisputable historical facts[184]. What the Roman Church chose to emphasize in its developing tradition about the two Apostles was (1) Paul's evangelizing and teaching in Rome and his departure from that city to Spain, and (2) Peter's

---

Scriptuarum" (in) *ANTIQUITATES ITALICAE MEDII AEVI*, Milan, 1740, Vol. 3, pg. 853. A photographic reproduction of the Latin Ms (*Ambrosiana Ms. I, 101 sup, fol. 10b*) is contained in H. Leclercq, "Muratorianum", *DACL*. 12,1; 1934, cols. 552-553.

180 English translation: H.J. Cadbury, "The Tradition", *BC*., Vol. 2; 1922; pg. 211.
181 *Contra* A.C. Sundberg who argues for a 4th Century date and an Eastern Church provenance (A.C. Sundberg, "Canon Muratori: a fourth Century List", *HTR*., Vol. 66; 1973; pg. 150).
182 Cf. S. Ritter, "Il frammento muratoriano", *RAC*., Vol. 3; 1926, pg. 258.
183 Certain late Arabic, Coptic and Syriac sources state that Luke, too, was martyred in Rome under Nero.
184 A.C. Vega, *op.cit.*, pg. 18.

subsequent arrival in Rome to lead the fight against the Roman Church's enemies (notably Simon Magus) and his passion. Paul's martyrdom was relatively de-emphasized (although it was not forgotten) in early Roman tradition. It is not surprising therefore that it was passed over in silence in the *Muratorian Canon*. It was only later Roman tradition which joined the two Apostles' ministries in Rome and linked them in violent deaths at the hands of a demoniacal Emperor.

Later Patristic literature attests, for the most part, to the historical reality of Paul's journey to Spain. In his letter to Principia Virgin, Jerome says that Paul was the *sagitta Domini*, the arrow of the Lord, which after having been shot from the Lord's bow from Jerusalem to Illyricum, proceeded to fly hither and thither and then hastened to go to the Spains, so that it might lay both East and West prostrate at the feet of the Master: *ad Hispanias ire festinat ut, velox sagitta, sub pedibus Domini sui Orientem Occidentemque prosternat*[185]. In his notice on Paul in *de Viris illustribus*, Jerome wrote that Paul had been released by Nero "so that the Gospel of Christ might be preached in the Western regions (*in Occidentis*) as well"[186]. Jerome also stressed the geographic universality of Paul's Apostolic ministry in his *Commentariorum in Isaiam Prophetam* and placed the Pauline missions to the Hellenistic East, to Rome and to Spain (*ad Hispanias*) within the context of the fulfillment of the Isaianic prophecies[187].

Athanasius of Alexandria evoked Paul's journey to Spain in one of the most deeply spiritual of his Epistles, his letter to Dracontius (354-355 A.D.), wherein the saintly Alexandrian Father exhorted his reader to the imitation of Paul:

> "This explains why the Saint was so zealous to preach as far as Illyricum, and not to shrink from proceeding to Rome, or even going as far as the Spains, in order that the more he laboured, so much greater the reward he might receive for that labour".[188]

Cyril of Jerusalem divided Paul's missionary activities into three distinct geographical spheres: from Jerusalem to Illyricum, his work in Rome and his mission to Spain:

> " ... and He fashioned his former persecutor into a herald and a good servant, who 'from Jerusalem round about as far as Illyricum completed the Gospel of Christ'; he instructed

---

185 Jerome, *Epistle* 65,12 (year 397 A.D.). Jerome used the plural *Spains*; this reflected later usage which tended to more sharply distinguish the three component parts of Spain: Tarraconensis, Baetica and Lusitania.
186 Jerome, *de Viris illustribus* 5.
187 Jerome, *Commentariorum in Isaiam Prophetam* 3 (130); 4,11 (163-164).
188 Athanasius of Alexandria, *Epistola ad Dracontium* 4.

imperial Rome and extended the zeal of his preaching even to Spain (μέχρι Σπανίας) sustaining countless conflicts and performing signs and wonders".[189]

In the *argumentum* to his *Commentary on the Epistle to the Hebrews*, John Chrysostom also noted a Spanish journey between Paul's two Roman captivities:

"He thus spent two years in Rome in chains when he was released. He then went to Spain and then departed for Judaea and at that time saw the Jews. And after that he went again to Rome and at that time he was put to death by Nero".[190]

In the *Commentary on the 2nd Epistle to Timothy*, John Chrysostom seems to allow the possibility that Paul went twice to Spain:

"For after he had been in Rome, he departed again to Spain, but whether he came thence into these parts again, we do not know. We see him however deserted by all".[191]

In the *Panegyrics of St. Paul*, the Greek Father noted that after completing a successful ministry in Rome, Paul "left it to go to Spain"[192]. He also alluded to the Spanish journey twice in his *Commentary on the Epistle to the Romans*[193].

In a passage which dealt with the Apostolic succession of the Roman episcopate, Epiphanius of Salamis noted that Peter and Paul left Rome to conduct further missions:

"They often travelled to other lands in order to preach Christ ... For Paul even reached Spain; (and) Peter made multiple visits to Pontus and Bithynia".[194]

As can be seen from the above sampler of Patristic references, the Fathers of the Church were quite convinced that Paul had indeed fulfilled his plan to go to Spain and preach there; that is to say that they understood the journey to be a historical reality. This understanding had been gleaned from the earliest and most reliable sources, probably the testimony of eyewitnesses. By the 4th Century Paul's journey to Spain had become firmly and immutably fixed in Holy Tradition.

---

189 Cyril of Jerusalem, *Catechesis* 17,26 (*de Spiritu Sancto*), (*trans.* L.P. McCauley, THE FATHERS OF THE CHURCH, Washington, 1970).
190 John Chrysostom, *In Epistolam ad Hebraeos*, argumentum 1,1.
191 John Chrysostom, *Commentarius in Epistolam secundam ad Timotheum*, 10,3.
192 John Chrysostom, *de Laudibus S. Pauli Apostoli* 7,9.
193 John Chrysostom, *In Epistolam ad Romanos* 29,3; 30,1.
194 Epiphanius of Salamis, *Adversus Octoginta Haereses* (*Panarium*) 27,6.

V,5. Paul's Journey to Spain in the early Christian Apocrypha

A) The Vercelli Acts of Peter

The first three chapters of the *Actus Petri Vercellensis* do not deal with the Apostle Peter (who is introduced into the narration only in Chapter 5) but with Paul's activities in Rome and with his departure for Spain.

Chapter I: The *Vercelli Acts of Peter* open with Paul's having a vision of the Lord who commands him to go to Spain:

> "At the time when Paul was sojourning in Rome and confirming many in the faith, it came also to pass that one by name Candida, the wife of Quartus that was over the prisons, heard Paul and paid heed to his words and believed. And when she had instructed her husband also and he believed, Quartus suffered Paul to go whither he would away from the city: to whom Paul said: If it be the will of God, he will reveal it unto me. And after Paul had fasted three days and asked of the Lord that which should be profitable for him, he saw a vision, even the Lord saying unto him: Arise, Paul, and become a physician in thy body (i.e. by going thither in person) to them that are in Spain".[195]

The Roman Christians lamented when they heard Paul had been instructed to go to Spain and they beseeched him not to absent himself from Rome for more than one year:

> "But the brethren lamented (and adjured) Paul by the coming of our Lord Jesus Christ, that he should not be absent above a year, saying: We know thy love for thy brethren; forget not us when thou art come thither, neither begin to forsake us, as little children without a mother".[196]

At this instant there was a Theophany and the voice of God sounded from Heaven announcing the Apostle's coming martyrdom:

> "And when they besought him long with tears, there came a sound from Heaven, and a great voice saying: Paul the servant of God is chosen to minister all the days of his life: by the hands of Nero the ungodly and wicked man shall he be perfected before your eyes".[197]

Chapter II: Paul celebrates the Eucharist and preaches to the Roman brethren. At the end of the chapter the brethren pray the Lord to restore Paul unto them whole.

---

[195] The Vercelli Acts of Peter 1, (in) M.R. James, *The Apocryphal New Testament*, Oxford, 1924, pg. 304.
[196] *Ibid.*
[197] *Ibid.*

Chapter III: Here Paul departs from Rome by ship from the harbour (of Ostia):

> "And when they told the brethren that had remained in the city, and the report was spread abroad, some on beasts, and some on foot, and others by way of the Tiber came down to the harbour, and were confirmed in the faith for three days, and on the fourth day until the fifth hour, praying together with Paul, and making the offering: and they put all that was needful on the ship and delivered him two young men, believers, to sail with him, and bade him farewell in the Lord and returned to Rome".[198]

Chapter IV: Simon Magus is introduced into the narrative. He is acclaimed as God in Italy and saviour of the Romans. He denounces the absent Paul and steals away the Apostle's converts, save a very few who pray the Lord for deliverance.

Chapter V: As the faithful Roman brethren were praying and fasting, the Lord was instructing Peter to leave Jerusalem and to go to Rome to defeat his old enemy, Simon Magus. The ministries of the two Apostles then were not concurrent in Rome; rather the calling of Peter to Rome is explained by the absence of Paul from that city at the very moment in which Simon Magus was ravaging the Church.

The *Acts of Peter* are, of course, colourful drama, the product of a wonderfully fertile literary mind. Yet in these introductory chapters of the *Acts of Peter* two key points stand out. Firstly the *Acts of Peter* relate that Paul went to Spain. Secondly they relate that Peter followed Paul to Rome; that is their Apostolic ministries in Rome were successive and not concurrent. These two key points reflect the Church's understanding of what happened to the two Apostles in the latter part of their ministries; they were a firm, historical nucleus embedded in a dramatic, edifying table about these men.

B) The Acts of Paul

There is no reference to a Spanish journey in the *Acta Pauli*. Ph. Vielhauer has formulated a whole hypothesis denying the historical reality of a Spanish journey on the basis of this silence:

> "One ought to bear in mind that not once did the *Acts of Paul* let its hero come to Spain and that in all of ancient Church literature, there is not a single legend about any activity by Paul in Spain ... "[199]

---

198 Vercelli Acts of Peter 3.
199 Ph. Vielhauer, *Geschichte der urchristlichen Literatur*, Berlin/New York, 1975; pg. 222.

Vielhauer's argumentation is captious. It is true that the *extant* text of the *Acta Pauli* is silent with regards to a Spanish journey. Still the question could be legitimately raised here if this silence were intended by the author of the *Acts of Paul* or if in fact it is due to a textual *lacuna*[200]. The text of the *Acta Pauli* is quite troubled in a goodly number of places as a result of its perturbated history and checkered manuscript tradition. Secondly Vielhauer seems to have dismissed much too summarily the story in the *Acts of Peter* which does in fact, as we have seen above, relate a Spanish journey. Thirdly Vielhauer goes on to dismiss the witness of, not only the *Acts of Peter*, but also of the *Muratorian Canon* and of Clement, asserting that they are "*lediglich Reflexe von Röm. 15,24;28*"[201]. In his view the aforementioned works appealed to Tradition and not to History to buttress their assertions. Vielhauer, however, made far too sweeping a generalization here for he did not take into account the different dates at which the three works were composed or what their theological goals or literary intent were. Clement's testimony, for one, is very ancient and quite likely is rooted in eyewitness accounts, his own or those of his contemporaries[202]. Once again, the silence of the *Acta Pauli* cannot be construed as indisputably indicating that Paul never made the journey to Spain.

C) The Acts of Xanthippe, Polyxena and Rebecca

The visit of the Apostle Paul to Spain also figures in the *Acts of Xanthippe, Polyxena and Rebecca*[203]. According to this tale, Xanthippe lived during the reign of Claudius and was the wife of one Probus, the ruler of Spain. When Paul came to Spain, Xanthippe was baptized and her maiden sister, Polyxena, was converted as well.

---

200 M.R. James writes: "There has been great dispute about these three chapters [i.e. the first three of the *Vercelli Acts of Peter*], whether they are not an excerpt from the *Acts of Paul*, or whether they are an addition made by the writer of the Greek original of the *Vercelli Acts*." (M.R. James, *The Apocryphal New Testament*, *op.cit.*, pg. 306).
201 Ph. Vielhauer, *op,cit.*, pg. 222.
202 Even Vielhauer was forced to admit that Clement had Spain in mind: "Zweifellos meint Clemens mit der 'Grenze des Westens' Spanien ...". As this evidence is quite contradictory to the hypothesis he formulated that Paul never went to Spain, the German scholar added: "... jedoch ob er diese Lokalangabe stadtrömischer 'Tradition' oder dem Röm. verdankt, lässt sich kaum entscheiden" (Ph. Vielhauer, *op.cit.*, pg. 222).
203 *The Acts of Xanthippe, Polyxena and Rebecca, editio princeps*: M.R. James, *Apocrypha Anecdota*, Texts and Studies II,3; Cambridge, 1893. James' edition is based on the 11th C. manuscript *Cod. Par. Gr. 1458*.

Chapter Four
Narratives of Paul's Martyrdom in Christian Apocryphal Literature

I. The *Acta Pauli*: From the Historical Paul to the Paul of Faith

The 2nd Century witnessed the birth and development of a whole *corpus* of Christian apocryphal literature. This included the composition of apocryphal acts of the various Apostles; writings which not only took in accounts of their travels, preaching and miracles, but also incorporated older, oral stories of their deaths. The more Christianity spread and simultaneously developed a sense of its own unique history, the more the need was felt to expand on the canonical *Acts of the Apostles*. Luke's second volume dealt mainly with the missions of Peter and Paul — and not even with the whole of these — and contained little or nothing about the other Apostles. Moreover Luke's account contained no mention of Peter's or Paul's martyrdoms in Rome, a subject of endless fascination to the expanding Christian Church. Thus there arose a desire to fill this *lacuna* by completing, as it were, the narrative begun in the canonical Acts, but which Luke expressly had left unfinished for literary and especially political reasons.

The *Acta Pauli* (Πράξεις Παύλου) of which the *Martyrium Pauli* (Μαρτύριον τοῦ Ἀποστόλου Παύλου) forms the concluding and culminating segment, was composed in the third quarter of the 2nd Century[1]. It was the work of a Christian author — nay, novelist would be a more appropriate designation — who composed it largely out of his own pious imagination, although availing himself at diverse points in his narrative of existing sources of information. These would include not only the canonical Acts and the Pauline Epistles (which, however, the author transformed radically), but especially local

---

1 M. Erbetta, *Gli apocrifi del nuovo Testamento*, 1966, Vol. 2, pg. 255-256. M.R. James dates them at c. 160 A.D., that is after the composition of the *Acts of John*, but before that of the *Acts of Peter* (M.R. James, *op.cit.*, pg. 270). L. Vouaux dates them at 160-170 A.D. (L. Vouaux, *Les Actes de Paul*, Paris, 1913, pg. 111).

I. The Acta Pauli

traditions about the Apostle's life and death which had been circulating independently in a much older, more rudimentary, oral form[2]:

> "In order to compose these works, the authors were able to count on some solid traditions, on different literary forms, both biblical and profane, on a few spicy details expected by the readership and on the authors' own theological convictions. But it was especially contemporary Christianity, that of the authors and not that of the Apostles, which explains the genesis and nature of these legends".[3]

Tertullian relates that the author of the *Acta Pauli* was a Presbyter of the Church of Asia. He further notes that the compilation of the *Acta Pauli* cost the author his ecclesiastical post, but it did not entail his excommunication from the confessing community as a heretic[4]. Indeed while Tertullian insists on the non-canonicity of the *Acta Pauli*, he does not condemn them[5]. Quite simply, for Tertullian as for Hippolytus and Origen, the *Acta Pauli* "were far from being considered a heretical work; they were not canonical, but were read and valued"[6].

D.R. MacDonald has quite appropriately characterized the *Acta Pauli* as the "earliest, most extensive and most influential of the apocryphal Acts that shaped the subsequent Pauline legend"[7]. In the canonical Acts, Luke had traced

---

2 W. Rordorf stresses the early date that the different segments of the *Acta Pauli* could have: "It is in no way settled that the *Acts of Paul* first originated in the second half of the 2nd Century; for at least parts of it could have already been composed in the first half of that century" (W. Rordorf, "Die neronische Christenverfolgung im Spiegel der apokryphen Paulusakten", *NTS*. Vol. 28; 1982; pg. 366). D.R. MacDonald has convincingly argued that at least four stories in the *Acta Pauli* once circulated orally; that is the story of Thecla, of Paul and the baptized lion, of the Apostle's martyrdom in Rome as well as the fragmentary tale of Frontina in the Philippi segment: "All four stories peak in the near-death or death of one of the protangonists - Thecla, Frontina, or Paul. Thecla miraculously escapes the pyre and later a host of beasts. Paul escapes execution in Ephesus with the lion and in Philippi with Frontina, but finally succumbs to the sword in Rome" (D.R. MacDonald, "Apocryphal and Canonical Narratives about Paul", (in) PAUL AND THE LEGACIES OF PAUL, Dallas, 1990; pg. 62).

3 F. Bovon, "La vie des Apôtres: traditions bibliques et narrations apocryphes", *LES ACTES APOCRYPHES DES APOTRES*, Geneva, 1981; pg. 154-155.

4 Tertullian, *de Baptismo* 17.

5 Cf. Eusebius, *HE*. 3,3.5 and 3,25.4 wherein Eusebius places the *Acta Pauli* ἐν τοῖς νόθοις. Cf. E. Plümacher, "Apokryphe Apostelakten", *RE. Supplementband* 15; 1978; col. 29.

6 L. Moraldi, *Apocrifi del nuovo Testamento*, Turin, 1971. Vol. 2, pg. 1062. Cf. W. Schneemelcher, "Die Apostelgeschichte des Lukas und die Acta Pauli", (in) *GESAMMELTE AUFSATZE ZUM NEUEN TESTAMENT UND ZUR PATRISTIK*, Thessalonica, 1974; pg. 206.

7 D.R. MacDonald, *op.cit.*, pg. 60. J. Quasten has given a pertinent description of the importance of the apocryphal Acts in general: "The Apocrypha are of the utmost importance for the Church historian in as much as they supply valuable information about tendencies and customs which characterize the early Church. Moreover, they represent the beginnings

Paul's apostolic trajectory from his calling on the road to Damascus to the end of his two-year stay in Rome. In the century separating the composition of the canonical Acts from that of the apocryphal Acts, a considerable extension of the Pauline legend had occurred. Stories of Paul's different missions and miracles as well as the narrative of his martyrdom had begun to circulate rather widely. These tales were clearly not dependent on Luke's work. The Presbyter collected, revised and fitted this material into his composition[8]; his work reflected above all the theological concerns, dogmatic struggles, customs, mentality and spirituality of the Church of his own day and not that of Paul's time. As such, the *Acta Pauli* not only laid claim on an older, independent Pauline tradition, but in fact the massive work itself became the seminal piece of literature vehiculating that tradition[9]. This apocryphal tradition, now codified, as it were, in the Presbyter's compilation, viewed, understood and presented Paul in quite a different manner than did the canonical Acts or the Pastoral Epistles[10]. Indeed the theological and literary intentions, the treatment of sources and the historical perceptions are quite dissimilar in the *Acta Pauli*[11]. Luke had taken great pains to depict Paul as a loyal Roman subject and the

---

of Christian legends, folk stories and romantic literature. They are indispensable to folk stories and romantic literature. They are indispensable to the understanding of Christian art. The mosaics of Santa Maria Maggiore in Rome and the reliefs of ancient Christian sarcophagi owe their inspiration to them. The miniatures of the liturgical books and the stained-glass windows of the cathedrals of the Middle Ages would be indecipherable without reference to the stories of these Apocrypha. (...) Accordingly we possess in them a picturesque and firsthand source on Christian thought" (J. Quasten, *Patrology*, Vol. I: *The Beginnings of Patristic Literature*, Utrecht/Brussels, 1950; pg. 106).

8 W. Schneemelcher, "Die Apostelgeschichte des Lukas und die Acta Pauli", *op.cit.*, pg. 221.

9 W. Rordorf writes: "Die Paulusakten sind ein selbständiger Versuch, das Leben des Missionars Paulus von Anfang bis Ende darzustellen" (W. Rordorf, "Was wissen wir über Plan und Absicht der Paulusakten?", (in) *OECUMENICA ET PATRISTICA*, Chambésy-Geneva, 1989; pg. 73).

10 Cf. W. Schneemelcher: "In diesen Paulusakten wird, unter Benutzung mancher älterer Legenden, dass in den Gemeinden Kleinasiens verbreitete und wirksame Paulusbild gezeichnet. Dieses Bild ist antignostisch. (...) Besonders am Herzen liegt dem Verfasser der Paulusakten zweifellos der Auferstehungsglaube und die Forderung der geschlechtlichen Enthaltsamkeit" (W. Schneemelcher, "Paulus in der griechischen Kirche des zweiten Jahrhunderts", *ZK.*, Vol. 75; 1964; pg. 12). R. Kasser notes: "The *Acta Pauli* very closely reflect the tendencies in popular Christianity in the 2nd Century. The Apostle is depicted as an ascetic, a preacher of chastity. This image corresponded very well to the aspirations of the public to which it was addressed. This is why the book had some success even though its author had been formally condemned (R. Kasser, "Acta Pauli 1959", *RHPR*, Tome 40, 1960; pg. 46, note 8).

11 W. Schneemelcher, "Die Acta Pauli—neue Funde und neue Aufgaben", (in) *GESAMMELTE AUFSATZE ZUM NEUEN TESTAMENT UND ZUR PATRISTIK*, *op.cit.*, pg. 200-201. Cf. D.R. MacDonald, *op.cit.*, pg. 57.

nascent Church as entirely friendly to the State and to the ruling imperial family. He had downplayed the troubling subjects of persecution and martyrdom and had striven to present the Principate as being benign in its treatment of the newly-founded Church. The Pastorals had transmitted the image of Paul as an elderly, fatigued man quite passively awaiting death in his obscure Roman dungeon. There is no mention of Nero, no confrontation with the Emperor at the trial, no preaching or miracles. Rather Paul was depicted as meditating on his approaching death under its sacrificial aspect; there is a clear intentional assimilation of Paul's coming Passion to that of Christ's. The *Martyrium Pauli*, on the other hand, depicts Paul as a dynamic figure, who directly challenges the tyrannical ruler hearing his case and who goes to his death defiantly, warmly embracing martyrdom. The relationship between Paul and Nero is confrontational to the extreme; that between the Church and Roman State overtly hostile and inimical. The *Paul of faith*, the Apostle of the legend, has acquired quite a precise image in the apocryphal tradition: that of a challenger to State authority, an enemy of the Emperor and a seeker after martyrdom. This image bears little resemblance — indeed it is quite alien — to the image of the *historical Paul* as he is understood from his own Epistles and from the canonical Acts.

II. The '*Martyrion Tou Hagiou Apostolou Paulou*' and the '*Passio Pauli Fragmentum*'

II,1. The Text

The text of the Μαρτύριον τοῦ ἁγίου 'Αποστόλου Παύλου[12] in 7 Chapters was given by R.A. Lipsius in his great work *ACTA APOSTOLORUM APOCRYPHA*, Leipzig, 1891, Vol. I starting page 104. Lipsius' edition is mainly based on Greek Ms. *Patmos 48*, St. John's Monastery, 9th Century (*P Patmius*), at times corrected or supplemented by Greek Ms. *Athos 79*, Vatopedi Monastery, 10—11th Centuries (*A Batopaedianus*)[13]. Another precious witness is the *Papyrus Hamburg* (*H*), which contains part of the *Martyrdom of Paul*. This was edited by W. Schubart and C. Schmidt, *ACTA PAULI:* NACH DEM PAPYRUS DER HAMBURGER STAATS- UND UNIVERSITATS BIBLIOTHEK, Hamburg, 1936, pg. 103—104. The *P. Hamburg* dates from c. 300 A.D.[14].

---

12 The title did not exist in the original text as the martyrdom tale had formed the concluding part of the larger *Acta Pauli*. It dates from the time when the tale was separated from the *Acta Pauli* and began to circulate independently.
13 *BHG*[3]. 1451; 1452.
14 C. Schmidt made a signal contribution to research on the Christian Apocrypha when he

The Latin version, *Passio Pauli Fragmentum*, the *recensio brevior* in 3 Chapters, is given by Lipsius in the above mentioned work, starting on page 105[15]. The text presented in his edition is according to the Latin Ms. *Munich 4554* (8-9th Centuries) collated with two other later Latin Mss., much inferior in quality: *Munich 22020* (12th Century) and *Munich 19642* (15th Century). Lipsius designates these three Mss. as M^1, M^2, and M^3 respectively.

The English translation of the 7-chapter Greek *Martyrion*, which we have reproduced integrally here below, is by M.R. James, *THE APOCRYPHAL NEW TESTAMENT*, op.cit., pg. 293—296.

The Martyrdom of the Holy Apostle Paul in 7 Chapters.

Chapter I

"Now there were awaiting Paul at Rome Luke from Galatia and Titus from Dalmatia[16]: whom when Paul saw he was glad: and hired a grange outside Rome[17], wherein with the brethren he taught the word of truth, and he became noised abroad and many souls were added unto the Lord, so that there was a rumour throughout all Rome, and much people came unto him from the household of Caesar[18], believing, and there was great joy.

And a certain Patroclus, a cup-bearer[19] of Caesar, came at even unto the grange, and not being able because of the press to enter in to Paul, he sat in a high window and listened to him teaching the word of God. But whereas the evil devil envied the love of the brethren, Patroclus fell down from the window and died[20], and forthwith it was told unto Nero.

---

pieced together and published the Heidelberg Coptic Papyrus (*co: Coptic version* of the *Papyrus Heidelberg*) in *ACTA PAULI: UBERSETZUNG, UNTERSUCHUNGEN UND KOPTISCHER TEXT* (Heidelberger Koptischen Papyrushandschrift 1). Leipzig, 2nd. Edition, 1905, pg. 121.

15 *BHL.* 6571.
16 Cf. 2 Tim. 4,10-11: "Crescens has gone to Galatia, Titus to Dalmatia. Luke alone is with me". Cf. the *Acts of Titus*, where "Titus, Timothy and Luke remained with Paul the Apostle until his consummation under Nero" (μέχρι τῆς ὑπὸ Νέρωνος τελειώσεως αὐτοῦ) (M.R. James, "The Acts of Titus and the Acts of Paul", *JTS*, Vol. 6; 1905; pg. 551;554).
17 ἔξω 'Ρώμης ὅρριον μισθώσασθαι/*conduxit sibi extra Urbem horreum*. The Western text of Acts 28,16 reads ἔξω τῆς παρεμβολῆς.
18 Cf. Phil 4,22: "All the saints greet you, especially those of Caesar's household". The author of the *Martyrium Pauli* expands the notice by adding "much people" to "Caesar's household".
19 οἰνοχόος/*pincerna*.
20 Cf. Acts 20,9-12 where Paul resurrects Eutychus at Troas. The story of the death and

But Paul perceiving it by the spirit said: Men and brethren, the evil one hath gained occasion to tempt you: go out of the house and ye shall find a lad fallen from the height and now ready to give up the ghost; take him up and bring him hither to me. And they went and brought him; and when the people saw it they were troubled. But Paul said: Now, brethren, let your faith appear; come all of you and let us weep unto our Lord Jesus Christ, that this lad may live and we continue in quietness. And when all had lamented, the lad received his spirit again, and they sat him on a beast and sent him back alive, together with the rest that were of Caesar's household".

Chapter II

"But Nero, when he heard of the death of Patroclus, was sore grieved, and when he came in from the bath he commanded another to be set over the wine. But his servants told him, saying: Caesar, Patroclus liveth and standeth at the table. And Caesar, hearing that Patroclus lived, was affrighted and would not go in. But when he went in, he saw Patroclus, and was beside himself, and said: Patroclus, livest thou? And he said: I live, Caesar. And he said: Who is he that made thee to live? And the lad, full of the mind of faith, said: Christ Jesus, the King of the ages. And Caesar was troubled and said: Shall he, then, be King of the ages and overthrow all kingdoms? Patroclus saith unto him: Yea, he overthroweth all kingdoms and he alone shall be forever, and there shall be no kingdom that shall escape him. And he smote him on the face and said: Patroclus, art thou also a soldier of that King? And he said: Yea, Lord Caesar, for he raised me when I was dead. And Barsabas Justus of the broad feet, and Urion the Cappadocian, and Festus the Galatian, Caesar's chief men[21], said: We also are soldiers of the King of the ages. And he shut them up in prison, having grievously tormented them, whom he loved much, and commanded the soldiers of the great King to be sought out, and set forth a decree[22] to this effect, that all that were found to be Christians and soldiers of Christ should be slain".

Chapter III

"And among many others Paul also was brought, bound: unto whom all his fellow-prisoners gave heed; so that Caesar perceived that he was over the

---

resurrection of Eutychus obviously served as the model for the episode of Paul and Patroclus.
21 οἱ πρῶτοι τοῦ Νέρωνος/*ministri Caesaris*.
22 προέθηκεν διάταγμα/*posuit edictum*.

camp²³. And he said to him: Thou that art the great King's man, but my prisoner, how thoughtest thou well to come by stealth into the government of the Romans and levy soldiers out of my province? But Paul, filled with the Holy Ghost, said before them all: O Caesar, not only out of thy province do we levy soldiers, but out of the whole world. For so hath it been ordained unto us, that no man should be refused who wisheth to serve my King. And if it like thee also to serve him, it is not wealth nor the splendour that is now in this life that shall save thee, but if thou submit and entreat him, thou shalt be saved; for in one day he shall fight against the world with fire. And when Caesar heard that, he commanded all the prisoners to be burned with fire²⁴, but Paul to be beheaded after the law of the Romans²⁵.

But Paul kept not silence concerning the word, but communicated with Longus the prefect²⁵ and Cestus the centurion²⁷.

Nero therefore went on in Rome, slaying many Christians without a hearing²⁸, by the working of the evil one; so that the Romans stood before the palace and cried: It sufficeth, Caesar! for the men are our own!²⁹. Thou destroyest the strength of the Romans! Then at that he was persuaded and ceased, and commanded that no man should touch any Christian, until he should learn thoroughly concerning them³⁰."

Chapter IV

"Then was Paul brought unto him after the decree; and he abode by his word that he should be beheaded. And Paul said: Caesar, it is not for a little space that I live unto my King; and if thou behead me, this will I do: I will arise and show myself unto thee that I am not dead but live unto my Lord Jesus Christ, who cometh to judge the world.

---

23 ὅτι ἐκεῖνος ἐπὶ τῶν στρατοπέδων ἐστίν/ *quod ipse esset dux super milites Christi*. Cf. Acts 24,5, where Paul is called "a ringleader of the sect of the Nazarenes".

24 πυρὶ κατακαῆναι/*exuri*.

25 τὸν δὲ Παῦλον τραχηλοκοπηθῆναι τῷ νόμῳ τῶν Ῥωμαίων/*ipsum autem plecti iudicavit secundum leges Romanas*.

26 πραιφέκτῳ — transliteration of *Praefectus*.

27 κεντυρίωνι — transliteration of *Centurion*.

28 ἀκρίτως — unjudged, untried, without trial. The cry for a regular legal procedure was a permanent one of the Christian apologists.

29 Cf. Tacitus, *Ann*. 15,44: "Hence, in spite of a guilt which had earned the most exemplary punishment, there arose a sentiment of pity, due to the impression that they were being sacrificed not for the welfare of the State, but to the ferocity of a single man". (*trans*. J. Jackson, *Loeb*, 1962).

30 μέχρις ἂν διαγνοῖ τὰ περὶ αὐτῶν. A very similar legal formulation appears in Hadrian's *Rescript* to Minucius Fundanus (Eusebius, *HE*. 4,8-9; Justin Martyr, *I Apology* 68) and in Trajan's answer to Pliny (Pliny, *Ep*. 10,97).

But Longus and Cestus said unto Paul: Whence have ye this King, that ye believe in him and will not change your mind, even unto death? And Paul communicated unto them the word and said: Ye men that are in this ignorance and error, change your mind and be saved from the fire that cometh upon the world: for we serve not, as ye suppose, a King that cometh from the earth, but from heaven, even the living God, who because of the iniquities that are done in this world, cometh as a judge; and blessed is that man who shall believe in him and shall live forever when he cometh to burn the world and purge it thoroughly. Then they beseeching him said: We entreat thee, help us, and we will let thee go. But he answered and said: I am not a deserter of Christ, but a lawful soldier of the living God: if I had known that I should die, O Longus and Cestus, I would have done it, but seeing that I live unto God and love myself, I go unto the Lord, to come with him in the glory of his Father. They say unto him: How then shall we live when thou art beheaded?"

Chapter V

"And while they yet spake thus, Nero sent one Parthenius and Pheres to see if Paul were already beheaded; and they found him yet alive. And he called them to him and said: Believe on the living God, which raiseth me and all them that believe on him from the dead. And they said: We go now unto Nero; but when thou diest and risest again, then will we believe on thy God. And as Longus and Cestus entreated him yet more concerning salvation, he saith to them: Come quickly unto my grave in the morning and ye shall find two men praying, Titus and Luke. They shall give you the seal in the Lord.

Then Paul stood with his face to the east and lifted up his hands unto heaven and prayed a long time, and in his prayer he conversed in the Hebrew tongue with the fathers[31], and then stretched forth his neck without speaking. And when the executioner[32] struck off his head, milk spurted upon the cloak of the soldier[33]. And the soldier and all that were there present when they saw it marvelled and glorified God which had given such glory unto Paul [34]: and they went and told Caesar what was done".

---

31 Cf. Mt. 27,46.
32 ὁ σπεκουλάτωρ.
33 γάλα ἐπύτισεν εἰς τοὺς χιτῶνας τοῦ στρατιώτου.
34 Cf. Mt. 27,54; Mk. 15,39 and Lk 23,47 for the Centurion's reaction to Jesus' death.

Chapter VI

"And when he heard it, while he marvelled long and was in perplexity, Paul came about the ninth hour, when many philosophers and the centurion were standing with Caesar, and stood before them all and said: Caesar, behold, I, Paul the soldier of God, am not dead, but live in my God. But unto thee shall many evils befall and great punishment, thou wretched man, because thou hast shed unjustly the blood of the righteous, not many days hence. And having so said, Paul departed from him. But Nero hearing it and being greatly troubled commanded the prisoners to be loosed, and Patroclus also and Barsabas and them that were with him."

Chapter VII

"And as Paul charged them, Longus and Cestus the centurion went early in the morning[35] and approached with fear unto the grave of Paul[36]. And when they were come thither they saw two men praying, and Paul betwixt them, so that they beholding the wondrous marvel were amazed, but Titus and Luke being stricken with the fear of man when they saw Longus and Cestus coming toward them, turned to flight. But they pursued after them, saying: We pursue you not for death but for life, that ye may give it unto us, as Paul promised us, whom we saw just now standing betwixt you and praying. And when they heard that, Titus and Luke rejoiced and gave them the seal in the Lord, glorifying the God and Father of our Lord Jesus Christ.

Unto whom be glory world without end. Amen".

II,2. Commentary

The image of Paul, which the Presbyter draws in the *Martyrium Pauli* (*MP*), bears little resemblance to that of the New Testament Paul. In this apocryphal text, the Apostle himself is to some extent the Great Revealer. He becomes the image of Christ's divinity on earth, a veritable icon of the invisible Saviour. God's power is concentrated on the Apostle's strength and not on his weakness; an emphasis quite in contrast to Paul's own theology[37]. Indeed the portrayal of Paul as the mighty and invincible one in this 2nd Century apocrypha is quite un-Pauline, if not totally anti-Pauline.

---

35 ὁ ὄρθρος — dawn, first light. The same word appears in Lk. 24,1.
36 τῷ τάφῳ Παύλου. The text does not identify the tomb's location.
37 F. Bovon, "La Vie des Apôtres", *op.cit.*, pg. 152-153.

Chapter I

The author of the MP notes the presence of Luke and Titus in Rome, although his precisions differ from the information contained in 2 Tim. 4,10-11, where it is Crescens and not Luke who is associated with Galatia (Gaul)[38].

Twin personages are very frequently encountered in the folk narrative. These characters speak and act in synchronism; their *personae* are rather blurred and depicted in low relief. In the MP there are three sets of 'twins': (a) Luke and Titus, who are introduced at the beginning of the account, (b) Longus and Cestus, who appear throughout the narrative, and (c) Parthenius and Pheres. The presence of Luke and Titus is meant to show that Paul was not alone in the great city, but was surrounded by his chiefest disciples.

Save for the mention of Nero and the city of Rome, there is no specific chronological or geographical data given in the text. The account is much more concerned with Paul's mighty challenge to Nero, his preaching, exemplary death and resurrection.

From the legal point of view, Paul is presented as a free missionary and not as an appellant prisoner under house arrest awaiting his case to be heard by the imperial tribunal. The Presbyter was unconcerned with the Apostle's legal trials and tribulations. For him, Paul was in Rome — the crowning point in his ministry — not primarily for judicial reasons, but to fulfill and perfect his Apostolate, that is to save many souls in that city and to die there a glorious martyr's death:

> "We have here the witness of a Presbyter of Asia Minor to the Roman Christian community at the time of Marcus Aurelius. (...) According to the Presbyter, the number of Christians in Rome could not be counted. This was then how the Roman community was spoken of in far away Asia Minor about the year 180 A.D. The author of the *Acta Pauli*, who had named so many cities and had recounted the Apostle's activities in so many places, never spoke in like manner about any other community. Rome was already considered in the second half of the 2nd Century A.D. as Christendom's principal community[39].

---

38 The *MP* is silent insofar as Crescens is concerned. The Presbyter highlights the persons of Luke and Titus who join the Apostle in Rome, work with him there and who are still associated with him even after his martyrdom. Cf. J. Rohde, "Pastoralbriefe und Acta Pauli", *Studia Evangelica V; TU.* 103, Berlin, 1968; pg. 308.

39 A. von Harnack, *Analecta zur ältesten Geschichte des Christentums in Rom; TU.* 28,2, Leipzig, 1905; pg. 6. Cf. Clement, *EpCor.* 6,1 where the Roman community is already described as an immense number of the elect (πολὺ πλῆθος ἐκλεκτῶν).

Chapter II

It is the conversion of Patroclus, Nero's cup-bearer, which sets off the chain of events culminating in Paul's death. The Apostle's sermon in Rome before the brethren would have been essentially encratic. Thus Patroclus' conversion would have entailed his vowing himself to a life of sexual continence.

Patroclus was not the only member of Caesar's household to be converted by the power of Paul's preaching. The *MP* also mentions by name Barnabas Justus, Urion the Cappadocian and Festus the Galatian, all termed *ministri Caesaris*. Later the Prefect Longus and the Centurion Cestus were also converted. The idea that Christianity had already gained converts in Ceasar's household as early as the Apostolic period is a constant theme in the N.T. apocrypha and re-appears in Patristic writings[40].

In addition to its marked encratism, the *MP* also stresses the theme of resurrection. In fact the text contains accounts of two resurrections: first Patroclus' and then Paul's.

Chapter 2 also marks the beginning of the persecution which would soon engulf Paul. The persecution is not connected to the great fire of 64 A.D., but is presented by the Presbyter as being Nero's vengeful reaction to the conversion of Patroclus and the other *ministri Caesaris*. The first to be imprisoned were these men and Paul; subsequently by imperial edict all the Christians of Rome were ordered to be rounded up. The totality of the action takes place in Rome, so there is no indication that this particular persecution spread beyond the City. The text draws a striking portrait of Nero which depicts him in both human and demoniacal terms: "Nero's feelings are well noted. He went progressively from pain to stupefaction, to fear, to anger, then fury and finally to vengeance"[41].

Chapter III

This chapter records the first of Paul's appearances before Nero who was previously unacquainted with the Apostle. There was no formal introduction of the Apostle before the imperial tribunal; a legalism which appears in the Gospels, the canonical Acts and throughout later martyrological literature[42]. Paul is described as being over the Christian camp. In Acts 24,5, Tertullus the

---

40 E.g. John Chrysostom, *Contra Oppugnatores Vitae monasticae* 1,3; *in Epistolam II ad Timotheum*, Homilia 3,1; 10,3; *Acta Apostolorum*, Homilia 46.
41 L. Vouaux, *op.cit.*, pg. 291.
42 The portrayal of Jesus' being formally introduced into Pontius Pilate's court is a constant theme of the early Christian Passion sarcophagi.

rhetor termed Paul a "ringleader of the sect of the Nazarenes" in laying down the formal accusation against the Apostle before the Procurator Felix[43].

The Presbyter is careful to make a clear, juridical distinction between Paul and the other Christian prisoners. Nero condemns the other prisoners to be burned at the stake, while Paul, a Roman citizen, is to be beheaded according to the legal usage of the Romans: τὸν δὲ Παῦλον τραχηλοκοπηθῆναι τῷ νόμῳ τῶν 'Ρωμαίων /*ipsum autem plecti iudicavit secundum leges Romanas*. —

τραχηλοκοπέω — to behead, to decapitate. The verb can also mean cutting one's throat. Cf. τραχηλοκοπία = *decollatio*.

In Plutarch the verb was used to denote the punishment for treason: Tarquin decapitated his sons for conspiring to betray him in his war with the Romans[44]. In the *Arrian Discourses*, Epictetus gives a chilling account of a decapitation carried out under Nero:

> "Are you willing to stretch out your neck as did a certain Lateranus at Rome when Nero ordered him to be beheaded? For he stretched out his neck and received the blow, but, as it was a feeble one, he shrank back for an instant, and then stretched out his neck again".[45]

The great interest of this chapter lies in its portrayal of the relationship between Paul and Nero. The historical Paul fully accepted the authority of the Roman court system and particularly the Emperor's right to judge him. This is clear from his appeal to Caesar (Acts 25,10-12), which is a manifestation of his confidence in the equity of the Roman legal system, and from his own remarks in Rm. 13,1-7. Later martyrological literature tended to present the martyr as far more detached from the political and judicial aspects of his own case. Indeed the martyr is more often than not depicted as a rebel or dissident, whose preaching was a direct challenge to the vested authorities. In the *MP*, the Apostle shows little obedience to or respect for his Prince. The Paul of the *MP*, in contrast to the historical Paul, is quite unmindful of the Emperor's criminal jurisdiction and refuses any recognition of the legitimacy of his earthly power and authority. The Presbyter stresses the confrontational in Paul's relationship with Nero: the Apostle refuses his authority, the Christian Kingdom is plainly proposed as an alternative to the Roman Empire; thus in the Presbyter's view

---

43 Cf. H.W. Tajra, *op.cit.*, pg. 118 ff.
44 Plutarch, *Moralia* 308 D.
45 Epictetus, *Arrian Discourses* 1,1.19 (*trans.* W.A. Oldham, *Loeb*, 1961). Cf. Artemidorus Daldianus, *Onirocriticus* 1,35. Cf. *P. Fay*, 2,III.24. This curious papyrus, a lurid poem in which the action seems to be laid in hell, gives a stark description of corpses beheaded or having their throats cut.

a Christian soldier cannot be a Roman citizen[46]. There is a total incompatibility between the two. The conflict between Paul and Nero was thus not merely political or juridical in the *MP*, for the Presbyter conceived of it as being essentially eschatological. It was the struggle between the demoniacal, represented by Nero, and the celestial, represented by Paul:

> "There is not the slightest glimmer of humanity in him [the judge], only a blind will to demonstrate the innate evil of which he is capable. Or to use an image: the dialogue between the accused and the accuser, the latter so often identified with the Emperor, is a dialogue between an intrinsically holy being, already smiling and happy about the celestial seat awaiting him in Heaven, and a demon disguised as a human, who, governed as he is by the impulse of a ferocious and irrational hate, tries in vain to deal a heavy blow to the other."[47]

Chapters IV and V

The custom of praying facing the East is attested from the end of the 2nd Century. The Fathers, mentioned in the passage, are the great figures of the Old Testament. The text in the *P. Hamburg* has Paul praying to God the Father into Whose Hands he commends his spirit. Only at the end of that prayer does the Apostle converse with the Old Testament Fathers in Hebrew[48].

The Presbyter added a new detail to the martyrdom tradition. He relates that when Paul was decapitated *milk* flowed out of his body splattering his executioner's cloak:

> "That Paul was decapitated in Rome under Nero was already a general tradition of the Church which the author of the Acts of Paul simply took over in my opinion. However that milk spurted forth from Paul's neck instead of blood when he was decapitated is a legend which must be attributed to the author-novelist. It was at this point that this legend made its way into official tradition".[49]

The image of milk flowing from Paul's body is a beautifully poetic creation. It is the sign of immortality. It is the milk which nourishes the Church[50]. It is by this miracle that the soldiers and other witnesses to Paul's death were won over to Christ. The image of the flowing milk re-appears in the successive re-workings of the original *MP* and it made a powerful impression on certain of the Church Fathers[51].

---

46 Cf. W. Rordorf, "Die neronische Christenverfolgung im Spiegel der apokryphen Paulusakten", *op.cit.*, pg. 367-368.
47 S. Pezzella, *Gli Atti dei Martiri*. Introduzione a una storia dell'antica agiografia, Rome, 1965; pg. 153.
48 Cf. Lk. 23,46 where Jesus prays to the Father; Acts 7,59 where Stephen prays to Jesus.
49 C. Schmidt, *op.cit.*, pg. 121.
50 Cf. 1 Cor. 3,2.
51 E.g. Macarius Magnes, *Apocriticus* 4,14; Gregory of Tours, *de Gloria Beatorum Martyrum* 1,29.

Chapter VI

This chapter recounts Paul's resurrection appearance to Nero to whom he predicts great woe. As a consequence of that miraculous occurrence, Nero orders the persecution stopped and the release of those previously arrested, including the cup-bearer Patroclus.

Chapter VII

This Presbyter gives no details as to the place of Paul's tomb or its appearance. His main interest in this concluding chapter is a second resurrection appearance by Paul and the baptism of Longus and Cestus by Titus and Luke:

> "The author's major interest seems to have been to 'finish', as it were, the conclusion of Luke's Acts. So he relates not only the Apostle's martyrdom and death, but also his resurrection; the latter in an exaggerated imitation of the synoptic narratives of Jesus' graveside appearances".[52]

II,3. Historical Value

The question which concerns us here is whether there is any historical kernel to be discerned in the text of the *MP* or whether this martyrdom tale is all the Presbyter's invention. What is, in fact, the relationship between the historical traditions in circulation about the martyrdom (especially at Rome) and the literary and doctrinal goals which the Ephesian Presbyter set for himself? Can anything of historical value be extracted from the text?

At first glance, the *MP* gives the impression of forming a comprehensive and cohesive literary unit. Nonetheless, as Prof. Schneemelcher has pointed out, the textual presentation is rather unskillful and the story flows rather awkwardly in a number of places. Quite obviously, the different sequences such as the story of Patroclus, the conversion of Longus and Cestus, and the actual account of Paul's death originally had nothing to do with one another, but rather were grouped together into a literary unit by the author[53]. The

---

52 A. Lindemann, *Paulus im ältesten Christentum*, Tübingen, 1979, pg. 70. Cf. *Acts of Peter* 40 (= *Martyrium Petri* 11) in which the martyred Peter appears to his faithful disciple Marcellus, the man who had previously embalmed Peter's body and laid it in his own costly sepulchre; *Acts of Thomas* 169, where Thomas appears to Siphon and Iuzanes while they were sitting atop his tomb following his martyrdom.

53 W. Schneemelcher, "Paulusakten", *NEUTESTAMENTLICHE APOKRYPHEN*, Tübingen, 3rd Ed., 1964; Vol. 2, pg. 238. Cf. E. Plümacher, *op.cit.*, col. 29.

Presbyter, however, was not merely a compiler, but an author as well. As such he proceeded to re-work and transform these different sequences in order to make them conform to his overall literary and theological goals. In addition he also composed from his own imagination whole scenes which he inserted into the overall text. The question remains open, however, as to how much he depended on Roman tradition in compiling and composing his work.

For L. Vouaux, the apocryphal text is its author's invention and devoid of any historical value:

> "One would have to confine oneself to the historical existence of the principal character; the Apostle and Missionary, and that is all. As for the rest, there would be nothing to be found save uncertainties and disappointments".[54]

Vouaux is rather pessimistic and hypercritical in his evaluation of the text's historicity. It is true, of course, that in the *Acta Pauli*, the Apostle's life and death were recounted in a fashion reminiscent of pagan romances. As J. Quasten, however, has pointed out, "sometimes an historical tradition appears at the bottom of all those miraculous and fantastic stories"[55]. Not everything was pure invention; but, once again, it behooves us to recall that the Presbyter was a *novelist* and not a historian. He was more concerned with fulfilling his literary and theological aims and much less in a factual accounting of Paul's *curriculum vitae* or of his violent death. L. Moraldi writes:

> I think that the author was not concerned with writing history, but rather he mixed together history, legend and local traditions in such a way that it is nearly impossible to extract from the account what is historical: i.e. of differentiating between the mythological and legendary on the one hand and the historical on the other".[56]

We would conclude that the Presbyter, who composed his work scarcely more than a century after Paul's death, took historical reminiscences which were circulating independently (both orally and in writing) and grouped them together into a new aggregate. He re-worked this assemblage, transforming it and fitting it to his goals. He added new material of his own to it. His work represented an enormous milestone in the development of the Paul-legend, forming as it did, the basis for the whole later Paul-tradition: apocryphal, Patristic and iconographical. The historical Paul was eclipsed and obscured in this dynamic process of poetic creation, compilation and composition. The recovery of a historical nucleus to the story is therefore rendered all the more difficult.

---

54 L. Vouaux, *op.cit.*, pg. 119.
55 J. Quasten, *op.cit.*, Vol. I, pg. 129.
56 L. Moraldi, *op.cit.*, pg. 1078.

II. The 'Martyrion Tou Hagiou Apostolou Paulou'

The following chart presents what is likely to have been the historical core of the story of Paul's martyrdom. In a parallel column there is a schema of the changes which the Presbyter wrought in that story and which in their turn, form the basis or the core of the later and more developed Paul-legend:

A) Historical core forming the substratum for the martyrdom tradition:	B) Accretions or re-working by the author of the *MP:*
1. The localization of Paul's death in Rome.	The author re-interates this information, but gives no further topographical data as to the exact place of martyrdom or to Paul's burial place.
2. The situating of Paul's death under Nero.	This is also re-iterated by the author, but he gives no other chronological evidence as to when exactly in the 14 year reign of Nero Paul's death took place.
3. Paul was a Roman citizen.	The author of the *MP* used Paul's Roman citizenship to distinguish Paul from the other prisoners and to introduce the chastisement of decapitation into the narrative.
4. Paul's death was a violent one and occurred at the conclusion of some sort of legal proceeding at the level of the imperial tribunal.	The author of the *MP* fleshes this out to Nero's personally condemning Paul to be beheaded. He thereby develops the drama of a personal confrontation between Apostle and Emperor. The decapitation itself is enveloped in the miraculous (theme of the flowing milk).
5. Paul's arrest was due to the success of his preaching.	The author expands this to a conversion of large segments of Nero's household. Paul's preaching is essentially encratic and stresses the resurrection and final judgement. Paul is arrested in the context of the great persecution which the very success of his mission had provoked. Paul's arrest and martyrdom are the culminating point of the persecution after which it ceases.
6. Peter was unconnected with Paul's ministry in Rome.	The author seems to know nothing of a joint Petro-Pauline ministry in Rome and even less of a joint martyrdom.

III. The 'Martyrion Tou Hagiou Apostolou Paulou': Versions

III,1. The Syriac Version

The Syriac version (*sy*) of the Greek *MP* was edited by F. Nau in his seminal article, "La version syriaque inédite des Martyres de S. Pierre, S. Paul et S. Luc", *ROC.*, Vol. 3; 1898. Nau also gives a French translation of the 10th Century Syriac manuscript *addit. 12.172* (British Museum), which had previously been unpublished.

While the Syriac *addit. 12.172* has not greatly departed from the general story line of the *P Patmius* text, it does contain a number of variants and additions. These interpolations led Nau to conclude that Syriac *addit. 12.172* is to be situated between the *P Patmius* text and the later Ps-Linus Latin paraphrase, *Passio Sancti Pauli Apostoli* (4th—5th C.) insofar as the development of the Paul legend is concerned.

Nau also studied another Syriac text, Manuscript *14.732* (British Museum) which likewise contains a segment of the *MP*. This text has even more variants than does *12.172*. Nau has concluded that the one was not a mere transcription of the other, but indicated the existence of independently circulating legends and traditions about Paul's martyrdom[57].

We shall now give a resumé of the Syriac version of the *MP* along with Nau's French translation of the actual martyrdom.

Martyre de Paul, apôtre élu du Messie

The text opens by mentioning that Titus is from Dalmatia, but Luke is from Judaea (and not Galatia). The Syriac indicates quite clearly that Paul came to Rome as a prisoner; it mentions a centurion who accompanied him from Caesarea to Rome[58]. As Nero was absent from Rome, Paul took a house in the country outside the city while waiting to witness before him. Luke and Titus come to Paul; they had previously been converted by Peter, now dead. Paul conducts his mission from this country house. His preaching was so powerful that many of his listeners became Christians. He worked miracles and healed the sick. He is surrounded by a vast number of disciples and converts.

Among the converts are many from Nero's household. The Emperor's cupbearer, Patricius, comes to hear Paul, falls from the window and is resurrected. Patricius returns to the palace and proclaims his faith to Nero as

---

57 F. Nau, *op.cit.*, pg. 40.
58 Doubtlessly to align the story contained in the *sy.* with the canonical Acts.

do four of the Emperor's eunuchs: Barsabas, Justus, Festus and Cestus (Here then is a considerable modification of the *MP*). Nero orders all five locked up and tortured, and all Christians in Rome to be rounded up and killed.

Paul is arrested along with other of his co-religionists. He is recognized as Paul, the "soldier of the Messiah". Paul preaches his sermon to Nero. The Emperor in a rage orders the prisoners burned alive and Paul to be decapitated "according to the law of the Romans". The centurions (not Prefect) Longus and Cestus are charged with beating and then beheading Paul.

A great crowd accompanies the three men to see the decapitation. Paul preaches to the crowd. That day "an immense quantity" of Christians are killed in Rome. This leads to a riot before the palace. Nero orders the massacre stopped. Paul is brought once again before Nero. He preaches a second sermon whereupon Nero renews the order to kill him.

Paul, Longus and Cestus once again head toward the place of execution. Paul preaches to the two Centurions. They offer to let him escape. Nero sends two more soldiers to see if Paul is dead. The Apostle preaches to them on the resurrection. Longus and Cestus ask to be baptized. Paul orders them to come to his tomb to be baptized by Luke and Titus. Paul, having arrived at the place of execution (no name mentioned) turns to the East and prays in Hebrew. After the prayer he preaches to the crowd, many of whom are converted. This final sermon is an addition to the old *MP* account. Also added in the Syriac is a brief description of Paul: "Or Paul était d'un extérieur agréable, sa figure rayonnait la gloire du Messie et il était aimé de tous ceux qui le voyaient".

The two soldiers sent by Nero return to him to tell him that Paul is still alive. The Emperor in a furor sends "a cruel soldier" to execute Paul:

> "Paul tendit la tête sans mot dire à ce bourreau qui la trancha sans miséricorde, et, ô prodige admirable que Dieu accomplit dans le corps pur de son saint apôtre! Il sortit de son corps du lait avec le sang qui jaillit sur les habits du bourreau qui avait coupé sa tête vénérée. A la vue de ce prodige la foule qui l'entourait se mit à louer Dieu et beaucoup crurent en Notre Seigneur Jésus-Christ".[59]

The resurrected Paul appears to Nero to whom he predicts great woe. Nero releases the remaining Christian prisoners. The following day Longus and Cestus go to Paul's tomb and are baptized by Luke and Titus. The Syriac text adds a chronological precision:

> "Or la tête du bienheureux apôtre saint Paul fut tranchée pour le nom de Notre Seigneur Jésus-Christ, vrai Dieu, dans la grande Rome, le troisième jour avant les calendes de juillet selon les Romains. Ce qui fait chez les Egyptiens le cinq du mois d'Abib et chez les Syriens

---

59 F. Nau, pg. 56.

le 29 Khaziram, c'est-à-dire le même mois que Saint Pierre, prince des apôtres, trois ans après son départ de ce monde, sous l'Empereur Néron ..."[60]

The Syriac text ends: "Fin du martyre du saint élu et apôtre Paul. Que sa prière nous aide!".

III,2. The Armenian Version

The Armenian Version of the *MP* was recently presented by Dom Louis Leloir in French translation in the *Ecrits Apocryphes sur les Apôtres*: Traduction de l'édition arménienne de Venise I: Pierre, Paul André, Jacques, Jean in the *Series Apocryphorum* (No. 3) of the *Corpus Christianorum*, 1986, pg. 77-86[61]. The text, entitled *Le Martyre du Saint Apôtre Paul*, is the Armenian translation of the Greek *MP* and rests on a sole witness: *Armenian Ms. 653* (Venice). Leloir notes that the Armenian version very often supports the reading in *P Patmius* over *A Batopaedianus* and that the Armenian version has the most affinities with the Coptic version. It tends to be brief, concise and characterized more often by omissions than by additions.

Le Martyre du Saint Apôtre Paul

In the main the Armenian version follows the story line of the Greek *MP*. There are only a few variants from it:

Chapter 1: Titus arrives from Dalmatia, Luke from Galilee. The cup-bearer, Patroclus, is mentioned by name, but all reference to Caesar's household is omitted.

Chapter 2: The text names five "grand chamberlains of the king": Barsabas, Justus, Ovrion, Laynotn and Festus.

Chapter 3: Nero orders the killing of the Christians at Rome at the instigation of the evil one.

Chapter 4: The text omits any title for Longus and Kretes.

Chapter 5: Nero sends Partenes and Phares to see if Paul has been decapitated. The chapter concludes with the account of the martyrdom itself:

"Alors Paul, debout face à l'Orient, pria longuement, parla en hébreu aux hommes, puis étendit le cou et ne dit plus rien. Et, lorsque le bourreau eut tranché sa tête, du lait jaillit sur ses vêtements; dans l'admiration, <le bourreau> glorifia Dieu, qui avait donné une telle gloire à Paul, puis, s'en allant, il raconta à l'empereur ce qui s'était passé".

---

60 *Ibid.*, pg. 57.
61 *BHO.* 885.

The Armenian account then differs from the *MP* in two respects: (a) Paul speaks in Hebrew to the men, (b) the executioner, perceiving the great miracle of the milk, glorifies God. This is in contrast to the Syriac, where the executioner was presented as a cruel man without mercy.

Chapter 6: Paul appears to Nero. He predicts much grief will befall the Emperor because he has shed righteous blood. Nero orders all the Christian captives to be released.

Chapter 7: The Armenian Version gives the following chronological notice, which places Paul's martyrdom in the year 66 A.D.:

> "C'est sous Néron, empereur des Romains, trente-six ans après la Passion du Sauveur, que l'apôtre Paul subit le martyre; sa tête fut tranchée par le glaive. Il avait combattu le bon combat dans la ville de Rome; le saint apôtre mourut de son martyre l'an soixante-six après l'avènement du Rédempteur, notre Seigneur, le septième jour du mois de Panemon, comme l'appellent les Romains, le troisième jour avant les calendes de juillet, c'est-à-dire le mois de Margats. Et moi j'ai noté avec certitude le moment du martyre de l'apôtre Paul".

III,3. The Coptic Version

A) The Coptic martyrdom was translated into Italian and published by Ignazio Guidi in his important article, "Gli atti apocrifi degli Apostoli nei testi copti", *GIORNALE DELLA SOCIETA ASIATICA ITALIANA*, Florence, Vol. 2; 1888, pg. 36-37. The translation is based on manuscripts which Guidi found in the old Museo Borgiano della Propaganda in Rome.

Guidi fully comprehended the great importance of these early Coptic apocryphal texts. "These texts", he wrote, "being relatively ancient, represent, at least in part, the old forms of these Acts"[62]. From the Coptic version sprang the much later and considerably expanded Arabic and Ethiopic versions (13th-14th C.). For Guidi the whole of these texts forms a distinct class within the Christian apocryphal writings, a class which the Italian scholar called "*il gruppo proprio del Patriarcato alessandrino*[63].

The earliest Coptic-Saidic texts were direct translations of the Greek. Such is the case of the *Martyrdom of St. Paul* presented below, which dates from the 5th-6th C. Later there was an expansion of this textual tradition both by the creation of local legends imitating the older Greek models as well as by compilations of diverse versions and tales circulating independently. Finally legends were created which did not at all imitate the old Greek models, but were

---

62 I. Guidi, *op.cit.*, pg. 1.
63 *Ibid.*, pg. 2.

totally original Coptic creations completely rooted in the ethos of that ancient Christian culture.

"*The Martyrdom of St. Paul, Apostle of Jesus Christ, which he consummated in Rome, under Emperor Nero, the 5th of Epêp. In the peace of God. Amen*".[64]

Chapter I. Luke came from Galatia. Paul converted many in Rome, but the mention of Caesar's household is omitted. It is Patroclus' conversion which infuriates Nero and induces the Emperor to seek vengeance on the Christian community.

Chapter II. Patroclus proclaims his faith to Nero who then orders the Christians to be rounded up and put to death.

Chapter III. Paul is arrested with many other Roman Christians. The text breaks off in the middle of his sermon to Nero.

B) As we mentioned above, the German scholar, C. Schmidt edited the Coptic version of the Heidelberg papyrus. This text is in very fragmentary condition. The extant pieces closely follow the Greek *Martyrium Pauli*[65].

The text basically starts at the appearance of the resurrected Patroclus in the imperial palace. The whole description of Paul's death is unfortunately lost; the text breaking off at the words (in German translation) "*stand Paulus, [gewendet nach] Osten, (und) er betete...*" and not resuming till the account of Paul's resurrection appearance to Nero[66].

IV. The 'Passio Sancti Pauli Apostoli' (Pseudo-Linus)[67]

The *Passio Sancti Pauli Apostoli*, in 19 chapters, is a 4th-5th Century work falsely attributed to Pope St. Linus. The text was not a translation of the Greek *MP*, but rather a developed paraphrase written in Latin at Rome "in the specific interest of the Roman Church"[68]. The relatively elevated number of extant manuscripts is a tell-tale sign that the Ps-Linus text circulated widely in its time and enjoyed great popularity in Church circles.

---

64 *BHO.* 886.
65 *BHO.* 882.
66 C. Schmidt, *Acta Pauli: Ubersetzung, Untersuchungen und koptischer Text; op.cit.*, s. 53; 56-57; pg. 89.
67 *BHL.* 6570. Latin text in Lipsius, pg. 23-44.
68 C. Schmidt, *op.cit.*, pg. 121.

The *Passio Sancti Pauli Apostoli* is a significant milestone in the history of the development of the Paul-legend in that it marked a clear Romanization of the original story of Paul's death:

> "At the same period in which the Church was piously receiving the chains of Peter, Christian society began to contour in a more precise way both the Acts of Peter and the Acts of Paul. The Church strove to historize those legendary narratives which were composed of novelistic *topoi* and placed in a vague and stereotyped *décor* that hardly recalled Rome. (...) The Romans did not re-write the Acts, they added glosses which related some aspect of the apostolic sojourns, stressed the martyrdom narratives or developed specific episodes ...".[69]

The *Passio Sancti Pauli Apostoli* thus introduced some novel and dramatic elements into the older story of Paul's martyrdom. Some of these additions were already independently circulating legends which the paraphraser incorporated into his work. For the most part, however, they were pieces which he himself composed and which reflected the Roman ambience of his own time.

Chapter I: The first chapter stresses Paul's success in evangelizing Caesar's household. It also evokes the relationship Paul supposedly had entered into with Seneca: their friendship, dialogue and correspondence. The historical Paul had, of course, appeared in the court of Seneca's brother, Lucius Iunius Gallio, when the latter was Proconsul of Achaia[70]. The fact that both Paul and Seneca were victims of Nero's tyranny gave rise to a tradition within Roman Christianity that the two men were personally acquainted with one another and had entertained a vigorous correspondence[71].

Chapter II relates the conversion of Patroclus, described as the *deliciosus et pincerna regis*, and his fall from the window.

Chapter III presents a more elaborate account of Patroclus' resurrection (through Paul's intercession) than did the old *MP*.

Chapter IV: Patroclus proclaims his Christian faith before Nero.

---

69 C. Pietri, *Roma Christiana*, Rome, 1976; Vol. II, pg. 1545-1546.
70 Acts 18,12ff.
71 Cf. Jerome, *de Vir. ill.* 12; Augustine, *Ep.* 153,5.14. J.N. Sevenster, in his magisterial work on the two men, comments: "Accordingly in the writings of the New Testament and in those of Seneca there is nothing to prove that the Apostle and the philosopher ever met each other. Neither is there any historically trustworthy evidence that they were familiar with each other's writings. It is understandable that not everyone has found it easy to resign himself to this, so that various traditions have sprung up concerning meetings said to have taken place between them and a correspondence they are supposed to have carried on with each other". (J.N. Sevenster, *Paul and Seneca*. Leiden, 1961; pg. 10).

Chapter V: Arrest and torture of Patroclus and the other chief men of Nero who had proclaimed their faith in Christ the King. Nero issues an *edictum* ordering the massive arrest of the Roman Christians who are subjected to torture without a legal hearing (*sine interrogatione omnes Christi milites per tormenta varia punirentur*).

Chapter VI: Paul's first appearance before Nero. The Emperor perceives that Paul is the group's leader (*ipsum magni regis militibus praesidere*). The Apostle tries in vain to convert Nero with a powerful sermon.

Chapter VII: Nero is infuriated beyond all measure. He orders the prisoners to be burned alive. Paul, however, as a Roman citizen, in virtue of the laws governing crimes of majesty, is sentenced to be decapitated (*Paulum autem senatus consultu tamquam maiestatis reum capite secundum Romanas leges truncari*)[72]. Paul is then remitted to *two* Prefects, Longinus and Megistus, assisted by the Centurion Acestus. Paul's execution is to take place outside the city walls and is to be public for the divertissement of whatever crowd might gather (*ut illum extra Urbem ducentes et populo spectaculum de eius occisione praebentes decollari praeciperent*). Simultaneously, the chief men and the lictors were sent out to seize all the Christians they could find and to kill them forthwith. This provokes a riot in front of the palace; the Romans demanding that these cruel measures be abrogated. Nero, frightened by the riot, issues another *edictum* which states that no one can touch the Christians unless he initiates proper legal proceedings against them.

Chapter VIII relates Paul's second appearance before Nero. There is a violent argument between the two men. Before being led away to be martyred, Paul promises to re-appear before Nero.

Chapter IX: Longinus, Megistus and Acestus question Paul as to his God's identity and nature while the procession is making its way to the *locus passionis*.

Chapters X and XI relates Paul's sermon to his captors.

Chapter XII: Paul is acclaimed by the many listeners following the procession to the *locus passionis*. The Apostle's three captors offer to release

---

[72] The paraphraser's account notes that while it was Nero who ordered Paul's death, the execution was carried out in virtue of a *Senatus Consultum*.

him and to become his servants, but Paul refuses to escape death, preferring to attain the crown of justice.

Chapter XIII: Nero sends Parthenius and Ferita to see if Paul is dead. Paul concludes his sermon.

Chapter XIV: The procession, surrounded by an enormous crowd, approaches the *locus passionis*. At the city gate (*ad portam Urbis Romae*)[73], Paul sees a faithful Christian matron by the name of Plautilla. Paul asks Plautilla to lend him her scarf to use as a blindfold during the actual execution. She is then ordered by Paul to await him at the same spot after his death. Parthenius and Ferita mock and insult Plautilla and call Paul an imposter and *magus*.

Plautilla

The paraphraser describes Plautilla as particularly devoted to the Apostles: *apostolorum ferventissimam dilectricem et religionis divinae cultricem*. This is the first time that this personage appeared in the Paul legend[74].

The story of Paul and Plautilla bears close relationship to the pious legends circulating about the matron Veronica, who was said to have wiped the face of Christ on His way to Calvary and on whose scarf the Saviour's image was miraculously imprinted[75].

Chapter XV: Longinus, Megistus and Acestus press Paul on the subject of their own salvation. Paul responds by telling them that some Christian men will come to gather up his body and bury it (*viri fideles rapient et sepelient corpus meum*). The three officials are to note the place of burial and on the following day to betake themselves there and receive Baptism from Luke and Titus. Again there is no geographical indication as to the location of the *locus sepulchri*.

---

73 There is no precise topographical information given to where the *locus passionis* was situated nor does the paraphraser give any specific indication as to which city gate he meant.
74 Plautilla does not figure in the mediaeval martyrologies of Usuard, Ado, Rhabanus Maurus or Notker nor in the earlier Christian martyrological calendars which preceded them. She is, however, mentioned in the *Martyrologium Romanum* for 20 May: *"Romae sanctae Plautillae feminae consularis, matris beatae Flaviae Domitillae, quae a sancto Petro apostolo baptizata omnium virtutem laude refulgens quievit in pace"*.
75 Cf. Lk. 23, 27 which forms the point of departure for the later Veronica legend: "And there followed Him a great multitude of the people, and of women who bewailed and lamented Him".

Chapter XVI gives the account of the martyrdom itself:

"And having pronounced these words, the Apostle reached the place of martyrdom. He turned toward the East and, with his hands raised to Heaven, prayed tearfully for a long time in Hebrew, giving thanks to God. When he had finished the prayer in his ancestral language, he bade farewell to the brethren and blessed them. And when he had blindfolded his eyes with Plautilla's scarf, he knelt on the ground on both knees and extended his neck. The executioner raised high his arm, struck with great force, and cut off Paul's head. The head, no sooner severed from the body, proclaimed the Name of the Lord Jesus Christ in a clear voice in Hebrew. Immediately a stream of milk flowed out of his body onto the soldier's clothing and then the blood flowed. But the scarf with which his eyes had been bound — as someone wanted to remove it — could not be found. At the moment of the decapitation, there shone forth from Heaven a light so blinding, accompanied by a smell so sweet, that human eyes were incapable of bearing it nor could a human tongue describe this scent. All those who were present, witnesses of God's grace in the blessed Apostle, were stupefied — praising and confessing at length the Lord Jesus Christ, eternal and invincible King, whom the great doctor, teacher of the nations, had preached".

Chapter XVII: Parthenius and Ferita are hastening to tell Nero of the Apostle's death when they espy Plautilla at the city gate. Their derision is turned into stupefaction when she produces the scarf stained with Paul's blood. Paul had come to her with a large group of others all dressed in white. Giving her back the scarf she had previously lent him, Paul promised to show her at the moment of her own approaching death the glory of the invincible King[76].

Chapter XVIII: Nero was astonished hearing the report of Parthenius and Ferita. Paul appears to Nero to whom he prophesied total destruction. Release of Patroclus and the other Christians of Nero's household from prison.

Chapter XIX: Longinus, Megistus and Acestus return the following day to Paul's sepulchre. Paul is praying with Luke and Titus, but disappears. The two disciples baptize the three officials.

---

76 Cf. L. Vouaux, *op.cit.*, pg. 307: "Here no doubt there has been borrowing from a martyrdom tale because Paul's last words clearly announce Plautilla's approaching death".

Chapter Five
Paul's Martyrdom in later Christian Apocryphal Literature

I. The Pseudo-Marcellus Re-Working of the Tale of Paul's Martyrdom

I,1. Introduction

The Ps-Marcellus re-working of the earlier apocryphal accounts of Paul's martyrdom is preserved in three different recensions, which Lipsius presented in his *Acta Apostolorum Apocrypha* (pgs. 117-222):

A) *The Martyrdom of the Holy Apostles Peter and Paul* (Μαρτύριον τῶν ἁγίων ἀποστόλων Πέτρου καὶ Παύλου) in 67 chapters, is established upon a single Greek manuscript, Venice, *Marciana 37*[1].

B) *The Passio Sanctorum Apostolorum Petri et Pauli*, in 66 chapters, is the Latin recension of the above *Martyrion*, and is established upon numerous Latin manuscripts[2].

C) *The Acts of the Holy Apostles Peter and Paul* (Πράξεις τῶν ἁγίων ἀποστόλων Πέτρου καὶ Παύλου) in 88 chapters, figures in all the Greek manuscripts, except the *Marciana 37*[3]. This work is more commonly referred to by its Latin title, *Acta Petri et Pauli*, by which name it will also be designated in this chapter.

There exist both an Armenian Version and an Armenian Abridgment of the *Acta Petri et Pauli*[3a]. The Version is a fairly literal translation of the Greek text. The Abridgment, on the other hand, has no equivalent in Greet and is a pure production of Armenian tradition, wherein lie its value and interest. This text was established for the most part on two manuscripts: Venice Armenian *Ms.*

---

[1] *BHG*[3]. 1491.
[2] *BHL.* 6657; 6658; 6659.
[3] *BHG*[3]. 1490.
[3a] *BHO.* 959 (Version); *BHO.* 962 (Abridgment).

569 (basic source) and Venice Armenian *Ms. 1447* (auxiliary source). Dom Leloir presents the French translation of both the Version and the Abridgment (*op.cit.*, pgs. 1-34).

The first 21 Chapters of the *Acta* relate Paul's journey from Malta to Rome and are a later adjunction. Erbetta dates these first 21 Chapters as 9th Century; the remainder, Chapters 22-88, as having been produced sometime between 450 and 550 A.D.[4]. Thus Chapter 22 of the *Acta* equals Chapter 1 of the *Martyrion* and the *Passio*, the story line of the three recensions being virtually the same except for characteristic additions or omissions. The most significant addition insofar as our purposes here are concerned occurs in *Acta* 80 (= *Martyrion* and *Passio* 59) in which the very terse account of Paul's death, which the latter two recensions give, is significantly expanded in the *Acta* by bringing in the legend of Paul and the pious woman Perpetua. Indeed the story of Perpetua's deeds and martyrdom greatly impacts the whole concluding part of the *Acta*.

I,2. The *Acta Petri et Pauli* : Text

Chapters 1-21 do not appear in either the *Martyrion* or the *Passio* as they are of much later date. They relate the story of Paul's journey from Malta to Rome.

Chapter 1 states that Paul's purpose in coming to Rome was his desire to be received in audience by Nero. The point of departure for his journey to Rome was Gaudomeletis.

Chapter 3: presents the Roman Jews as going to Nero to supplicate him to prevent Paul from reaching Rome. Peter is already in Rome and according to the Jews had already grievously afflicted their community by his words and deeds.

Chapter 4: Nero agrees to their request and orders his officials to prevent Paul from reaching Rome. He also calls on Simon Magus to help in the same cause by using his magical powers against Paul.

---

4 M. Erbetta, *op.cit.*, Vol. II, pg. 178. J. Flamion dates the *Martyrdom* and *Passio* to c. 550 A.D., that is after the composition of the *Acts of Nereus and Achilleus*. Flamion considers the *Acta*, which he termed the *textus graecus vulgatus*, to be a second recension of Ps-Marcellus dating from the early mediaeval period (J. Flamion, "Les Actes apocryphes de Pierre", *RHE*, Tome 11; 1910; pg. 465). For L. Vouaux, Ps-Marcellus can be dated as 6th C., the *textus graecus vulgatus* as 7th C. in its developed parts (L. Vouaux, *Les Actes de Pierre*, Paris, 1992; pg. 176).

I. The Pseudo-Marcellus Re-Working

Chapter 5: The Gentile Roman Christians send a letter to Paul warning him of the Jewish intrigues. Paul is termed the "true servant of our Lord Jesus Christ and brother of Peter, first of the Apostles". The letter states the belief of the Gentile Roman Christians that God does not wish the "two great lights" Peter and Paul to be separated in this the ultimate phase of their missionary career.

Chapters 6-21 relate the journey from Malta to Rome. Chap. 9 narrates the story of the decapitation of Dioscoros, the captain of the vessel on which Paul was voyaging. He was decapitated at Puteoli; being bald he was mistaken for Paul and his head was sent to Nero.

Chapter 22: Paul arrives in Rome (according to the *Martyrion* 1 he arrived from Spain). Appeal by the Roman Jews to Paul, as an Orthodox Jew, to fight Peter, who is preaching against the Mosaic Law.

Chapter 23: Paul calls for obedience to Peter's teaching.

Chapter 24: Peter goes to Paul. They meet and exchange the kiss of peace.

Chapter 26: A great commotion (μεγάλη ταραχή; *(Passio* 5 reads *infinita conturbatio)* between the Judeo and Gentile Christians before Paul's door (τῶν θυρῶν τοῦ Παύλου; *(Passio* 5 reads *ante fores Pauli*). The Armenian version makes a clearer distinction: it was the Jews, and not the Judeo-Christians, who were arguing with the Gentile Christians before Paul's door[5].

Chapters 28-29: Paul quiets the crowd, Peter preaches the mystery of Christ.

Chapter 31: Many are converted by Peter's sermon, including Livia, Nero's wife and the wife of the Prefect Agrippa (named as Agrippina in the *Martyrion* 10 and *Passio* 10). Because of Paul's teaching many soldiers spurned military life and turned to God, likewise members of Caesar's household (ἀπὸ τοῦ κοιτῶνος); *(Passio* 10 = *ex cubiculo regis*).

Chapter 32: Simon Magus at Nero's palace.

---

5 Cf. L. Leloir, *op.cit.,* pg. 4: "the [Armenian] account speaks consistently of Jews rather than Judeo-Christians. The translator might very well have preferred to leave unmentioned conflicts within the Christian community itself".

Chapter 36: Simon Magus warns Nero that if Peter and Paul are not driven away, his kingdom will not last. In the *Martyrion* 15 and *Passio* 15, Simon Magus proclaims himself son of god.

Chapter 37: Here begins a segment covering several chapters which deals with the struggle between Simon Magus and Peter and Paul before Nero. (*Passio* 16 reads: *Hi sunt discipuli illius Nazareni, quibus iam non est tam bene, ut sint de plebe Iudaeorum*).

Chapter 39: Nero asks who the Christ is.

Chapters 40-42: reading of Pontius Pilate's letter to Emperor Tiberius.

Chapters 43-53: Peter struggles against Simon Magus.

Chapters 54-59: Paul outlines his doctrine to Nero.

Chapter 60: Peter explains the essence of Paul's Apostolic ministry to Nero.

Chapters 61-69: Nero expresses his perplexity as to which of the two parties, Simon Magus or the Apostles, is right.

Chapters 70-71: Simon Magus announces that he will ascend into heaven.

Chapter 72: Nero builds a tower on the Field of Mars from which Simon is to fly[6].

Chapter 73: Peter condemns Simon Magus; Paul kneels to pray[7].

---

[6] The Field of Mars has no tie to the Petro-Pauline tradition. Flamion writes: "the choice of this site could have been suggested by a new idea which the author had of Simon's flight — depicted especially as a show and a prodigy of aviation. In order to dramatize the scene, he had to have the magician start off at some distance from the via Sacra, the flight's terminal point as consecrated by local tradition" (J. Flamion, *op.cit.*, pg. 465).

[7] Legend has it that ruts were formed in the pavement by the impression of the two Apostles' knees as they were praying at the via Sacra for the bringing to naught of Simon Magus' pretensions. Cf. Gregory of Tours, *de Gloria beatorum Martyrum* 1,28: "There exists still today in the City of Rome a stone with two fossettes. It was on this stone that the two blessed Apostles knelt when they prayed to the Lord against Simon Magus. The rainwater which collects in them is sought by the sick, who recover their health once they have partaken thereof".

Pope Paul I (757-767) had a Church constructed at this site on the via Sacra in honour of the Apostles' victory. Cf. the notice in the *Liber Pontificalis*, which reads:

Chapter 75: Simon flies.

Chapter 77: Peter conjures the demons holding Simon Magus aloft to let him fall. Simon immediately plunges to earth, landing on the via Sacra and breaking into four pieces[8].

    Hic fecit noviter ecclesiam infra hanc civitatem Romanam in via Sacra iuxta templum Rome in honore sanctorum apostolorum Petri et Pauli, ubi ipsi beatissimi principes apostolorum, tempore quo pro Christi nomine martyrio coronati sunt, dum Redemptori nostro funderent preces, propria genua flectere visi sunt; in quo loco usque actenus eorum genua pro testimonio omnis in postremo venture generationis in quodam fortissimo silice esse noscuntur designata (L.P. I, pg. 465).

    The topographical indications would point to a smallish Church situated between the Church of Sts. Cosma and Damian and the Basilica of Maxentius. H. Grisar has identified this Church with the Church of St. Peter's at the Forum, which the *Itinerary of Einsiedeln* mentions (H. Grisar, *Histoire de Rome et des Papes au Moyen Age*, Paris 1906; Vol. I,1; pg. 189). The *fortissimus silex* itself is now in the adjoining Church of Santa Francesca Romana where it is venerated as an Apostolic relic. It is clear that the story of the two Apostles' struggle with Simon Magus was so popular and the legend so rooted in the people's piety that it came to be considered as an historical fact. Paul I was thus practically constrained, as it were, to construct a Church on this site in the Forum to honour so wondrous an event (cf. A. Dufourcq, *Etude sur les Gesta Martyrum romains*, Paris, 1900, Vol. I, pg. 389, note 1; L. Duchesne, "Notes sur la topographie de Rome au Moyen-Age", *MELANGES D'ARCHEOLOGIE ET D'HISTOIRE*, Paris/Rome, Vol. 6; 1886; pg. 29).

8 The tale of Peter and Paul's struggle with Simon and the latter's dramatic death fascinated generations of early Christians. Hippolytus of Rome related Peter's struggle with Simon Magus in Rome after the magician tried to deceive the faithful. Hippolytus' account mentions no flight. Simon, instead, has himself buried alive promising to resurrect on the third day. He dies sealed in his tomb ... *non enim erat Christus* (*Philosophumena* 6,20). The Syriac *Didascalia Apostolorum* (early 3rd. C.) already related the story of Simon's flight and his fall which was attributed to Peter's intervention (Ch. 24). Eusebius devotes a chapter to Simon Magus whom he depicted as being a mortal enemy to the Roman Church and the first heresiarch. (*HE*. 2,13). Arnobius of Sicca mentioned Simon's flight, (this time in a chariot of fire) and his crash consequent to Peter's prayer (*adversus Nationes* 2,12). Cyril of Jerusalem associated both Peter and Paul in the struggle with Simon Magus. Cyril writes that when Simon was flying about in the air held up by the demons, "the servants of God knelt" and prayed that the magician would be confounded. Cyril used this story in his exegesis of Jesus' sentence in Mt. 18,19; "if two of you agree on earth about anything they ask, it will be done for them by my Father in Heaven". Thus Cyril of Jerusalem strongly insists on the union and complete accord (συμφωνία) of the two Apostles in their titanic struggle against this potent foe of the Roman Church. (*Catechesis* 4,15: *de uno Deo*). Finally Maximinus the Arian in his sermon, *de passione Sancti Petri et Pauli*, notes that the flight and death of Simon Magus had as its direct consequence the martyrdom of Peter and Paul:

    Victores igitur sancti et gloriosi apostoli ab impio Nerone ducuntur ad mortem. Ducebantur ad temporalem mortem, sed a Christo ducebantur ad vitam aeternam. Paulus capite caeditur, qui ut caput in sese Christi servaret totiens contra hostes inprobos dimicaverat. Petrus vero transversus cruci figitur: sic enim se ipse cruci figi rogaverat, ut

Chapters 78-83 relate the martyrdoms of Peter and Paul.

Chapter 78: Nero, wrathful at the Apostles, has them chained. He orders Simon Magus' body to be treated with care while awaiting his promised resurrection in three days. Nero blames Peter for the magician's death[9].

Chapter 79: Nero consults the Prefect Agrippa about putting the two Apostles to death. Nero orders Peter and Paul to be whipped and then to die in the Naumachia along with their followers:

ἀνδρώπους ἀδρησκεύτους κακῶς ἀπολέσθαι χρή. κινάραις οὖν σιδηραῖς τυφθέντας κελεύω αὐτοὺς ἐν τῷ ναυμαχίῳ τόπῳ ἀναλωθῆναι, καὶ πάντας τοὺς τοιούτους κακῶς συντελεσθῆναι

The *Martyrion* 58 reads:

ἀνδρώπους θρησκεύοντας κακῶς χρή ἀποθανεῖν.ὅθεν κελεύω τούτους κινάρας σιδηρᾶς λαβόντας ἐν τῷ ναυμαχίῳ ἀναλωθῆναι

The *Passio* 58:

> Homines inreligiosos necesse est male perdere, et ideo cardis ferreis acceptis iubeo eos in Naumachia consumi et omnes huiuscemodo homines male consummari.

Agrippa opines that Paul appears innocent of homicide and that it was Peter alone who was responsible for Simon Magus's death. Thus Peter should be crucified for the homicide he perpetrated, whereas Paul should be decapitated as an irreligionist: ὡς ἀθρήσκευτον ὄντα τὴν κεφαλὴν ἀποτμηθῆναι . (Here the *Passio* 58 reads *iustum est Paulo inreligioso caput amputari*)[10].

Chapter 80: The Apostles are led away to their respective places of execution. *Passio* 59 gives a very abbreviated account of Paul's martyrdom: *Et deducti sunt Petrus et Paulus a conspectu Neronis. Paulus decollatus est in via Ostiensi ... .* Contrariwise the account in the later *Acta Petri et Pauli* has been considerably expanded and the place of Paul's death shifted to the demesne of the Aquae Salviae:

> "The sentence having been handed down, Peter and Paul were removed from Nero's presence. Paul was led, chained, to the place where he was to be decapitated, three miles from the City, by an escort of three soldiers of noble blood.

---

inclinato capite vestigia Domini Iesu Christi, quae semper fuerat subsecutus, et in ipsa passione adoraret (*Sermo* 11; (in) *PL.* Suppl. 1; 1958, col. 754).

9 Cf. the parallel account in Isidore of Seville, *Chronicon* 70.
10 The Armenian version reads *agitator* rather than irreligionist.

When they were about an arrow's flight from the city gate, there came to them a pious woman who, when she saw Paul in chains, was greatly moved and burst into tears. The woman's name was Perpetua and she had only one eye. Seeing her weeping, Paul said to her: 'Give me your scarf and at my return I shall give it back to you'. She took her scarf and immediately gave it to him. The soldiers approached the woman and said to her: 'Woman, why do you wish to lose your scarf? Do you not know that he is on his way to be decapitated?' But Perpetua answered them: 'I beseech you, by Caesar's soul, to cover his eyes with this scarf when you behead him'. And so it was.

They beheaded him at the demesne of the Aquae Salviae, near the pine-tree. According to God's will, before the soldiers returned, the scarf, soaked with blood, was restituted to the woman and as soon as she put it on, her eye was suddenly opened".[11]

Chapter 81: Peter is crucified head down.

Chapter 82-83: Peter preaches from his cross and then dies.

Chapter 84: Marcellus buries Peter (here *Passio* 63 reads *sub terebinthum iuxta Naumachiam in locum qui appellatur Vaticanus*). The three soldiers, who had formed Paul's escort, are converted by the miracle of Perpetua's scarf. Perpetua is imprisoned. While in prison she meets Potentiana, the sister of Nero's wife. Secretly she instructs Nero's wife about the Christian faith. Nero's wife is convinced and consequently flees the palace along with the wives of certain Senators. Perpetua, Potentiana and the three noble soldiers are martyred.

Here then the *Acta Petri et Pauli* have gone beyond the stories of the deaths of the two principal Apostles to encompass an amalgamation of legends circulating about different martyrs of the Roman Church. All these legends sprang from a particularly rich and fecund local tradition. They were elaborated according to a common literary procedure and shared the same literary ideal and theological aim.

Chapters 85-86: The revolt against Nero is described. The Emperor's downfall is presented as divine punishment for his ordering the slayings of Peter and Paul.

Chapter 87: relates the attempted theft of the two Apostles' bodies by persons from the Greek East. It tells of the Apostles' temporary burial at the Catacombs on the via Appia (i.e. San Sebastiano ad Catacumbas).

---

11 The Armenian abridgement adds two further details to this account: (a) when Paul was beheaded milk flowed from his body along with blood, and (b) Perpetua's scarf was restituted by holy angels.

Chapter 88: marks the recension's end and closes with a short liturgical calendar:

"The way of the holy Apostles and Martyrs of Christ, Peter and Paul, came to an end on the 29th of June; that of the three soldiers on the 2nd of July and that of Saints Perpetua and Potentiana on the 8th of the same month".

I,3 Commentary

The Ps-Marcellus account of Peter and Paul's martyrdoms is the product of a later, more developed, Roman tradition which very consciously and very purposefully strove to link the two Apostles in Rome. As such the account stressed their close companionship, their joint preaching and their total accord as to matters of faith and doctrine. Ps-Marcellus depicted their titanic struggle with Simon Magus in the most dramatic of terms and linked the magician's death to their martyrdoms. The text is a hallmark of the flowering of the Roman tradition regarding Peter and Paul: a tradition which held them to be the joint founders of the Church of Rome, which conceived of their Roman ministry as having been jointly undertaken and fulfilled in perfect harmony; a tradition which understood their deaths to have occurred at one and the same time (although not in the same place nor by the same means of execution). In short this more developed Roman Christian tradition twinned Peter and Paul as joint founders of the new, Christian, Rome, just as the older Romans had twinned Romulus and Remus as joint founders of the old, pagan, Rome.

The Ps-Marcellus text thus marks a striking evolution in the development of the Paul legend:

A) The old *Acta Pauli* and *Acta Petri* had never linked the Apostles in Rome. Indeed the beginning of the *Vercelli Acts of Peter* clearly placed the arrival, ministry and death of Peter in between Paul's two sojourns in Rome and not concurrently with one or the other of them.

B) The Ps-Linus tradition drew Peter and Paul closer together, but did not join them in martyrdom.

C) It was Ps-Marcellus which twinned the Apostles in a joint Roman ministry, in the struggle against Simon Magus and in death:

"There was no one at the end of the second century who did not accept as an historical truth not only Paul's sojourn and death at Rome, but also Peter's. From that point there grew up an entirely natural tendency to intertwine the tales of their martyrdoms even though the accounts of these had previously been related in independent works".[12]

Thus the author of Ps-Marcellus re-adapted and re-worked the older accounts, paraphrasing parts, making considerable additions, incorporating independently circulating legends and finally placing in his text material of his own creation:

> "Ps-Marcellus ... gathered together all the essentials of the preceding narrations. In the East it supplanted the parallel work of the Byzantine chronographer John Malalas, who had put a year's distance between the martyrdoms of the two Apostles".[13]

Ps-Marcellus was eminently successful in codifying and historizing the later, more-developed Paul-legend. Henceforth the information it contained was no longer considered in Church circles to be merely an edifying tale or entertaining piece of hagiographical literature high in drama, but was widely accepted as pure historical narration.

II. Excursus 1: *The Aquae Salviae as Paul's Locus Passionis: a Late Adjunction to the Paul Legend*

The different recensions of Ps-Marcellus highlight another difficulty, that is the precise identification of Paul's *locus passionis*. Both the *Martyrion* and the *Passio*, reflecting older Roman tradition, locate Paul's death and burial at the via Ostiense (i.e. at the place where the major basilica of San Paolo fuori le Mura now stands):

Martyrion 59: καὶ ὁ μὲν Παῦλος ἀπετμήθη τὴν κεφαλὴν ἐν τῇ Ὀστησίᾳ ὁδῷ
Passio 59: *Paulus decollatus est in via Ostiensi.*

In its entry for Pope Cornelius (251-253 A.D.), the *Liber Pontificalis* relates that Lucina buried Paul *in predio suo, via Ostense, iuxta locum ubi decollatus est*[14]. In the same passage there is parallel phrasing with regards to Peter. Here Cornelius is said to have buried that Apostle's body *iuxta locum ubi crucifixus*

---

12 L. Vouaux, *Les Actes de Pierre, op.cit.,* pg. 30.
13 L. Moraldi, *op.cit.,* pg. 972. In the *Chronographia* 10, John Malalas had clearly separated Peter and Paul. In his account Peter alone fought Simon Magus and was crucified as a consequence. John Malalas related Paul's execution after Peter's and in the tersest and most succinct of terms: καὶ ἐμαρτύρησε καὶ αὐτὸς ἀποτμηθεὶς τὴν κεφαλὴν τῇ πρὸ γ´ Καλανδῶν Ἰουλίων ἐπὶ τῆς ὑπατείας Νέρωνος καὶ Λεντούλου.
14 *LP.* Vol. I, pg. 150.

est, i.e. the Vatican. In both cases the preposition *iuxta* indicates a very immediate proximity. Thus with Paul the phrase *iuxta locum ubi decollatus est* indicates the via Ostiense site. It would be totally inappropriate in designating the distance between the via Ostiense and the Aquae Salviae, now the Abbey of the Three Fountains (*tre fontane*) which is just East of the via Laurentina.

The later *Acta Petri et Pauli*, however, clearly state in Chap. 80 that Paul was beheaded, not at the via Ostiense site where the older tradition had consistently located it, but at the "*massa* called Aquae Salviae near the pine tree":

> ἀπεκεφάλισαν δὲ αὐτὸν εἰς μάσσαν καλουμένην Ἄκουαι Σαλβίας, πλησίον τοῦ δένδρου τοῦ στροβίλου.

This new tradition that Paul was decapitated at the Aquae Salviae and his mortal remains then transported to the via Ostiense site for burial enjoyed an immediate and lasting success. Indeed it was even given Pontifical approval by Gregory the Great whom one finds attesting thereto in his letter to the sub-Deacon Felix (604 A.D.):

> "Valde incongruum esse ac durissimum videretur ut illa ei specialiter possessio non serviret, in qua palmam sumens martyrii capite est truncatus ut viveret, utile indicamus eadem massam quae Aquas Salvias nuncupatur, cum omnibus fundis suis ..."[15]

A) Massa

The word *massa* designates here a piece or parcel of land; a demesne, landed property or estate. This is a late usage of this term[16].

B) the pine-tree

The mention of the terebinth tree (to indicate Peter's grave) and the pine-tree (to designate Paul's) was a precise topographical indication which made sense only for the recension's author and his contemporaries[17].

The tradition associating the Aquae Salviae site with Paul's martyrdom came into existence after the composition of the *Martyrion* and the *Passio* (early 6th C.), but before the redaction of the *Acta Petri et Pauli* (late 6th C.). The tale was not born of the apocryphal tradition, although it found its expression there[18]. It was a tradition which was born and took shape in the

---

15 Gregory the Great, *Registri Epistolarum* XIV,14.
16 Cf. CIL 6, 25144; *CIL*. 14, 3482.
17 Cf. J.P. Kirsch, "Der Ort des Martyriums des Hl. Paulus", *RQS*, Vol. 2; 1888; pg. 237.
18 Cf. G.B. de Rossi, "Recenti scoperte nella chiesa alle Acque Salvie dedicata alla memoria

monastic milieu of Byzantine Rome. The many Eastern monks residing in Rome at that time assured its transmission, not only in Rome itself, but also in the Byzantine world[19]. It was due to the influence of the Cilician monks resident at the Abbey of the Three Fountains that the legend made its way into the *Acta Petri et Pauli*, as well as into Gregory's letter to Felix and into the 7th C. itineraries[20].

What might explain the sudden birth of this new tradition concerning Paul's *locus passionis*, a tradition which rapidly supplanted the older tradition that had been transmitted for centuries from one generation to the next? The mediaeval chronicler, Benedict of Soracte (c. 1000 A.D.), provided a clue to the answer. He ascribed the foundation of a Church and a Monastery at the Aquae Salviae to the Byzantine general, Narses, who ruled Rome from 548 to 567 A.D. and who brought Italy firmly under Justinian's rule. Narses built or restored a number of public works and public buildings during his rule. He also was responsible for the erection of a number of religious edifices in Rome:

"Narsus vero patricius fecit ecclesia cum monasterium Beati Pauli Apostoli, qui dicitur ad Aquas Salvias, reliquiae Beati Anastasii martyris adductae venerantur".[21]

Benedict of Soracte was a late witness whose testimony has to be used with great caution. That is all the more so in this particular example as the first solid historical record of the Monastery was not that of its foundation by Narses, but the notice that one of its Abbots, Georgius, a Cilician, attended the Lateran Synod of 649 A.D.[22]. What Benedict of Soracte did do was to point the way to this Byzantine connexion by repeating in his *Chronicon* the standard story of the Monastery's foundation. The story itself, as related by Benedict, is probably less than historically accurate. It had been elaborated by the first monks who came to live at the Monastery and had been transmitted for centuries by successive generations of Eastern monks who were still in

---

del martirio dell'Apostolo Paolo", *BAC.* 7; 1869; pg. 86. Speaking of the *Acta Petri et Pauli* as the source of this tradition, the great archeologist says: "One cannot reasonably imagine that from this impure source was derived the Roman tradition asserted with such certainty by the great Gregory as to the site of Paul's martyrdom". De Rossi concludes: "Nor do I see any indication that any other written apocrypha even unknown to us could have been at the origin of the tradition under discussion here".

19 Cf. V. Capocci, "Sulla tradizione del martirio di San Paolo alle Acque Salvie", *ATTI DELLO .VIII° CONGRESSO INTERNAZIONALE DI STUDI BIZANTINI (1951)*, Rome, 1953; pg. 11-19.

20 Cf. G. Ferrari, *Early Roman Monasteries*, Vatican City, 1957; pg. 36, note 1.

21 Benedict of Soracte, *Chronicon* 9 (*PL.* 139, col. 15). St. Anastasius was a Persian, martyred in his homeland in 628, whose head was later translated to Rome.

22 Abbot Georgius is noted as having come from the *Monasterium de Cilicia qui ponitur in Aquas Salvias*. There is no mention of either Paul or Anastasius Martyr.

residence at the Monastery in Benedict's time. The monks would have been very happy indeed to have had as the founder of their Monastery a glorious Byzantine general [23]. Moreover, as the monks were Cilicians — in fact the monastery was known as the *Monasterium de Cilicia in Aquas Salvias* — it was natural for them to try to link the site to the great Apostle who hailed precisely from Cilicia:

> "The Cilician monks of St. Anastasius naturally saw in Paul a compatriot and so venerated him in an especial way. The Apostle figured among the eponyms of their convent. It is, moreover, thanks to their influence that the Greek *Acta Petri et Pauli* (7th C.), a re-working of the Greek *Martyrion* (end 5th-beginning 6th C.), incorporated the tradition, already in circulation in Gregory the Great's time, that St. Paul had been decapitated at the Aquae Salviae and not at the via Ostiense site".[24]

The story associating the Aquae Salviae site with Paul's death is completely unhistorical. It was a legend elaborated by the resident Cilician monks, who particularly venerated Paul, to confer greater glory and renown on their new monastic foundation by linking the site on which it was build to Paul's martyrdom.

III. *The Passio Apostolorum Petri et Pauli (Pseudo-Hegesippus)*

The Latin *Passio Apostolorum Petri et Pauli* in 13 Chapters was compiled about the year 580 A.D.[25]. One of the principal sources for this brief work was Ps-Hegesippus, *de Excidio Urbis Hierosolymitanae* (especially Bk. III,2), a late 4th C. rhetorical re-working of Flavius Josephus' *Bellum Iudaicum*, which had formerly been attributed to St. Ambrose. At some points, the extract from *de Excidio Urbis Hierosolymitanae* is incorporated into the *Passio Apostolorum Petri et Pauli* almost word for word (e.g. the account of the resurrection of the young member of the imperial family). At other points the *Passio Apostolorum Petri et Pauli* becomes an amalgamation of several sources. One of these other sources is Ps-Marcellus with which the *Passio Apostolorum Petri et Pauli* coincides in several places.

The *Passio Apostolorum Petri et Pauli* (as had the extract from *de Excidio Urbis Hierosolymitanae*) almost exclusively centers on Peter. It is he who

---

23 G.B. de Rossi, "Oratorio e monastero di S. Paolo Apostolo alle Acque Salvie costruiti da Narsete patrizio", *NBAC.* 4,5; 1887; pg. 80). Cf. F. Antonelli, "I primi monasteri di monaci orientali in Roma (b) Monastero di S. Vincenzo e Anastasio ad Aquas Salvias", *RAC.* Vol. 5; 1928; pg. 111-112.

24 J.M. Sansterre, *Les moines grecs et orientaux à Rome aux époques byzantine et carolingienne*, Brussels, 1983; Vol. I, pg. 152.

25 M. Erbetta, *op.cit.*, Vol. II, pg. 193.

struggles against Simon Magus, resurrects the young man and who is the beneficiary of the Christophany. Paul appears in the work as an accessary figure whose presence and importance in the narration is much diminished.

The manuscript tradition for the *Passio Apostolorum Petri et Pauli* is rather exiguous, an indication that the text was not widely distributed. The Latin edition is in Lipsius, pg. 223-234. Lipsius based his edition by and large on London *Latin addit. 11.880*, a 9th C. manuscript, supplemented by *Bybl. sedil Florentinae eccles. 132*, which dates to the 11th C.[26]

The *Passio Apostolorum Petri et Pauli*

Chapter 1: Peter and Paul, *discipuli Domini nostri Iesu Christi*[27] arrived *together* in Rome *secundum voluntatem Dei* and were received by some of the Roman faithful. The two Apostles began to frequent the house of a relative of Pontius Pilate, whom they had known when Pilate was Prefect of Judaea[28]. The chapter also contains an account of Simon Magus' arrest, which Nero had ordered, his miraculous disappearance from prison and his appearance to the Emperor as the latter was about to sacrifice to the gods. The friendship of the evil pair, Simon Magus and Nero, is contrasted to the friendship and *concordia* of the holy twins, Peter and Paul.

Chapter 2: Simon proclaims to Nero that he is the Christ.

Chapter 3: Magical appearance of Simon Magus in the Roman Senate. Deepening relationship between Nero and the magician.

Chapter 4: Pontius Pilate's relative denounces Simon Magus in the Senate as a false Christ and prays Nero to send for Peter and Paul to confront the magician.

Chapter 5: Simon Magus assimilated to the god Janus.

Chapter 6: Peter and Paul appear before Nero and the Senate and denounce Simon Magus.

---

26 *BHL.* 6667.
27 *De exc. Hieros.* III,2 reads *doctores Christianorum.*
28 This represents a further enlargening of the Pontius Pilate legend. In Ps-Marcellus only Pontius Pilate's letter to Tiberius was read. Here the Apostles frequent one of his relatives in Rome.

Chapters 7-9: Struggle between Peter and Simon Magus. The magician is confounded when the holy Apostle resurrects a member of the imperial family.

Chapter 10: Simon asks Nero to construct a wooden tower on the Capitoline from which he would ascend to heaven.[29] Both Peter and Paul kneel to pray foreseeing their end to be near: *adpropinquat enim de mundo transitus noster*, says Paul.

Chapter 11: Simon Magus flies. Peter calls on the demons to let him fall. The magician plunges to earth and is broken in twain. Despite this he does not die at once, but is taken to Ariccia and dies there: *cum diabolo eius anima discessit in gehennam.*

Chapter 12 relates Peter's arrest. Nero seeks a way of killing Peter and issues an order for both Apostles' arrest. It is Peter who is being aimed at in particular as it was he who was deemed responsible for Simon Magus' death. The Christian community persuades Peter to flee Rome. The famous *Quo Vadis* scene ensues. Peter understands his meeting with Christ outside the walls of Rome as a sign of his own impending death. He returns to Rome and is arrested the following day *cum conservo suo Paulo.* Paul's arrest is not described and his presence is much minimalized.

Chapter 13 is an account of the two Apostles' deaths:

"Now Nero had kept Simon's body thinking that he would be resurrected as in the past. Seeing, however, that it was already decomposing and was full of pus, he ordered it to be covered. Then full of wrath against Peter and Paul, he ordered Clement, the Urban Prefect: 'Father Clement, these people are total atheists and could completely ruin our religion if we allow them to live'. (...) The Prefect Clement replied: 'O most excellent Emperor, as Paul is not incredulous, he should die in a diverse manner'. The Emperor: 'How do you wish them to die?' The Prefect Clement thereupon delivered the verdict: 'Paul, in contumacy to the Roman Empire, is to be punished by capital sentence (*Paulus contumax contra Romanum imperium capitali sententia puniatur*). Peter, on the other hand, by his casting of spells, has committed a murder and is to be crucified'. Peter asked that he be crucified upside down as he considered himself unworthy to be crucified in the same way as his Lord and Master had been, Jesus Christ, the Son of God".[30]

---

29 The pagan Romans considered the Capitoline to be their sacred mountain.
30 The account of the two Apostles' deaths in *de Excidio Urbis Hierosolymitanae* is much briefer. The whole episode involving the Prefect Clement does not appear nor does the chronological note. The text merely says: *et ipse [Petrus] et Paulus, alter cruce, alter gladio necati sunt* (*de Exc. Hieros.* III,2).

The chapter concludes with a peculiar chronological note: *passi sunt autem tertio kalendarum Iuliarum, Nerone bis et Pisone consulibus.* This places the martyrdoms, not at the end of Nero's reign which was the date retained by Tradition, but at its beginning for Nero's second Consulate, which he shared with Piso, occurred in 57 A.D.

IV. The Historiae Apostolicae of Pseudo-Abdias: Vol. II: The Passion of St. Paul

The *Historiae Apostolicae* (6-7th C.) is a collection of stories about the various Apostles written in the Latin language. It is divided into 10 books and goes under the name of Abdias, the legendary disciple of the Apostles Simon and Jude and later Bishop of Babylon. Book 2 of the *Historiae Apostolicae* treats St. Paul[31].

Originally the collection only included the *passiones* of each of the ten Apostles treated. Later the *virtutes*, accounts of their *gesta*, were added to the passions. The literary milieu of the *Historiae Apostolicae* is to be situated in the Frankish ecclesiastical world of the later 6th C. Much of the material in the collection, and especially the Passions of Peter, Paul, John, Andrew and Thomas, is derived, however, from much older sources:

> "The chief interest of Ps-Abdias lies in the information the work provides on the legends which were circulating about the Apostles in the 6th C. Frankish world as well as in the preservation of some of the ancientmost apocryphal Acts, although in a derivative way".[32]

From the compositional point of view, the *Historiae Apostolicae* is a rather heteroclite work. It takes ancient traditions about the Apostles — including some Biblical references to them — and amalgamates these traditions with newer tales and legends. The new literary pieces created by this process are thus eminently fitted to fulfilling the overall work's objective. That goal is to present each of the Apostle's deeds and the accounts of his death in a plausible and realistic way for the edification of the Church community.

The account is composed of eight Chapters. The first six relate Paul's earlier life and are quite clearly derived from the information recorded in the canonical *Acts of the Apostles.*

Chapter I: The Damascus Road and the Baptism of Paul.

---

31 *BHL.* 6574.
32 P. Batiffol, "Abdias, évêque de Babylone", *DICT. THEOL. CATH.*, Vol. I; 1909; col. 24.

Chapter II: Saul begins his preaching ministry in Damascus and goes with Barnabas to Jerusalem.

Chapter III: Saul, now Paul, conducts a mission to Lystra and Philippi.

Chapter IV: Paul in Ephesus. The author stresses that he is a miracle-worker. Paul raises Eutychus from the dead after the latter's fall from the window.

Chapter V: Paul in Malta.
Paul arrives in Rome where he is *released* from his chains. Ps-Abdias thus continues the apocryphal tradition that Paul was a free missionary in Rome.

Chapter VI: Detailed account of Paul's *disputatio* with the Roman Jews in his rented house. Reiteration of the information contained in the last two verses of the canonical Acts.
Paul remains alive and in *libera custodia* in Rome after the crucifixion of Peter and the death of Simon Magus. The text notes that "divine Providence had deprived him, however, of the crown of martyrdom the same day as Peter in order that all peoples could come through him to know the Gospel". Thus Ps-Abdias refuses the tradition that Peter and Paul died on the same day in the same year, placing Peter's death two years before Paul's.

Chapters VII and VIII touch directly on Paul's martyrdom.

Chapter VII: Ps-Abdias notes that Paul was accused not only of introducing a new *superstitio*, but of seditious activity against the Emperor. He was convoked and interrogated by Nero personally and asked to give an account of his teaching. The remainder of Chapter VII gives an account of Paul's sermon to Nero.

Chapter VIII: the final climactic chapter gives an account of Paul's martyrdom:

> "The Emperor Nero was astonished by these words of Paul. Afterwards, however, he became irritated and pronounced against him a sentence of death by decapitation. As the news of Paul's death tarried in reaching him, Nero sent two of his guards, Ferega and Parthemius. They went and found Paul who was teaching the people — assembled in the great wonder of Christ — freely and outspokenly. When Paul saw them approaching, he exhorted them as follows: 'Come, children, and believe too in God. Thus your souls shall be saved, and He, with the coming of His only-begotten Son, will raise me and all who believe in Him and will set them in His eternal Kingdom'. They answered: 'Paul, first we are going to Nero to tell him of your end; in the meantime pray for us, that we may believe in the God whom you are preaching'. In fact they beseeched Paul to baptize them in order

to be saved. The Apostle said to them: 'In a short while return here to my grave. You shall find two men praying, Titus and Luke. They will succeed me in imparting the sign of Salvation'.

Having said this, soldiers arrived who took him and led him outside the city. Having arrived at the place of martyrdom, Paul turned toward the East. He raised his hands and eyes to Heaven and prayed for a long time. The prayer finished, he kissed the brethren, who had accompanied him, and after having bid them farewell, he knelt down, made the sign of the cross and offered his head to the executioner. When the head was severed, the sword became soaked with milk instead of blood, so much so that the right arm of the striker was bathed in milk. The bystanders witnessed this event, amazed, and magnified God who had bestowed such glory on His Apostle. Lucina, a servant of Christ, buried his body, full of aromatic spices, on her own property on the via Ostiense at the second mile-stone from the city.

Paul was martyred the 29th of June, two years after the death of Peter, under the reign of Our Lord Jesus Christ, to whom with the eternal Father and the Holy Spirit, belongs all honour and glory forever. Amen."

The Ps-Abdias account of Paul's martyrdom differs in a number of places from the previous apocryphal narratives which treated his death:

A) Paul is accused of sedition and of a dangerous brand of proselytism which is disturbing the established order. His sermon irritates Nero and this leads to his condemnation. Ps-Abdias de-emphasizes the theme of the conversion of members of Nero's household as being the major factor motivating Nero's desire for vengeance.

B) Longus and Cestus disappear from the narrative along with the other Christian *ministri Caesaris*. It is Ferega and Parthemius who participate in Paul's execution and whom Luke and Titus baptize the day after Paul's martyrdom.

C) The text adds small, dramatic details to the account of Paul's final moments on earth: he kisses the brethren, bids them farewell and makes the sign of the cross.

D) Ps-Abdias lays considerable emphasis on the theme of milk flowing from the slain Apostle's body and the praise of God resulting from this miraculous occurrence.

E) The figure of the pious woman (Plautilla/Perpetua) who lends her scarf to Paul, disappears from the story. Attention is centered on Lucina, a devout Roman matron, who buries Paul's body on her property.

V. Excursus 2: Lucina Buries Paul

There is no other figure quite like Lucina in the early Christian martyrological legends. She appeared at different times and in different centuries in the stories of a number of martyrs. Yet she is depicted in the same, standard way: busy at work caring for and burying the bodies of those who died the glorious death. The burials usually take place *in praedio suo* or *in agro suo*. These, however, are not always in the same area of Rome, but change location to the different places at which the various martyrs are thought to have been slain.

A) Paul

1. *Ps-Abdias 8* relates that Lucina buried Paul: "Lucina, a servant of Christ, buried his body, embalmed with aromatic spices on her property on the via Ostiense, at the second mile-stone from the City".

2. The *Vita Cornelii (Felician Abridgement,* 6th C.) gives the same information.

> "Hic temporibus suis rogatus a quendam matronam corpora apostolorum beati Petri et Pauli de Catacumbas levavit noctu; primum quidem corpus beati Pauli accepto beata Lucina posuit in predio suo, via Ostense, iuxta locum ubi decollatus est; ...[33].

B) Pope Cornelius, martyred in 253 A.D.

The *Vita Cornelii* concludes with the notice that Lucina buried the martyred Pontiff himself, by night, ... *in cripta cimiterium Calesti, via Appia, in predio suo*[34].

C) Processus and Martinianus, martyrs

In the *Passio SS. Processi et Martiniani*, Lucina reappears in much the same way. This *Passio* relates the decapitation and burial of these two early Roman martyrs. According to legend, these two men had been Peter and Paul's jailers when they were incarcerated in the Mamertinum. Peter had converted and baptized them during his nine month imprisonment there. After their martyrdom, Lucina took their bodies and having embalmed them with aromatic spices, laid them to rest on her own property, this time adjoining the via Aurelia near the site traditionally associated with their deaths.

---

[33] *LP.* Vol. I, pg. 64-66. According to the notice, it was Cornelius himself who buried Peter's body *inter corpora sanctorum, in templum Apollinis, in monte Aureo, in Vaticanum palatii Neronis* ... .

[34] *LP.* Vol. I, pp. 66.

"... sepelivitque in praedio suo in harenario iuxta locum: ubi decollati sunt sub die sexto nonas Iulias via Aurelia...[35].

D) Sebastian Martyr

The *Passio S. Sebastiani* also mentions Lucina. Here the slain Sebastian appears in a dream to the pious matron and orders her to inter his body, not on her property, but at the Catacombs along the via Appia, *iuxta vestigia apostolorum*[36]:

"Beatus itaque Sebastianus apparuit in somno sanctae Lucinae cuidam religiosissimae matronae dicens. In cloaca illa quae est iuxta circum invenies corpus meum pendens in gunfo. Hoc itaque dum tu levaveris perduces ad catacumbas: et sepelies me in initio criptae iuxta vestigia apostolorum. Statim beata Lucina cum servis suis medio noctis abiit: et elevans eum imposuit in pagone suo: perduxitque ad locum: et ibi ubi ipse imperaverat sepellivit".[37]

A plurality of persons lie behind Lucina. G.B. de Rossi noted that Lucina was an *agnomen*, an epithet or additional *cognomen*, derived from the Latin noun *lux*, rather than a personal or family name[38]. Lucina, thus, was taken by hagiographers as a prototype "whenever there was an occasion to highlight the burial of a martyr's mortal remains by a pious matron"[39]. Lucina was a totally legendary person: her importance lies in the fact that she was a striking symbol of Christian feminine piety[40]. Lucina was many people. As her legend developed and as the many people indicated by her name became concretized into one, sole, person, Lucina, this person was shifted back in time and became the individual who buried Paul.

It is clear that a Lucina in the sense of a real, historical individual who buried Paul, never existed[41]. Yet it must not be forgotten that Paul had indeed been

---

35 *Passio SS. Processi et Martiniani*, text in Mombritius Vol. II, pg. 404.
36 *Iuxta vestigia apostolorum* is a reference to the old, but unhistorical, tradition that the bodies of Peter and Paul were removed from their original resting places at the Vatican and at the via Ostiense in the year 258 (during the Valerianic persecution) and placed *ad Catacumbas* for safe keeping till the peace of the Church.
37 *Passio S. Sebastiani*, text in Mombritius, Vol. II, pg. 476.
38 G.B. de Rossi, *Roma sotterranea cristiana*, Rome, Vol. I, 1864; pg. 315.
39 G. Belvederi, "Le cripte di Lucina", *RAC.* Vol. 21; 1944-1945; pg. 122.
40 A. Ferrua, "Iuxta coemeterium Callisti", *RENDICONTI DEGLI ATTI DELLA PONTIFICIA ACCADEMIA ROMANA DI ARCHEOLOGIA*, Vol. 20; 1943-1944; pg. 110.
41 Very early on Lucina was considered by the Church community to have been an historical person. As such she made her way into the great mediaeval martyrologies. Thus Ado introduces her into his calendar for 30 June: *Natalis Lucinae, discipulae Apostolorum* (*Martyrologium of Ado, PL.* 123). So too Usuard: *Romae, natalis beatissimae Lucinae discipulae Apostolorum* (*Martyrologium of Usuard, PL.* 124); and Notker: *II kal, iul. natalis*

buried at the via Ostiense near the place at which he was martyred. He was buried in a *columbarium* along that road, a *columbarium* which had a legal proprietor. It was likely that proprietor (or perhaps a member of his family) who betook himself to the authorities and requested Paul's mortal remains. He then effectuated the burial in his own family tomb. The early Roman Church, ever mindful of this unknown person's deed of love and piety, attributed his act of fellowship to Lucina.

VI. Later Accounts of Paul's Martyrdom from the Eastern Christian Tradition

VI,1. An Armenian *Martyrium:* Martyre des principaux (et) glorieux Apôtres Saint Pierre et Saint Paul

This narrative in 14 Chapters has no equivalent in Greek and is likely to have been the product of pure Armenian tradition[42]. It is based on Venice *Armenian Ms. 346.* A like account appears in the Armenian *Synaxary of ter Israel* in its entry for the Feast of the Martyrdom of the great and glorious Apostles Saints Peter and Paul: 23 Margats (= 29 June)[43].

As in many of the texts bearing both Apostles' names, this narrative is principally focussed on Peter (i.e. Chapters 1-8; Chapters 6 and 7 relate Peter's martyrdom and burial). Chapters 9 to 14 are devoted to Paul. The story of his martyrdom (Chapter 12) is much more succinct than the parallel story of Peter's death.

Chapter 9 outlines Paul's earlier life and career,

Chapters 10-11 provide a number of curious indications, amendments and additions to the standard tale of Paul's life and death. The first is that Paul preached and taught in exactly sixty-five cities and provinces, which the text then enumerates. Secondly the account does demarcate two distinct Pauline journeys to Rome. On the first of these, the Apostle arrived in the City in

---

beatissimae Lucinae, quae ab apostolis baptizata est et instructa ... (*Martyrologium of Notker, PL.* 131).

42 *BHO,* 963. Commentary and French translation in LeLoir, *op.cit.,* pgs 55-63.

43 G. Bayan (ed.), *Le Synaxaire arménien de ter Israël, PO.* 21; 1930; the account of Paul's martyrdom is on pgs. 634-635. The text appearing in the Armenian Synaxary is based on Paris *Armenian Ms. 180.*

chains; on the second, he was apparently a free missionary. The Armenian *Martyrium* identifies the *second* of these visits with the two-year stay mentioned in the concluding verses of the canonical Acts. Thus Paul's first visit to Rome had occurred earlier in his Apostolic career. Finally the Armenian text places Paul's martyrdom at the end of this second stay in Rome. The text explains that the account of Paul's martyrdom is missing from the canonical Acts because Luke had left Rome before Paul's death and as he was not an eyewitness to it, he left it unreported in Acts.

Chapter 12 relates the actual martyrdom, which is given here below in Dom Leloir's French translation; pg. 62-63:

> Comparaissant devant le roi Néron, Paul lui faisait de dignes réponses, mais Néron s'emporta comme un chien enragé. Il tua d'abord sa tante et son épouse Octaviana, puis sa mère Agrippine, parce qu'elles avaient cru dans le Christ; il fit de même avec beaucoup d'autres de ses parents. Ensuite, par toute la terre, il persécuta les chrétiens et s'efforça de tuer les apôtres. Il fit comparaître Paul devant lui et, vu que, par son enseignement, il avait converti beaucoup <d'hommes> à la connaissance de Dieu, il le condamna à mort; sur son ordre, on lui coupa la tête, et il en jaillit du sang et du lait.

This little passage is a splendid example of how new legends built upon and expanded older legends. First the text greatly amplifies the idea that there were Christian converts in Caesar's household. Christian penetration of the palace was no longer restricted to Nero's cup-bearer or to some of his chief men; according to the text members of the imperial family, including Nero's wife and his mother, Agrippina, were also Christian converts. Their deaths are explained as having been caused by their belief in Christ. Secondly Paul's own death was made parallel to those of Octaviana and Agrippina: all died for the faith, they as pious women, he as evangelist. Thirdly the Neronian persecution was not limited to the Christians living in Rome, but was said by the text to be Empire-wide.

Chapter 13: As elsewhere in the Armenian apocryphal and liturgical tradition, a physical description of Paul was inserted here immediately after the account of his martyrdom.

Chapter 14 mentions the 29th of June as being the two Apostles' feast day and concludes with a doxology.

VI,2. A Syriac Chronicle: Fragments pertaining to the legend of Paul's head

This brief fragment of an ancient Syriac chronicle was first edited by F. Nau in 1896[44]. The fragments are extant on a 10th C. British Museum manuscript, *Syriac Ms. 14642*. This is a very precious document in that it contains one of the most ancient versions of the legend of Paul's head; a legend which was greatly enlarged in subsequent centuries by the additions of many interpolations and elaborations.

The text in its present form is a compilation of different chronicles clumsily joined together. Thus one sees the notice of Paul's martyrdom joined to an account of Peter's crucifixion which in turn is joined to the legend of Paul's head. This has troubled the text to a certain extent and has generated some conflicting information.

Below is F. Nau's French translation of the legend of Paul's head (pg. 404 of his article cited above):

> "La douzième année de Néron qui est l'an 375 d'Alexandre, Paul fut martyrisé à Rome par l'ordre de Néron le 5 Thomouz. La même année, Pierre subit aussi le martyre, crucifié la tête en bas, le 28 du premier Conoun[45]. Beaucoup de fidèles moururent aussi ce même jour; Marc alla durant la nuit avec des frères descendre Simon son maitre de la croix; il prit aussi le corps de Paul[46], mais comme il faisait sombre, il ne put trouver la tête[47]. Un homme zélé sortit de Rome au matin, rassembla les corps et les membres dispersés des martyres, ainsi que la tête de Paul, et les cacha dans un certain lieu."

> "Longtemps après, un pâtre qui avait là une étable de brebis, prit la tête de Paul qu'il avait trouvée, et la plaça au-dessus de son étable; pendant la nuit il vit comme un feu brûler au-dessus de la tête. Ce fait fut raconté et arriva jusqu'à saint Evariste, évêque de Rome à cette époque[48]:

---

44 F. Nau, "Fragments d'une chronique syriaque inédite relatifs surtout à Saint Pierre et à Saint Paul", *ROC*, Vol. 1; 1896; pg. 396-405.

45 Here the author is using a tradition that the two Apostles died on separate dates in the same year. As we saw earlier, *Syriac Ms. 12172* places their martyrdoms on the same date in separate years.

46 Here the author used a newer tradition which placed the two martyrdoms on the same day in the same year.

47 Cf. P. Peeters, "Notes sur la légende des Apôtres S. Pierre et S. Paul dans la littérature syrienne", *ANAL. BOLL.*, Tome 21; 1902; pg. 128-129, who writes: "The compiler had in hand a text related to the Latin (or Frankish) recension. In this recension it is stated that St. Paul's head was not found immediately after his execution: *propter multitudinem occisorum qui interfecti sunt illa die*. That is the explanation which the Syriac Chronicle's compiler had begun to transcribe textually in accordance with the original. But in his clumsy effort to join the tale of St. Peter's martyrdom to the text, he left the sentence unfinished and added another explanation a bit further on: *qua nox erat*".

48 Evaristus was Clement's successor as Bishop of Rome (c. 99-107 A.D.).

Les clercs dirent que c'était la tête de Paul, mais d'autres trouvèrent qu'il ne convenait pas de la mettre sans plus ample recherche près des corps des saints. Après une longue discussion, ils firent l'office des vêpres durant la nuit, et au matin ils trouvèrent que la tête était montée à sa place et que la vertèbre coupée par le glaive adhérait au crâne. Tous crurent et louèrent Dieu."

Chapter Six
Paul's Martyrdom in Patristic Literature

The period between the years 60 and 70 A.D. was one of the most traumatic in all Church history. That decade witnessed the martyrdoms of Peter, Paul and James; the disappearance of its chief Apostles decapitated the Church. In Rome the horrendous persecution of the Church ordered by Nero in the aftermath of the Great Fire of 64 A.D. left the Church there decimated. Finally the destruction of Jerusalem caused a tremendous upheaval and occasioned the flight of that city's Christian community to Pella:

> "Thus within a few years the whole situation was transformed; ... Suddenly a power-vacuum came into being, which was also, and this is more important, a theological vacuum".[1]

All these terrible blows impacted the way the early Fathers treated the Apostles' lives and deaths. Their approach was very cautious. They were usually quite reticent to give any information about the Apostles which did not figure in Scripture[1a]. They tended to abord the subject of the Apostles' deaths in a vague way; indeed silence was more often than not the chief characteristic of their approach. This was especially the case insofar as the martyrdoms of Peter and Paul were concerned.

The apocryphal acts of the Apostles greatly affected the Fathers' writings. After the year 200 A.D., the Fathers began to utilize this *corpus* of writings more and more in their treatment of the final days of Peter and Paul. Therefore one cannot really speak of an independent Patristic tradition insofar as the martyrdoms of Peter and Paul were concerned. Patristic writing on this painful subject was an emanation of the apocryphal tradition and wholly dependent on it.

---

1 C.K. Barrett, "Pauline Controversies in the post-Pauline Period", *op.cit.*, pg. 235.

1a Cf. A. Lindemann, who writes "The Church's *external history* between c. 70 A.D. and the middle of the 2nd. Century lies in darkness, although it was during this very period of time that, with the exception of the Pauline Epistles, all the New Testament writings and numerous other Christian texts were produced" (A. Lindemann, *op.cit.*, p. 2).

I. The Apostolic Fathers

I,1. Clement of Rome

Epistle to the Corinthians 5[2] (c. 95 A.D.)

"But, to cease from the examples of old time, let us come to those who contended in the days nearest to us; let us take the noble examples of our own generation. Through jealousy and envy (διὰ ζῆλον καὶ φθόνον) the greatest and most righteous pillars of the Church (οἱ μέγιστοι καὶ δικαιότατοι στύλοι) were persecuted and contended unto death. Let us set before our eyes the good Apostles (τοὺς ἀγαθοὺς ἀποστόλους): Peter, who because of unrighteous jealousy suffered not one or two but many trials, and having thus given his testimony (μαρτυρήσας) went to the glorious place which was his due. Through jealousy and strife (διὰ ζῆλον καὶ ἔριν) Paul showed the way to the prize of endurance; seven times he was in bonds, he was exiled (φυγαδευθείς), he was stoned, he was a herald both in the East and in the West, he gained the noble fame of his faith, he taught righteousness to all the world, and when he had reached the limits of the West he gave his testimony before the rulers (καὶ μαρτυρήσας ἐπὶ τῶν ἡγουμένων), and thus passed from the world and was taken up into the Holy Place (καὶ εἰς τὸν ἅγιον τόπον ἐπορεύθη), — the greatest example of endurance".

Commentary

The great value of Clement's text lies in the fact that it is a very early — almost contemporary — witness to the *historic reality* of Paul's violent death, even though, for its own reasons, it supplies no details as to the circumstances surrounding that death. Clement's epistle shows that from the ancientmost time Roman tradition held that Paul had been legally tried and executed in Rome during Nero's reign[3].

---

2 Greek text in *PG*. 1, col. 217-220. The Latin Version is very ancient, going back to the first half of the 2nd C. It was edited by G. Morin, "Codex Namurcensis", *ANECDOTA MAREDSOLANA*, Vol. II; 1894. The English translation given above is by K. Lake, *Loeb*, 1912.

3 Cf. J.D. Quinn, "Paul's last Captivity", *STUDIA BIBLICA III*, 1978; pg. 290; cf. A. Lindemann, *op.cit.*, pg. 76.

A) διὰ ζῆλον καὶ φθόνον/διὰ ζῆλον καὶ ἔριν (LatinVersion=*propter zelum et invidiam/propter zelum et contentionem*)

Clement understood the martyrdoms of Peter and Paul to have basically resulted from bitter contention and rivalry between the Roman Jewish community and the nascent Christian Church. This fierce strife had impacted the Christian community in that it sharpened the divisions between Judeo and Gentile Christians; divisions which caused Paul much grief and great harm[4].

Clement sharply contrasts the feelings of jealousy, hate, contention and rivalry entertained by the two Apostles' foes with their greatness, righteousness, holiness and nobility[5]. The struggle then is between forces of sin and darkness on the one hand and righteousness and light on the other.

The text concentrates on Peter and Paul "the great pillars of the Church" and leaves the other Apostles in obscurity. Luke, writing about twenty years before Clement, had already pointed the way by centering the *Acts of the Apostles* mainly, although not exclusively on the Apostolic ministries of Peter and Paul. Clement obviously went a step further by joining together the two Apostolic ministries in a common witness and by blaming their violent deaths on the same enemies. The process of twinning Peter and Paul — considered as co-founders of both the Roman and Corinthian Churches — which became a hallmark of Roman tradition, found its first expression and impetus here in Clement's *Epistle to the Corinthians*. It is important to note that although Peter is mentioned before Paul in Clement's sequence of names, he devoted more attention to Paul, whose example is given greater prominence and developed more at length[5a]. This is in marked contrast to later Roman tradition which greatly minimized both Paul's role in the evangelization of Rome as well as his death.

B) φυγαδευθείς

φυγαδεύω — to banish, to exile, to live in banishment. This verb does not appear in the NT except in the variant reading of Acts 7,29[6]. The Latin Version translates by the participle *fugatus*. This word, of course, expresses the idea of banishment, but it is a less precise juridical term than *relegatus*.

Paul does not mention exile in his enumeration of his own sufferings (2 Cor. 11,25). The reference in Clement is probably to Paul's two-year house arrest in Rome, which, from a legal point of view, was an *internal* exile.

---

4 Cf. Phil. 1,15 where Paul contrasts διὰ φθόνον καὶ ἔριν with δι' εὐδοκίαν.
5 Cf. *supra*, pg. 80ff.
5a A. Lindemann, *op.cit.*, pg. 75-76.
6 The variant reading occurs in D for the most part as well as E and g.

C) καὶ μαρτυρήσας ἐπὶ τῶν ἡγουμένων (Latin Version = *et dato testimonio martirii sic a potentibus*)

1. μαρτυρέω

Clement's letter is a good example of the evolving use of the term μαρτυρέω in the early Church:

> "In the first verse there has been no mention of Peter's preaching, only of his sufferings. Hence it seems to be said that he suffered a martyr's death. But in what is said about Paul the *martyrein* seems to refer to his preaching, though this is, of course, the preaching of one who died for the sake of his ministry. The usage is thus fluid".[7]

2. οἱ ἡγούμενοι

This term originated in military vocabulary where it designated those in command (i.e. the leaders)[8]. As a generic term, it denotes rulers or leading men; this could be in both secular and in religious life[9]. As an official title, it was used of a provincial governor (*praeses provinciae*) or of a high, but nonetheless subordinate, official[10].

Clement used the term on a number of occasions in the *Epistle to the Corinthians*. In chapter 51, he distinguished between Pharaoh and the rulers of Egypt: "Pharaoh and his army and all the rulers of Egypt ... were sunk in the Red Sea". In *EpCor. 55*, he wrote: "many kings and rulers ... have followed the counsel of oracles". Again in *EpCor. 32*, he noted: "kings and rulers and governors in the succession of Judah". Clement used the term in its true sense to designate those who were subordinate to the chief ruler — in the above examples Pharaoh or kings — but never to designate the chief ruler himself.

In the passage at hand, Clement is referring to those high, though anonymous, officials at Rome who conducted Paul's trial and who had the power to hand down a sentence of death in his case; that is in the case of a Roman citizen accused of a crime of majesty. Clement's use of such a general term to designate Paul's judges would preclude Nero's participation in the trial. Indeed the earliest and most authentic Roman tradition knew of no appearance by Paul before Emperor Nero.

---

7 H. Strathmann, "Martys, ktl.", *ThWb*. Vol. 4; 1967, pg. 505.

8 Arndt and Gingrich, pg. 344.

9 Cf. Acts 7,10 which notes that Pharaoh, "king of Egypt, made him [Joseph] governor (ἡγούμενον) over Egypt and over all his household". Cf. Acts 15,22: "They sent Judas called Barsabbas, and Silas, leading men (ἄνδρας ἡγουμένους) among the brethren". In *EpCor 1*, Clement uses the term to designate the rulers of the Church of Corinth.

10 *LS*[9]. pg. 763.

D) οὕτως ἀπηλλάγη τοῦ κόσμου καὶ εἰς τὸν ἅγιον τόπον ἐπορεύθη (Latin Version = *liberavit se ab hoc seculo, et in sanctum locum receptus est*)

The martyr's reward is eternal life in Heaven with the Lord Jesus Christ. This blissful and blessed place is contrasted to the earth, violent and sinful, where the righteous and holy are slain[11].

I,2. Ignatius of Antioch

Epistle to the Ephesians 12 [12] (c. 110 A.D.)

"I know who I am and to whom I write. I am condemned, you have obtained mercy; I am in danger, you are established in safety; you are the passage for those who are being slain for the sake of God, fellow-initiates with Paul, who was sanctified, who gained a good report, who was right blessed (πάραδός ἐστε τῶν εἰς Θεὸν ἀναιρουμένων, Παύλου συμμύσται τοῦ ἡγιασμένου, τοῦ μεμαρτυρημένου, ἀξιομακαρίστου), in whose footsteps may I be found when I shall attain to God ...".

Commentary

In this passage Ignatius of Antioch alludes to Paul's martyrdom although the passage is more a portrait of Paul than a description of his death.

A) ἀναιρέω — to kill, to do away with, to destroy. Ignatius evokes in a powerful way the memory of those who were killed for the sake of God. The only victim mentioned directly by name is Paul[13].

B) ὁ συμμύστης — the one who is initiated with others, a fellow-initiate; one of the same faith, sharing the same opinion and way of life; a companion in the

---

11 V.C. Pfitzner notes the close correlation between this passage and the martyrdom accounts contained in *4 Maccabees* (V.C. Pfitzner, *op.cit.*, pg. 197).
12 Greek text in *PG.* 5, col. 656. The English translation is by K. Lake, *Loeb*, 1912.
13 Cf. Ignatius' *Epistle to the Romans* 4 where Peter is named (first) along with Paul in this letter addressed to the Roman Church: "I do not order you as did Peter and Paul; they were Apostles, I am a convict; they were free, I am even until now a slave". (*PG.* 5, col. 690; *trans.* K. Lake, *Loeb*, 1912).

same. The word does not appear in the NT, but it does occur in the lexicon of Gnosticism where it indicates a fellow-initiate into esoteric doctrines.

C) τοῦ ἡγιασμένου, τοῦ μεμαρτυρημένου. Ignatius describes Paul — one of those slain for the sake of God — with these two Perfect Passive Participles. They are evocative words which encapsulate Ignatius' thoughts on Paul. In Ignatius' view, the Apostle was sanctified through his death which perfected his Apostolic career. A. Lindemann has pointed out that the term ἡγιασμένος was not as a rule used by the early Christian writers to designate individual persons. Rather it was generally employed to refer to a group of Christians or the confessing community as such[13a]. Thus Ignatius' use of this term with reference to the martyred Paul is noteworthy.

Paul has gained a good report, he is the subject of testimony, a witness to be imitated. Soon Ignatius too will arrive in Rome to be perfected there as Paul had been a half century earlier.

D) ἀξιομακάριστος — worthily called blessed, right blessed. This is a rare word, peculiar to the Ignatian lexicon[13b]. Once again there are no details of Paul's martyrdom, just praise of his *blessed* figure.

Ignatius' theology of martyrdom is clear from his letters of which this passage is a good example. The disciple should imitate Christ unto death; he will become Christ's true follower when the world sees him no more. Ignatius' prayer is that he will be a fit sacrifice to the Lord. Because of his suffering, the martyr will be liberated by Christ and will find eternal life in and with Him:

> "True discipleship was also equated with death as a witness to the death and resurrection of Jesus and as a symbol of the bonds which bound disciple to Master".[14]

I,3. Polycarp of Smyrna

Epistle to the Philippians 9[15] (c. 130 A.D.)

"Now I beseech you all to obey the word of righteousness, and to endure with all the endurance which you also saw before your eyes, not only in the blessed Ignatius, and Zosimus, and Rufus, but also in others among yourselves, and in

---

13a A. Lindemann, *op.cit.*, pg. 84.
13b Ignatius had a fondness for ἄξιος -compounds. Cf. *Eph.* 4,1: ἀξιονόμαστος; *Eph.* 13,1: ἀξιόπλοκος.
14 W.H.C. Frend, *op.cit.*, pg. 198.
15 Greek text in *PG.* 5, cols. 1012-1013. English translation by K. Lake, *Loeb*, 1912.

Paul himself, and in the other Apostles; being persuaded that all of these 'ran not in vain', but in faith and righteousness, and that they are with the Lord in the 'place which is their due', with whom they also suffered. For they did not 'love this present world' but him who died on our behalf, and was raised by God for our sakes".

Commentary

Polycarp views the examples of the martyrs in much the same way as did Clement of Rome. He exhorts the Philippians to imitate the martyrs' patient endurance and suffering, whereby their deaths become assimilated to Christ's.

Paul is the only Apostle mentioned by name here; the other specific examples being Ignatius, Zosimus and Rufus[16].

II. The Fathers from Tertullian to the First Nicene Council

II,1. Tertullian

II,1a) *De Praescriptione Haereticorum* 36[17] (c. 200 A.D.)

"Come now, if you are ready to exercise your curiosity better in the business of your own salvation, run through the apostolic churches, where the very thrones of the Apostles preside to this day over their districts, where the authentic letters of the Apostles are still recited, bringing the voice and face of each one of them to mind. If Achaea is nearest to you, you have Corinth. If you are not far from Macedonia, you have Philippi and Thessalonica. If you can go to Asia, you have Ephesus. If you are close to Italy, you have Rome, the nearest authority for us also. How fortunate is that Church (*Ista quam felix Ecclesia!*) upon which the Apostles poured their whole teaching together with their blood, where Peter suffered like his Lord (*ubi Petrus passioni Dominicae adaequatur*), where Paul was crowned with John's death (*ubi Paulus Iohannis exitu*

---

[16] Clement writing to the Church of Corinth from Rome cited both Peter and Paul as examples. Ignatius, writing to Ephesus, mentioned only Paul, while in his letter to the Roman Church, he mentioned both Peter and Paul. Here Polycarp names Paul alone among the Apostles in his letter to the Church of Philippi.

[17] Latin text in *PL.* 2, cols. 58-60. The English translation is by S.L. Greenslade, *LCC.* Vol. 5; 1956.

coronatur), where the Apostle John, after he had been immersed in boiling oil without harm, was banished to an island ... ".

Commentary

De Praescriptione Haereticorum is one of Tertullian's most powerful works, not only because of its stunning refutation of heresy, but also because it "exhibits more than all his other works Tertullian's profound knowledge of Roman Law"[18].

A) *Ista quam felix Ecclesia*

Tertullian names five *ecclesiae apostolicae*, but it is on Rome that he lavishes the most attention. That Church's felicity and indeed its pre-eminence is due to the fact that *three* Apostles Peter, Paul and John taught there and that the first two were martyred in the City. Rome, then, is doubly apostolic, founded as it was on the doctrine taught by Peter and Paul and on the blood they shed there[19].

B) *ubi Petrus passioni Dominicae adaequatur, ubi Paulus Iohannis exitu coronatur*

Tertullian was the first Christian Father to specifically mention that Peter's death was by crucifixion and Paul's by decapitation. His decision to include these details was probably influenced by the recently-published and widely-circulated apocryphal *Acts of Peter* and apocryphal *Acts of Paul*[20].

II,1b) Tertullian

Adversus Gnosticos Scorpiace 15[21] (c. 213 A.D.)

"And should the heretic deny the truth which the historic narrative [i.e. the Acts] relates, let the imperial documents speak like the stones of Jerusalem! We have read the lives of the Caesars, how the faith was born in Rome before Nero

---

18 J. Quasten, *op.cit.*, Vol. II, pg. 269.
19 Cf. Irenaeus of Lyons, *Adversus Haereses* 3, 2-3.
20 Cf. W. Rordorf, Die neronische Christenverfolgung im Spiegel der apokryphen Paulusakten", *op.cit.*, pg. 372, note 14.
21 Latin text in *PL.* 2, col. 175.

stained it with blood. Peter was bound by another when he was led away to the cross. Paul was born into the Roman citizenship; but he was reborn therein by the nobility of his martyrdom (*tunc Paulus civitatis Romanae consequitur nativitatem, cum illic martyrii renascitur generositate*)."

Commentary

The *Scorpiace* defends the idea of martyrdom against Gnostic assailants who affirmed that it was unnecessary and not demanded by God. In Tertullian's view, martyrdom was a new birth and obtained life everlasting for the martyr. It was indeed necessary if there were no other way to avoid participating in idolatry or in another form of apostasy.

Tertullian carefully buttressed his arguments by an appeal to history and to the imperial documents (*instrumenta*) should his heretical adversaries refuse to believe the witness of the *Acts of the Apostles* (termed here the *commentarius*). The historical sources to which Tertullian referred his foes were likely to have encompassed Tacitus and Suetonius, both of whom had mentioned Nero's persecution of the Christians in their histories of the early Emperors. The *instrumenta* designated the totality of the legislation which had been passed and the imperial edicts or rescripts which had been promulgated against the Christians from the time of the first persecution of the Church under Nero till Tertullian's own time.

Paul had boasted of his having been born into the Roman citizenship during his interrogation by the tribune of Jerusalem, Claudius Lysias:

> "So the tribune came and said to him, 'Tell me, are you a Roman citizen?' And he said, 'Yes'. The tribune answered, 'I bought this citizenship for a large sum'. Paul said, 'But I was born a citizen'."[22]

But Tertullian dramatically transforms the whole concept of Paul's Roman citizenship. It is no longer merely a political or juridical state of being or status; rather that citizenship is spiritualized and given another dimension by the Christian writer. Paul attained true Roman citizenship in that, after having been one of the two founders of the new, Christian Rome and having taught his doctrine there, he culminated, fulfilled and accomplished his Apostolic ministry by laying down his life in that City as the Lord's veritable witness and faithful follower. *True Roman citizenship* attains its fullest dimension, then, in the new, Christian Rome, not in the old, pagan Rome whose rulers had persecuted and slain the Lord's followers and ensanguined His Church.

---

22 Acts 22,27-28.

II,2. Peter of Alexandria

De Poenitentia: Epistola Canonica 9 [23] (306 A.D.)

"Thus first Stephen, pressing on His footsteps, suffered martyrdom, being apprehended in Jerusalem by the transgressors, and being brought before the council, he was stoned, and glorified for the name of Christ, praying with these words, 'Lord, lay not this sin to their charge'. Thus James, in the second place, being of Herod apprehended, was beheaded with the sword. Thus Peter, the first of the Apostles, having been often apprehended, and thrown into prison, and treated with ignominy, was last of all crucified at Rome. Likewise also, the renowned (περιβόητος) Paul having been oftentimes delivered up and brought in peril of death, having endured many evils, and making his boast in his numerous persecutions and afflictions, in the same city was also himself beheaded (ἐν τῇ αὐτῇ πόλει καὶ αὐτὸς μαχαίρᾳ τὴν κεφαλὴν ἀπετμήθη); who, in the things in which he gloried, in these also ended his life ... ".

Commentary

Canon 9 of Peter of Alexandria's great disquisition, *de Poenitentia*, has as its theme the total disapprobation of those Christian rigorists — chiefest among which figured Peter's deadly enemies, the Meletian schismatics — who sought out the Roman authorities and actually invited martyrdom[24]. In doing so, the Bishop of Alexandria wrote, they not only were acting in a grievously sinful manner, but also acting in total opposition to the Saviour's own example as well as to the example of the early martyrs.

Peter of Alexandria, soon to be decapitated himself in the great persecution under Diocletian, mentions four martyrs by way of example: Stephen, the proto-martyr, James, Peter, whom he calls "the first of the Apostles" (ὁ πρόκριτος τῶν ἀποστόλων) and Paul, termed "the renowned".

A) περιβοήτος — the one much talked of, famous, noised abroad, renowned. This is a rather infrequent attributive as Paul was much more commonly referred to as the 'blessed' (μακάριος/*beatus*) in the ante-Nicene writings.

---

23 Greek text in *PG.* 18, cols. 484-485. The English translation is by J.B.H. Hawkins, *ANL.*, Vol. 14; 1869.
24 Meletius, Bishop of Lycopolis, who had tried to usurp Peter of Alexandria in his own diocese, started the Meletian Schism. Quasten notes: "He made himself a champion of rigorism and set up 'the church of the martyrs'.". (J. Quasten, *op.cit.*, Vol. II, pg. 113-114).

B) ἐν τῇ αὐτῇ πόλει καὶ αὐτὸς μαχαίρᾳ τὴν κεφαλὴν ἀπετμήθη

Peter of Alexandria accords Paul the longest description of the four martyrs. This is, in fact, quite characteristic of the Eastern tradition, which tended to lavish more attention on Paul than on Peter, in contrast to the Roman tradition which did the opposite and in which Paul generally played a diminished role. Peter of Alexandria did not relate details of Paul's martyrdom other than to say that he was beheaded at Rome. The text concentrates more on Paul's role as a model. The Apostle was the victim of much persecution and adversity. He was delivered up many times to the authorities, the last time being at Rome; but he never delivered *himself* up to them — never yielded to what Peter of Alexandria thinks was a diabolical temptation. Instead the Alexandrian father notes that in spite of his afflictions, Paul continued his ministry undaunted, he watched and he prayed.

II,3. Lactantius

de Mortibus Persecutorum 2[25] (between 316 and 321 A.D.)

"It was when Nero was already emperor that Peter arrived in Rome; after performing various miracles — which he did through the excellence of God Himself, since the power had been granted to him by God — he converted many to righteousness and established a faithful and steadfast temple to God.

This was reported to Nero; and when he noticed that not only at Rome but everywhere great numbers of people were daily abandoning the worship of idols and condemning the practice of the past by coming over to the new religion, Nero, abominable and criminal tyrant that he was (*ut erat execrabilis ac nocens tyrannus*), leapt into action to overturn the heavenly temple and to abolish righteousness (*prosilivit ad excidendum coeleste templum delendamque iustitiam*), and, first persecutor of the servants of God, he nailed Peter to the cross and slew Paul (*primus omnium persecutus Dei servos Petrum cruci affixit, Paulum interfecit*).

For this he did not go unpunished; God took note of the way in which His people were troubled. Cast down from the pinnacle of power and hurtled from the heights, the tyrant, powerless, suddenly disappeared; not even a place of burial was to be seen on the earth for so evil a beast (*tam malae bestiae*).

---

25 Latin text in *PL.* 7, cols. 195-198. The English translation is by J.L. Creed, Clarendon Press, Oxford, 1984.

Hence some crazed men believe that he has been borne away and kept alive (for the Sibyl declares that 'the matricide, though an exile, will come back from the ends of the earth'), so that, since he was the first persecutor, he may also be the last and herald the arrival of Antichrist (*et antichristi praecedat adventum*); it is not right to believe this; yet just as certain of our number maintain that two prophets have been borne away until the last days before the holy and eternal rule of Christ, in the same way they think that Nero too will come as the forerunner and herald of the devil (*praecursor diaboli ac praevius*) when he comes to lay waste the earth and overturn the human race."

Commentary

Lactantius' great work, *de Mortibus Persecutorum*, is the mighty and telling story of divine anger at and punishment of the wicked persecutors of the Church, in the first instance, Nero. Lactantius transforms Nero from an historical person into the very epitome of evil, into a mythical figure as forerunner of the Antichrist. Lactantius begins his remarkable portrait of the Emperor with an historical fact, Nero was the first to persecute God's servants: *primus omnium persecutus Dei servos*. Lactantius' hatred of Nero waxes: the Emperor was an execrable and criminal tyrant and an evil beast. He concludes by linking the Emperor to the very Antichrist. Nero will return, and his return will precede the Antichrist's advent *(antichristi praecedat adventum)*. In this Nero, as a totally evil figure, does nothing but the devil's work of whom he is the forerunner and herald *(praecursor diaboli ac praevius)*. Thus the martyrdoms of Peter and Paul were a significant event in a giant battle, first terrestrial, later to become cosmic, between the forces of good and evil. True in the first, terrestrial battle, the Emperor succeeded in killing Peter and Paul, but he, their murderer, was punished by God and deprived of his kingdom. Here, then, the deaths of Peter and Paul, are linked to Nero's overthrow in 68 A.D.; the Emperor's downfall being considered as divine punishment for so dastardly a deed as the shedding of the Apostles' blood.

A) *Petrum cruci affixit*

Lactantius concentrates much more on Peter than on Paul[26]. He places Peter's

---

26 Irenaeus of Lyons had spoken of a double apostolic origin for the See of Rome, one that was both Petrine and Pauline, and understood the apostolic succession to be a doctrinal and dogmatic guarantee (*Adversus Haereses* 3,2-3). By Lactantius' time, interest was more clearly focussed on the episcopal authority in itself and for the See of Rome, that meant first

arrival in Rome during Nero's reign[27] and makes of Peter the great evangelist of Rome. Indeed, according to Lactantius' account, it was the success of Peter's mission (and not of the Pauline mission) that induced Nero to initiate his great persecution of the Church: *prosilivit ad excidendum coeleste templum delendamque iustitiam.*

Lactantius limits his account of Peter's death to the simple words: *Petrum cruci affixit.*

B) *Paulum interfecit*

Paul plays a negligible role in Lactantius' account. Nothing is said of his ministry in Rome; indeed Lactantius attributes to Peter the successful mission in Rome which the earlier *MP* had attributed to Paul. Even the account of Paul's death is shorter and vaguer than that of Peter; Lactantius limits himself to saying; *Paulum interfecit*[28].

III. *Eusebius of Caesarea: The Tropaeum of St. Paul*

Historia Ecclesiastica 2,25[29] (c. 325 A.D.)

"In this way then was he [Nero] the first to be heralded as above all a fighter against God (θεομάχος), and raised up to slaughter against the Apostles. It is related that in his time Paul was beheaded in Rome itself, and that Peter likewise was crucified, and the title of 'Peter and Paul', which is still given to the cemeteries (κοιμητηρίων) there, confirms the story, no less than does a

---

and foremost Peter. Cf. Y. Congar, "S. Paul et l'autorité de l'Eglise romaine d'après la tradition", *ANALECTA BIBLICA* 17/18, Rome, 1963; Vol. I., pg. 493.

27 and not 25 years earlier as later legend would have it.

28 Lactantius makes another brief reference to Peter and Paul's martyrdoms in the *Divine Institutes*. Here the Latin author notes that just before His ascension, Our Lord gave His disciples the power to prophesy. When at Rome, according to Lactantius, Peter and Paul predicted the destruction of Jerusalem: "And so, after their decease, when Nero had put them to death (*Itaque post illorum obitum, cum eos Nero interemisset*), Vespasian destroyed the name and nation of the Jews, and did all things which they had foretold as about to come to pass". (*Divinarum Institutionum* 4,21; [*PL.* 6, col. 517] English translation by W. Fletcher, *ANL.* Vol. 21; 1871).

29 Greek text in *PG.* 20, cols. 208-209. The text of the Latin translation done by Rufinus of Aquileia at the beginning of the 5th C. is taken from the *GCS.*, Eusebius, II,1; Leipzig; 1903. The English translation is by K. Lake, *Loeb*, 1959.

writer of the Church (ἐκκλησιαστικὸς ἀνήρ) named Caius, who lived when Zephyrinus was Bishop of Rome. Caius in a written discussion with Proclus, the leader of the Montanists, speaks as follows of the places where the sacred relics of the Apostles in question are deposited (τὰ ἱερὰ σκηνώματα κατατέθειται): "But I can point out the trophies of the Apostles, for if you will go to the Vatican or to the Ostian Way you will find the trophies of those who founded this Church' (τὰ τρόπαια τῶν ταύτην ἱδρυσαμένων τὴν ἐκκλησίαν).

And that they both were martyred at the same time (κατὰ τὸν αὐτὸν ἄμφω καιρὸν ἐμαρτύρησαν) Dionysius, Bishop of Corinth, affirms in this passage of his correspondence with the Romans: 'By so great an admonition you bound together the foundations of the Romans and Corinthians by Peter and Paul, for both of them taught together in our Corinth and were our founders, and together also taught in Italy in the same place and were martyred at the same time'. And this may serve to confirm still further the facts narrated".

Commentary

In the passage cited above, Eusebius makes mention not only of the martyrdoms of Peter and Paul at the hands of Nero, but also of their burial places and especially of the *tropaea* which marked those burial places. Eusebius made use of two ancient sources in this section. The first of these primary sources was of direct Roman provenance, being an extract of the *Adversus Proclum*, a work composed by the Presbyter Caius, who lived in Rome during the pontificate of St. Zephyrinus (199-217 A.D.) and whom Eusebius describes as an ἐκκλησιαστικὸς ἀνήρ[30]. The second source which Eusebius used here was a passage from an epistle which Dionysius, Bishop of Corinth, wrote to the Roman Church[31].

A) The notice on the martyrdoms of Peter and Paul

1. κατὰ τὸν αὐτὸν ἄμφω καιρὸν ἐμαρτύρησαν (Rufinus: *eodem tempore ambo passi sunt*).

The long and cumulative process of twinning Peter and Paul was now complete. Here Eusebius, basing himself on the testimony of Caius and of

---

30 Rufinus: *scriptor antiquus*. In *HE*. 6,20, Eusebius described Caius as λογιώτατος. Caius was, of course, renowned in his time for his refusal to attribute the authorship of the 4th Gospel or of *Revelation* to St. John.

31 In the *Chronicon* 2, Eusebius placed Dionysius under the year 172 A.D. Dionysius' letter

Dionysius of Corinth, states that both Apostles founded the Church of Corinth, that both taught there, that both taught in Italy, that both founded the Church of Rome and that both were martyred in Rome at one and the same time[32].

It is, however, difficult to accept the notion, in view of all the contrariant evidence, that the tradition of a synchronous martyrdom of the two Apostles goes all the way back to the time of the historical Dionysius. It is much more likely that Eusebius took this idea of a synchronous martyrdom, which was gaining popularity in his own time, and embedded it into Dionysius' account.

One should also note how succinct the account of Peter and Paul's martyrdoms is especially when compared to the substantially longer and considerably more detailed relation of the martyrdom of James, which occurs just before this passage in *HE.* 2,23.

2. τῶν ταύτην ἱδρυσαμένων τὴν ἐκκλησίαν. (Rufinus: *quibus ex utraque parte statutis Romana communitur ecclesia*)

ἱδρύω — to set up, to establish, to found.

Eusebius, quoting Caius, asserts anew that Peter and Paul were the founders of the Roman Church. From the standpoint of pure historical fact, it is obvious that the introduction of Christianity into Rome pre-dated the Apostles' arrival in that city. Paul's *Epistle to the Romans* was addressed, after all, to a long-established and functioning Christian community. Yet from the standpoint of faith as received and taught by Tradition, the arrival, ministries and especially the martyrdoms of Peter and Paul were the seminal events which really constituted the Church of Rome. It was from their time, and not before, that an orderly and meetly ordained succession of Bishops originated. Peter and Paul's teaching had nurtured the Church of Rome; their blood had impregnated Roman soil. Other Churches could claim an Apostolic foundation — or even as Corinth, a double Apostolic foundation —, but Rome was unique in that it was also the site of the martyrdoms of Peter and Paul and of their burial places.

---

was in response to one by Soter, Bishop of Rome in which the Roman Pontiff chided Dionysius on certain doctrinal matters. The Bishop of Corinth was careful in his letter to stress the unity of the Corinthian and Roman Churches, both founded on the double apostolate of Peter and Paul.

32 In the *Chronicon* 2, Eusebius dated Peter and Paul's martyrdoms to the year 68 A.D., that is to Nero's last regnal year. Another tradition dates their deaths to Nero's 12th regnal year; cf. Epiphanius of Salamis, *Adversus Haereses* 27.

3. θεομάχος (Rufinus: *hostem divinitatis pietatisque*)

ὁ θεομάχος— the one who fights against God.

The word occurs relatively infrequently in the classical Greek writers and only once in the NT at Acts 5,39 during Gamaliel's speech to the Sanhedrin. The verb θεομαχέω occurs in 2 Macc. 7,19, where one of the seven brothers says to King Antiochus: "But do not think that thou shalt escape unpunished, for that thou hast attempted to fight against God".

Here Eusebius applied this epithet to Nero, the first of the persecutors, who after slaying the Apostles, was in turn divinely punished by revolution and death[33].

B) The notice on the Apostolic *tropaea*

1. κοιμητηρίων

τὸ κοιμητήριον — the sleeping-room, the burial place. Cf. the verb κοιμάω — to put to sleep; in the Passive and Middle Voices, to fall asleep; metaphorically, the sleep of death, to die[34]. The noun κοίμησις is a falling asleep in death; e.g. the *Dormition* of the Blessed Virgin[35].

The term κοιμητήριον was for the most part used in its collective, more familiar signification of an *area sepulcralis*, containing multiple resting-places for the dead[36]. It was also used to designate a *single* tomb or an individual family grave. This usage is attested in numerous cemeterial inscriptions, mostly from the Christian East[37].

---

33 Eusebius again affirms that Paul's martyrdom occurred under Nero in *HE.* 3,1, this time using Vol. 3 of Origen's *Explanationum Genesis* as his source: "What need be said of Paul, who fulfilled the Gospel of Christ from Jerusalem to Illyria and afterward was martyred in Rome under Nero?".
34 *LS⁹.* pgs. 967-968. Cf. 1 Cor. 15,18: to fall asleep in Christ.
35 Cf. Lampe, *Patr. Gr. Lex.*, pg. 760.
36 Cf. *Thesaurus Ling.Lat.*, Vol. III, col. 1411, where the Latin *coemeterium* is defined as the *locus sepulchrorum ubi requiescunt corpora.* Cf. Tertullian, *de Anima* 51. P. Testini notes that in Rome the term *coemeterium* eventually came to be synonymous with *ecclesia* because the great number of tombs in the suburban Churches transformed those edifices into veritable covered cemeteries (P. Testini, *op.cit.*, pg. 85).
37 Cf. C. Bayet, "Inscriptions chrétiennes de l'Attique", *BCH.*, Vol. I; 1877, who gives a number of Attic inscriptions in which the word κοιμητήριον designates individual sepulchres. Bayet notes that this usage is one of the distinctive traits of Attic Christian epigraphy (pg. 392).

Caius' text reflects the belief of the Roman Church that the mortal remains of Peter and Paul lay at the Vatican and at the via Ostiense. No cemetery at Rome bore the names of the two Apostles. Rather Eusebius used the term in its popular sense of single tombs. The text would indicate that by the latter half of the 2nd C., if not earlier, individual Christians or perhaps the Roman community as an entity, held legal rights to the graves of Peter and Paul, although, of course, at that early date, not to the entire burial areas in which those graves were located. Otherwise it is very difficult to imagine how and in what way the Roman faithful could have obtained permission to edify *tropaea* at the two grave sites[38].

2. τὰ ἱερα σκηνώματα κατατέθειται

The noun σκήνωμα is properly speaking a tent or tabernacle. In Acts 7,46, it designates the habitation, i.e. Temple, of God. More cogent to our purposes here is its usage in 2 Peter 1,13-14: "I think it right, as long as I am in this body, to arouse you by way of reminder, since I know that the putting off of my body will be soon, as our Lord Jesus Christ showed me". Here then the term designates the human body, or mortal flesh, as the corporal tabernacle for the *anima*. Eusebius purposely placed the term σκήνωμα in juxtaposition with Caius' term τρόπαιον, because he "... interpreted the τρόπαια of Caius in the sense of *tombs with mortal remains*"[39]. The verb κατατίθημι confirms this sense as it signifies here 'to deposit' or 'to lay in a tomb' as in Mk. 15.46.

3. τὰ τρόπαια

τὸ τρόπαιον — a trophy, a monument, be it in wood, bronze or stone, marking an enemy's defeat[40]. Indeed as a monument to a military victory it was very often erected on the battlefield itself.

In Christian usage, the term was frequently put into a correspondential relationship to the Cross of Christ. The idea of the *tropaeum crucis* underpinned the conception of the crucified Christ's death as being a victory over the devil and his empire[41]. The word thus contained a strong nuance of triumph.

---

38 It is possible that the proprietors of Paul's sepulchre on the via Ostiense resided on the nearby Mt. Aventino. Cf. P. Lampe, *op.cit.*, pg. 22-23.
39 C. Mohrmann, "A propos de deux mots controversés de la latinité chrétienne: Tropaeum-Nomen", *VC.*, Vol. 8; 1954; pg. 165.
40 *LS*[9]., pg. 1826.
41 C. Mohrmann, *op.cit.*, pg. 156.

C. Mohrmann notes that along side the *tropaeum crucis* image was another, yet rarer, and even more remarkable usage: "the Body of Christ Itself, after His resurrection was called a trophy and it was with this trophy that He ascended into Heaven"[42]. From this type of usage, the word *tropaeum* came to designate the martyr's victory: the martyr went to Heaven and there received the attributes of his victory, the crown and the palm (*tropaea victoriae*). The term also became a metonymic designation for the martyrs' bodies, the mortal instrument by which they gained the victory (*martyrum tropaea*). Finally the term could be used to designate the mortal remains or *reliquiae* of the martyrs.

The *tropaea* of which Caius spoke were true funerary monuments, and not merely cenotaphs, because the actual mortal remains of the Apostles were deemed as reposing therein[43]:

"When he spoke of the τρόπαια, Caius was, of course, thinking of very visible sepulchral monuments which could easily be pointed out (ἔχω δεῖξαι) and identified (εὑρήσεις). I would even say that he had very much alive before his own eyes the image of the monuments which in his time existed on the true tombs of Peter and Paul".[44]

IV. *Paul's Martyrdom in the Nicene and Post-Nicene Fathers*

IV, 1. John Chrysostom

It is most appropriate to start this section by St. John Chrysostom, Patriarch of Constantinople; of all the Church Fathers, his love for Paul was the noblest:

"Chrysostom's love for Paul sprang from a double source: from the sublime holiness and example of faithfulness of the Apostle even to martyrdom and from the doctrine of wisdom contained in Paul's epistles, which so wonderfully depict his soul and spirit".[45]

Chrysostom's understanding of Paul the man and Paul the Apostle, was probably the fullest of the Fathers. He grasped the very essence of Paul's

---

42 *Ibid*, pg. 157.
43 J. Ruysschaert, "Les documents littéraires de la double tradition romaine des tombes apostoliques", *RHE*. Vol. 52; 1957; pg. 795. Cf. Eusebius, *de Theophania* 4,7 (Syriac Version).
44 M. Guarducci, "I trofei degli Apostoli Pietro e Paolo", *RENDICONTI DEGLI ATTI DELLA PONTIFICIA ACCADEMIA ROMANA DI ARCHEOLOGIA* (Serie III), Vol. 55-56; 1982-1984; pg. 135.
45 M. di S. Maria, "San Paolo nella prospettiva di San Giovanni Crisostomo", (in) *Studiorum Paulinorum Congressus Internationalis Catholicus 1961*, Analecta Biblica 17/18, Rome, 1963; Vol. II, pg. 493.

doctrine and teaching and admired, and wished to imitate, the Apostle's absolute love for the Master. Paul was a model, a very great and virtuous one, who was to be imitated not only in his practice of the Christian virtues, but also for his fidelity to that Master, most especially in his laying down his life for the Lord and for the sake of His Church.

1a. *Contra Oppugnatores Vitae Monasticae,* 1,3[46]. (378-385A.D.)

"This Nero accused Paul (for it happened that both lived at the same time) in the same way that you accuse these holy men; for it was that Paul had converted Nero's concubine (whom he loved very much) to the true Word of the Faith and moreover had persuaded her to refrain from those impure relations that she was having with her consort. Nero accused him and called him the very names that you yourselves repeat, that is, a corrupter and a deceiver (λυμεῶνα καὶ πλάνον) and other names of like purport. Accordingly, Nero first had him chained, then as he could not prevent the Apostle from continuing his admonitions to the young woman, he finally had him killed (τέλος ἀπέκτεινε)".

1b. *In Epistolam Secundam ad Timotheum,* Homily 10,2[47]. (395 A.D.)

"He had stood before Nero and had escaped. But afterwards because he had converted his cup-bearer, he was beheaded".

1c. *Acta Apostolorum,* Homily 46[48]. (400 A.D.)

"He is said to have welcomed both Nero's cup-bearer and his concubine ... and drew them to right living".

Commentary

In these three passages, John Chrysostom states that Paul's martyrdom was a consequence of his successfully converting members of Nero's household to the Christian faith. As a result of their conversion, these new Christians had renounced their old lives and refused service in the palace, abstaining, most especially, from granting the Emperor any sexual favours. Their conduct had

---

46 Greek text in *PG.* 47, col. 323.
47 Greek text in *PG.* 62, col. 657.
48 Greek text in PG. 60, col. 325.

infuriated Nero, who, in revenge, ordered the Apostle's arrest and then execution.

In his commentary on 2 Timothy, John Chrysostom mentioned only Nero's cup-bearer, an obvious reminiscence of the story of Patroclus as recounted in the old *MP*. In his commentary on the *Acts of the Apostles*, he mentioned both the cup-bearer and a concubine[49], while in his tract *Contra Oppugnatores Vitae Monasticae*, only the concubine (ἡ παλλακίς).

The idea of the Christian evangelist successfully converting the wife, fiancée or concubine of a Roman official — resulting in strict sexual continence on the part of the converted woman and a consequent persecution of the preacher — is a constant literary theme in the various apocryphal writings on the Apostles. Although the story of Paul's converting Nero's concubine is a late legend totally lacking in any historical foundation, it is, nonetheless, a good example of how these characteristically encratic legends about the Apostle penetrated into Patristic writings where they were transformed from unhistorical fable into authoritative teaching[50].

A) λυμεῶνα καὶ πλάνον

ὁ πλάνος — vagabond, impostor, misleader, deceiver.

ὁ λυμεών — corrupter, destroyer.

These are strong terms which the Christian writers used to designate false teachers in general and more particularly the minions of the devil or of the Antichrist. Here John Chrysostom took this terminology, which he normally used in polemizing with his adversaries, and placed it in the context of the struggle between Paul and Nero.

B) ἀπέκτεινε

The verb ἀποκτείνω, a strong variant form of κτείνω, means to slay, kill, condemn to death or put to death. Paul used it in 1 Thess. 2,15: "... the Jews, who killed both the Lord Jesus and the prophets". John Chrysostom evokes Paul's violent death, but gives no further details as to its manner or circumstances.

---

49 Cf. the 12th Century Byzantine historian, Michael Glycas, (*Annalium* 3), where the cup-bearer and (male) concubine are one and the same person.

50 Cf. C. Schmidt, *op.cit.*, pg. 123. The appearance of a concubine in Chrysostom's homily was perhaps due to the influence of the *Acts of Peter* wherein it is written that that Apostle had converted four concubines of the Roman Prefect Agrippa (*Acts of Peter* 33); cf. also the tale of Xanthippe in *Acts of Peter* 33-35.

These texts are all variations on one theme, as it were. While Nero sleeps, the Apostle is converting members of his household. The more the Emperor persecutes Paul to prevent this, the more harm he does to himself. Finally by ordering the Apostle's arrest, imprisonment and execution, Nero condemns himself to the loss of his kingdom and his very life. Nero had the political power and judicial authority to chain, imprison and behead Paul, but it is really the Apostle who was victorious because his doctrine spread throughout the whole Roman Empire[51]. When he evoked the titanic, cosmic struggle between Paul and Nero, John Chrysostom did nothing other than illustrate the point that persecutions do far greater harm to the persecutors than to their saintly victims[52].

1d. *De Laudibus S. Pauli Apostoli*, Homily 4[53]. (beginning 5th C.)

"It came to pass that among those who fought the blessed Paul were certain at Rome who preached the same doctrine. With the intention of irritating Nero who was already warring on Paul, they took it upon themselves to preach, so that as the Word further spread and the number of disciples increased, the tyrant's anger would become more inflamed and the monster more furious".

Commentary

John Chrysostom sharply contrasts Paul and Nero and presents the Emperor as the Apostle's implacable foe[54]. In this panegyric, one of the great Church Father's most beautiful writings, Paul is portrayed as the very model of Christian perfection, the Lord's Apostle whose *kerygma* is accompanied by a marvellous and extraordinary power. Nero, by contrast, is the raging beast, the tyrant, the incarnation of the bad Emperor, the Antichrist's minion who is set to kill God's disciple[55]. Here too, the struggle between the two men is cosmic: the celestial versus the diabolical.

In this passage the great Patriarch returned to an older tradition concerning Paul's martyrdom. For here he recounts that Paul fell victim to Nero's wrath because of his success in evangelizing the Roman population. But John Chrysostom also emphasized another point, that Nero's antagonism was even

---

51 Cf. John Chrysostom, *ad Populum Antiochenum*, Homily 16.
52 Cf. John Chrysostom, *In Epistolam II Timotheum*, Homily 4.
53 Greek text in *PG.* 50, col. 493.
54 Cf. J. Rougé, "Néron à la fin du IVe et au début du Ve siècle", *Latomus*, Tome 37; 1978; pg. 80.
55 Cf. John Chrysostom, *In Epistolam ad Romanos*, Homily 2,6.

more kindled by the Apostle's enemies *within his own community*. These enemies are expressly described as men who took it upon themselves to preach the same doctrine (δόγμα) as Paul did in Rome. John Chrysostom is quite clear here. Paul's enemies among the Roman Christians were partly to blame for the Apostle's violent end.

IV,2. Asterius Amasenus

Homily 8 (in Sanctos Principes Apostolos Petrum et Paulum)[55a]
(c. 400 A.D.)

"And emulating Herod in his disposition, Nero had the Apostles imprisoned. And as in the case of John, he had present another in the likeness of Herodias, licentious and fond of pleasure by inclination, who desired the heads of Peter and Paul. Both received the crown of martyrdom; the former was crucified, while Paul was decapitated".

Commentary

This homily, one of a group of *encomia* on various martyrs, is characterized, not by any dogmatic speculations, but rather by a biographical and moralistic approach to the two Apostles.

Asterius treats the two Apostles separately: first Peter and then Paul. His homily is more weighted towards their early lives and initial contact with the Lord. Although he does conclude his account with an allusion to the Apostles' deaths, the homily generally maintains a festive note about it and is a goodly example of a developed rhetorical style.

The sermon is vehement in its denunciation of Nero and of his court. He was termed earlier on an "effeminate person" (θηλυδρίας) and not a "king of men". His entourage was depicted as totally depraved. Asterius' account of the end of the two Apostles is brief and their deaths are likened to the death of John the Baptist, with Nero being the replica of Herod and the Apostles crowned with the martyrdom with which John was crowned[55b].

The text is an exhortation to the pious reader to imitate the virtues of the two martyrs, who were perfect disciples of the Master.

55a Greek text in *PG.* 40, col. 300.
55b Cf. Tertullian, *de Praescriptione Haereticorum* 36: *ubi Paulus Iohannis exitu coronatur.*

IV,3. Jerome

Liber de Viris illustribus 5[56] (392-393 A.D.)

After noting that Nero had dismissed Paul at the conclusion of his first defence and that the Apostle had subsequently gone to preach the Gospel of Christ *in Occidentis*, thus momentarily escaping the "mouth of the lion", Jerome wrote about the martyrdom as follows:

" ... but obviously he felt that his martyrdom was imminent, for he wrote in the same Epistle [2 Tim. 4,6]: 'For I am already on the point of being sacrificed; the time of my departure has come'. Accordingly in the 14th year of Nero's reign, on the same day as Peter, in Rome, he was beheaded for Christ, and was buried at the via Ostiense, in that the 37th year after Our Lord's Passion".

Commentary

Jerome's account is very succinct. He limited himself to a chronological indication: that Paul was beheaded in 68 A.D. and to a geographical one: that Paul was slain in Rome and buried along the via Ostiense. The only other piece of information he added was that Peter had been martyred on the same day as Paul and buried in Rome *in Vaticano iuxta viam Triumphalem*[57].

The indication that both Apostles were martyred on the same day in the same year also re-appears in a passage in Jerome's *tractatus* on Psalm 96:

Tractatus de Psalmo XCVI (*Series Altera*) lines 176-183[58]

"If the Lord preserves the souls of his saints and frees them from the hands of sinners, how then were the martyrs overwhelmed by persecution? How then were Peter and Paul condemned to death on one day by the impious Nero, if the Lord preserves the souls of his saints? Consider carefully what is being said. The Lord preserves the souls of his saints, their souls, not their bodies."

---

56 Latin text in *PL.* 23, col. 647.
57 Jerome, *de Viris illustribus* 1.
58 Latin text in G. Morin, (ed.), "Sancti Hieronymi Presbyteri: Tractatus novissime reperti", *Anecdota Maredsolana*, Vol. III,3; 1903; also in *Corp.Christ.-Ser.Lat.*, Vol. 78, pgs. 440-446.

IV,4. Augustine of Hippo

Sermones (for the Feast of Saints Peter and Paul: 29 June)

Jerome had followed a later tradition of Roman provenance which placed the martyrdoms of both Peter and Paul on one and the same day. The earliest Roman tradition (2nd Century) had said nothing of a double martyrdom and it is obvious that the tradition which Jerome used was not based on historical fact. Nonetheless in the Roman liturgical calendar, the anniversary of the two martyrdoms was celebrated (and still is) on the same day, the 29th of June. This is a very ancient liturgical feast going back to at least the mid 3rd Century. By the 4th Century, the feast had developed into a magnificent liturgical celebration with Masses celebrated at the three "stations" of the two Apostles, that is, St. Peter's at the Vatican, St. Paul's on the via Ostiense and at St. Sebastian's at the Catacombs (via Appia)[58a].

Amongst St. Augustine's many sermons were several which he composed for the Feast of Saints Peter and Paul (*in Natali Apostolorum Petri et Pauli*). The blesséd Bishop of Hippo followed a different tradition than did Jerome. This tradition also placed the two martyrdoms on the same day, but in different (and successive) years. Peter's martyrdom was first; Paul's martyrdom took place on the anniversary of Peter's death, that is to say on his *dies natalis*, or date of birth in Heaven.

1a. *Sermo* 295,7[59]

"... although they suffered on different days, they were one. First Peter led the way, then Paul followed."

1b. *Sermo* 381[60]

After noting that the Fathers had handed down the tradition that the two Apostles did not suffer on one and the same day, Augustine wrote: "Accordingly Paul suffered on the date of Peter's birth (in Heaven)".

Augustine's sermons for this feast day are a veritable poetical play on the numbers *one* and *two*. There were two Apostles, Peter and Paul, who were martyred in two different years, but on the same (one) day. They were two in

---

58a Cf. Prudentius, *Peristephanon* 12.
59 Latin text in *PL.* 38, col. 1352.
60 Latin text in *PL.* 39, col. 1683.

number, but one in their witness, now the two have one *dies natalis* celebrated in one great liturgical feast.

IV,5. Sulpicius Severus

Chronicorum libri duo, 2.28-29[61] (c. 403 A.D.)

"Nero was the first who undertook to destroy the Christian Name (*hic primus Christianum nomen tollere aggressus est*) because vice is always the enemy of virtue and the conduct of the virtuous is considered as a reproach by the dishonest. At this time, the divine religion was in rapid development in Rome. Peter was Bishop there (*Petro ibi episcopatum gerente*) and Paul was also there, having appealed to Caesar against an unjust judgement of the Procurator [of Judaea], and many came together to hear him (*ad quem tum audiendum plures conveniebant*). They converted many to the worship of God, by the truth of what they said and by the miracles which they performed. Indeed it was at that time that Peter and Paul had their famous confrontation with Simon Magus. With the help of the art of magic, Simon, who thought himself divine, went up into the sky, supported by two demons. But the Apostles' prayers put the demons to flight and Simon, in the sight of all the people, fell back to earth and was killed.

During that time there was a great multitude of Christians at Rome (*interea abundante iam Christianorum multitudine*), when a fire broke out and burnt the city. Nero was at Antium, but general opinion accused the Emperor of the crime, as it was believed that he wanted to re-build the city. No matter what he did, he was unable to exculpate himself from the charge that he was responsible for the fire. So he channelled all the hatred onto the Christians, who, although innocent, were made to suffer the cruelest tortures. New manners of death were invented: they were covered with the skins of beasts and torn to pieces by the dogs; others were crucified or burnt alive. Many others, after day was done, were used as living torches by night. This was the beginning of a fierce persecution. From that time Christianity was proscribed and edicts were promulgated forbidding the profession of Christianity. It was then that Peter and Paul were condemned to death: of whom the one was beheaded by the sword (*quorum uni cervix gladio desecta*) and Peter was crucified."

---

[61] Latin text in *PL*. 20, col. 145.

Commentary

Sulpicius Severus' account is largely based on Tacitus and Eusebius[62].

A) Nero

The portrait which Sulpicius Severus draws of Nero reflected current tradition. The Emperor represents the forces of evil, a diabolical power closely associated with the Antichrist. Nero was the first of a series of bad Emperors (*persecutores*) who tried to destroy the Christian religion (*hic primus Christianum nomen tollere aggressus est*). His hatred for the Christians was not only due to their considerable number in Rome (*interea abundante iam Christianorum multitudine*)[63], which was the result of the intense evangelizing efforts of Paul and Peter, but also was due to the virtuous life which these Christians led and which the vice-ridden Emperor found so insupportable.

B) Simon Magus

Sulpicius Severus briefly alludes to the struggle between the two Apostles and Simon Magus in Rome; a struggle which ended with the magician's death. But the historian definitely diminishes the importance of that episode, which played such a primordial role in the apocryphal tradition, in his account of the Apostles' lives in Rome. He clearly separates Simon Magus' death from the martyrdoms of Peter and Paul. Whatever role the Apostles played in Simon Magus' downfall and death was not the reason for Nero's persecution of them.

---

62 Cf. G.K. van Andel, *The Christian Concept of History in the Chronicle of Sulpicius Severus*, Amsterdam, 1976, pgs. 40-52. On pg. 48, van Andel writes: "We might wonder why it should have been Tacitus who had such an influence on Severus' style and subject matter, for there was no particular interest in this writer in late Antiquity. It is easier to ask the question than to answer it, but I should point out that in Severus' time there was a greater interest in Tacitus than before or after. In addition to Severus, Orosius too read and used his works, and Ammianus Marcellinus wrote under his influence and in emulation of him in about the same period. Apart from this elusive matter for which fashion is too strong a term, there is also the fact that the somewhat gloomy view of the times which we find both in Sallust and in Tacitus is also to be found in Severus and that this trait appealed to him in both writers. And besides, a large part of Tacitus' subject matter was of enormous importance to Severus' own narrative".

63 Cf. Tacitus, *Ann*. 15,44: *multitudo ingens*.

C) Peter and Paul

While Sulpicius Severus twinned the two Apostles in accordance with current tradition, he clearly distinguished their respective ministries. Peter was the Bishop, the episcopal authority (*Petro ibi episcopatum gerente*). Paul was the great doctor, whose teaching drew many to the faith (*ad quem tum audiendum plures conveniebant*). Both Apostles performed miracles at Rome and converted many *ad cultum Dei*.

D) The Great Fire of 64 A.D. and the Deaths of Peter and Paul

Sulpicius Severus, using Tacitus as his source, clearly believes Nero to have been the true author of the Great Fire of 64 A.D. Like Tacitus, he reports that Nero tried to channel responsibility for the fire onto the Christians so as to divert attention from himself[64]. Thus in his view the first persecution of the Christians at Rome resulted from the Great Fire. Peter and Paul were caught up in that persecution along with many other members of the Roman Church.

Of the martyrdom itself, Sulpicius Severus furnishes only the barest minimum of information, basing himself in this largely on Eusebius. The two Apostles were condemned to death *tum Paulus ac Petrus capitis damnati*), Peter was crucified and Paul decapitated (*quorum uni cervix gladio desecta*).

IV,6. Orosius

Historiarum adversus Paganos 7,7[65] (417-418 A.D.)

"Moreover, he was so roused with cruel madness that he killed the greater part of the Senate, and almost annihilated the equestrian order. And he did not even refrain from parricides; without hesitation, he destroyed mother, brother, sister, wife, and all his other relatives and kinsmen. He increased this mass of

---

64 Van Andel writes: "The report of the persecution of the Christians under Nero *as a consequence of the fire* appears exclusively in Tacitus. We read about it in no other secular author nor in any of the Christian writers before Severus except for the pseudo-correspondence between Paul and Seneca which probably dates from the fourth century and is certainly earlier than 392: in Ep. XII the same connection is made between the fire and the persecution obviously on the basis of Tacitus' account combined with data from Suetonius' *Vita Neronis*. (pg. 48).

65 Latin text in *PL*. 31, col. 1078. The English translation is by R.J. Deferrari, *The Fathers of the Church*, Catholic University Press of America, Washington, 1964.

crime by his daring impiety against God (*impietas in Deum*). For he was the first at Rome to torture and inflict the penalty of death upon Christians, and he ordered them throughout all the provinces to be afflicted with like persecution; and in his attempt to wipe out the very Name, he killed the most blessed Apostles of Christ, Peter and Paul, one by the cross and the other by the sword (*ipsumque Nomen exstirpare conatus beatissimos Christi apostolos Petrum cruce, Paulum gladio occidit*)."

Commentary

Chapter 7 of Book 7 of Orosius' chief work, *Historiarum adversus Paganos*, contains a brief summary of Nero's reign. The short notice which Orosius inserts therein on the martyrdoms of Peter and Paul forms a significant element in the quite depreciatory description which he formulates of Nero's rule.

Orosius explained the martyrdoms of Peter and Paul, not as a consequence of their confounding Simon Magus, nor of their converting members of Nero's household, the reasons given in the apocryphal tradition; nor even, in the final analysis, as a result of the Great Fire of 64 A.D. Rather, the Iberian historian saw the martyrdoms as the culmination of a long and frightening series of murders ordered by Nero: first of all of Senators and knights, then of members of the imperial family, and finally in an act of defiant impiety against God, of members of the Roman Church and of its leaders, Peter and Paul.

Paul may have been convicted and executed under the majesty laws, for his alleged *impietas in Principem*, but Nero, by contrast, was guilty of something far worse, for his slaying the Apostles was an act of *impietas in Deum*. As such divine punishment did not tarry in afflicting the Emperor for Orosius concluded chapter 7 by recounting Nero's lamentable end:

> "When he was performing incredible evils to disturb, and even to destroy the state, he was pronounced a public enemy by the Senate, and fleeing more ignominiously, he killed himself four miles from the City, and in him the entire family of the Caesars came to an end".[66]

IV,7. Paul's decapitation and the milk-theme: Macarius Magnes and Gregory of Tours

The old apocryphal tradition that milk flowed from Paul's body when his head was severed was taken up anew by Macarius Magnes and Gregory of Tours.

---

[66] Orosius, *Hist. adv. Paganos*, 7,7; (English translation: R.J. Deferrari, *op.cit.*).

7a. Macarius Magnes

Apocriticus 4,14 [67] (c. 410 A.D.)

"For when his head was severed, blood and milk flowed forth; dainties, as it were, that enticed the serpent".

7b. Gregory of Tours

De Gloria Beatorum Martyrum 1,29 [68] (590 A.D.)

"As for Paul, he was put to death at Rome by the sword on the same day, a year later, as Peter had been martyred. From his holy body flowed forth milk and water. What is there astonishing about milk's flowing forth from the body of the man who had borne and weaned unbelieving nations with that spiritual milk and after having dissipated the darkness around them, had led them to the solid food of Holy Scriptures?"

Commentary

Macarius Magnes obviously borrowed from the apocryphal tradition when he mentioned both blood and milk. Gregory of Tours, for his part, mentioned not blood, but water. It is likely that the Gallic father had in mind that water which flowed from Christ's sacred body, when He was pierced by the soldier's spear[69]. The mention of both milk and solid food is a clear reference to 1 Cor. 3,1-2 where Paul wrote to that troubled and disunited community:

> "But, I, brethren, could not address you as spiritual men, but as men of the flesh, as babes in Christ. I fed you with milk, not solid food; for you were not ready for it; and even yet you are not ready".

V. *The Flowering of the Roman Tradition:*
Leo the Great: *In Natali Apostolorum Petri et Pauli*

Leo was Bishop of Rome from 440 to 461, a tense and crucial moment in the history of the City of Rome and of the Roman Church. It was a troubled time

---

67 Greek text: C. Blondel, (ed.), Paris, 1876 (*editio princeps*).
68 Latin text in *PL.* 71, col. 729.
69 Jn. 19,34.

of barbarian invasions, political, social and economic upheaval as well as a sorrowful moment for the Church what with increasing religious dissidence and the propagation of sects and diverse heresies.

From the very outset of his pontificate, Leo Magnus championed, with all his personal strength and charisma and the power of his office, an assertion of traditional orthodoxy in the line of the teachings of the Nicene Council. Doctrine was elaborated in clear and forceful terms, discipline was strengthened, liturgy was renewed and liturgical usage was tightened and fixed to a greater degree than hitherto.

Leo's magnificent sermon, *in Natali Apostolorum Petri et Pauli* (29 June 441 A.D.), has to be understood in this historical context. What concerned the Roman Pontiff was less the facts about the martyrdom of the two Apostles — he is vague as to the dates and circumstances — than the theological implications of and dogmatic assertions about their ministries and martyrdoms in Rome. For Leo, the true significance of the Apostolic ministries in Rome was contained in the concept of the primacy of the See of Rome, a doctrine about which Leo wrote considerably. Thus in the Pontiff's *Sermon*, Peter's role is greatly enhanced while Paul becomes a clearly ancillary figure:

Sermo 82,6: in Natali Apostolorum Petri et Paul [70]

"Thither came also thy [Peter's] blessed brother Apostle Paul, 'the vessel of election', and the special teacher of the Gentiles, and was associated with thee at a time when all innocence, all modesty, all freedom was in jeopardy under Nero's rule. Whose fury, inflamed by excess of all vices, hurled him headlong into such a fiery furnace of madness that he was the first to assail the Christian name with a general persecution, as if God's grace could be quenched by the death of saints, whose greatest gain it was to win eternal happiness by contempt of this fleeting life. 'Precious', therefore, 'in the eyes of the Lord is the death of His saints': nor can any degree of cruelty destroy the religion which is founded on the mystery of Christ's Cross. Persecution does not diminish but increase the Church, and the Lord's field is clothed with an ever richer crop, while the grains, which fall singly, spring up and are multiplied a hundred-fold. Hence how large a progeny has sprung up from these two Heaven-sown seeds is shown by the thousands of blessed martyrs, who, rivalling the Apostles' triumphs, have traversed the city far and wide in purple-clad and ruddy-gleaming throngs, and crowned it, as it were, with a single diadem of countless gems".

---

70 Latin text in *PL.* 54, cols. 425-426. The English translation is by C.L. Feltoe, *LNPF,* Vol. 12; 1895.

Commentary

Leo composed the sermon for the feast-day of the two Apostles and so his first point in the sermon is that the 29th of June should not only be celebrated everywhere in the world, but that the memory of the two Apostles should be particularly honoured in the City in which they fell[71]:

> "But, besides that reverence which today's festival has gained from all the world, it is to be honoured with special and peculiar exultation in our City (*speciali et propria nostrae Urbis exsultatione veneranda est*), that there may be a predominance of gladness on the day of their martyrdom in the place where the chief of the Apostles met their glorious end".[72]

Leo stresses the parallel between Peter and Paul on the one hand and Romulus and Remus on the other. Rome now has in the two martyred Apostles tutelary saints, who have effaced the founders of the pagan city. It was, in fact, Peter and Paul who were the real founders of Rome in that they led and integrated the city into the celestial Kingdom: *qui te regnis coelestibus inserendam*. This deed was far superior to the work of the enemy brothers, Romulus and Remus, who founded a merely human city:

> "These are thy holy Fathers and true shepherds, who gave thee claims to be numbered among the heavenly kingdoms, and built thee under much better and happier auspices than they, by whose zeal the first foundations of thy walls were laid: and of whom the one that gave thee thy name [i.e. Romulus] defiled thee with his brother's blood."[73].

It was Peter and Paul who bestowed on Rome its true glory and made of the Romans "a holy nation, a chosen people, a priestly and royal state"[74]. Because of the presence of the See of Peter, Rome is the very *caput orbis*, which attained a "wider sway by the worship of God than by earthly government"[75]. In Leo's view, the Christianity which Peter and Paul preached in Rome and the continuing presence of the See of Peter in that City, allowed Rome to fully accomplish its essential civilizing function, that is to fully realize its purpose in God's design.

Although this sermon was composed for the feast-day of both Apostles, the stress is much more on Peter than on Paul. It was Peter, the *princeps apostolici ordinis*, who was appointed to Rome as a consequence of the *divisio Apostolorum*[76], while Paul was labouring elsewhere:

---

[71] Leo himself made renovations in the Theodosian Basilica of St. Paul without the Walls and modified the liturgy celebrated there in honour of the bless{é}d Apostle.
[72] *Sermo* 82,1.
[73] *Sermo* 82,1.
[74] *Sermo* 82,1.
[75] *Sermo* 82,1.
[76] *Sermo* 82,3.

"To this City then, most blessed Apostle Peter, thou dost not fear to come, and when the Apostle Paul, the partner of thy glory, was still busied with regulating other churches, didst enter this forest of roaring beasts, this deep, stormy ocean with greater boldness than when thou didst walk upon the sea."[77]

Thus, says Leo, Peter was providentially prepared for his great mission of bringing the "trophy of Christ's Cross" (*tropaeum crucis Christi*) to Rome, "whither by the Divine fore-ordaining there accompanied thee the honour of great power and the glory of much suffering"[78]. In Leo's exultation of Peter as the one chosen by Christ to be the true founder of that Church which was now laying its claim to primacy over all other Churches, Paul is clearly a secondary figure: Peter's *co-apostolus*.

> "Peter *and* Paul were the founders of the Roman Church. It is their authority which confers on the authority of the Bishop of Rome, who is their heir, all its plenitude. However, the Bishop of Rome is not the successor or 'vicar' of Paul as he is of Peter, although there were Popes who called themselves 'vicar' of both. There is no succession of Paul in the sense of a succession on an episcopal throne. Insofar as Paul is concerned, it is more a question of a moral heritage or better still the heritage of a charisma: that of the edification of the Church by teaching as well as that of concern for all the Churches".[79]

Although Leo underlined Peter's importance throughout the sermon, it was nonetheless the feast-day of *both* Apostles and Leo is emphatic that no distinction ought to be drawn between the merits of the two Apostles, as he concludes his sermon (*Sermo* 82,7):

"And over this band, dearly beloved, whom God has set forth for our example in patience and for our confirmation in the Faith, there must be rejoicing everywhere in the commemoration of all the saints, but of these two Fathers' excellence we must rightly make our boast in louder joy, for God's grace has raised them to so high a place among the members of the Church, that He has set them like the twin light of the eyes in the body, whose Head is Christ. About their merits and virtues, which pass all power of speech, we must not make distinctions, because they were equal in their election, alike in their toils, undivided in their death (*quia illos et electio pares, et labor similes, et finis fecit aequales*). But as we have proved for ourselves, and our forefathers maintained, we believe, and are sure that, amid all the toils of this life, we must always be assisted in obtaining God's mercy by the prayers of special interceders, that we may be raised by the Apostles' merits in proportion as we are weighed down by our own sins. Through our Lord Jesus Christ, who with the Father and the Holy Spirit, is one God, world without end".

---

77 *Sermo* 82,4.
78 *Sermo* 82,5.
79 Y. Congar, *op.cit.*, pg. 500.

Chapter Seven
An Afterword

I

The story of Paul's final days in Rome and the exact circumstances of his death and burial are to a very great extent shrouded in obscurity. Luke, who composed the *Acts of the Apostles* a mere handful of years after Paul's death, maintained an eloquent silence about the Apostle's violent end. This was, however, a studied, deliberate and purposeful omission as the painful events leading to — and the circumstances surrounding — Paul's execution were impossible to accommodate with the specific pro-Roman, and irenic apologetic aims, which the Evangelist had set for his composition. The Pastoral Epistles do no more than allude to certain conditions characterizing Paul's last imprisonment. Although the martyrdom's imminence is clearly evoked, the Pastorals focus on assimilating the Apostle's death to Jesus' sacrifice on the Cross, and thus offer no further details about it. St. Clement of Rome, St. Ignatius of Antioch and other very early Christian writers, while surely in possession of authentic historical tradition concerning Paul's death, refer to it in a vague, general and cursory way, subserviating its narration to their own immediate apologetic goals and specific literary objectives.

The *Acta Pauli*, as well as the subsequent apocryphal works descended therefrom, essentially re-invented the Apostle, as it were, creating a vibrantly dramatic, though entirely legendary Paul, thereby obscuring the historical Paul to an even greater degree. The *Martyrium Pauli* presents the Apostle as a defiant missionary, directly and consciously challenging the authority of the Roman State and indeed of the Emperor Nero himself. Paul is presented as actively seeking martyrdom, in fact provoking the Emperor to such an extent that martyrdom could be the only outcome of their meeting. This image of Paul created by the apocryphal tradition could scarcely have been more dissonant to the person of the historical Paul as he is understood from his own *corpus* of Epistles.

Finally the Patristic tradition used the figure of Paul for a variety of doctrinal or polemical purposes. His martyrdom became part of the arsenal which the Fathers used to confute heresies and other doctrinal deviations. The martyrdom was repeatedly mentioned, cited as a most worthy example, gloried in, but rarely were more than the meagerest details given as to how Paul's death and burial unfolded. Paul's person also became part of the struggle for primacy among the various Patriarchal Sees. Roman tradition generally enhanced Peter's role in the evangelization of Rome and the establishment of the Church in that city, thus reducing Paul to the role of an ancillary figure. Contrariwise, the Eastern Patristic tradition tended to stress the figure of Paul considerably more. A perfect example of this is the primordial role which the martyred Paul played in the thought and writings of one of the greatest Fathers, St. John Chrysostom.

II

Despite the manifest difficulties with the literary sources, as discussed in this book and briefly outlined above, it is not altogether impossible to reconstruct a few facts about Paul's final days in Rome and the circumstances of his death:

A) *The tradition that Paul died in Rome and not in another city can be accepted as historically accurate.* All the sources are concordant in pointing to Rome as the site of his martyrdom; there being no rival claims.

B) *It is quite certain that Paul's death occurred during Nero's reign (54-68 A.D.)..* Later Patristic tradition generally dated Paul's death to Nero's last regnal year in order to firmly link Paul's martyrdom with the Emperor's downfall; this latter event being understood by the later Fathers as an act of divine punishment for his ordering the slayings of both Peter and Paul. Other early sources place the martyrdom in the immediate wake of the Great Fire of 64 A.D. But the arguments supporting these dates are largely theological or apologetic. The juridical sequence of events would tend to support an earlier date, that is one *before* the Great Fire. As such we have retained the date of 63 A.D. (or beginning 64) as the most plausible date for Paul's death. Paul, in any case, would not have been martyred at the same time as Peter as the twinning of the two Apostles' martyrdoms is a late tradition.

C) *Paul was martyred*: that is he was formerly accused, arrested, tried, legally condemned and executed. There are no indications whatsoever that he died a natural death or for some unknown reason took his own life.

The likeliest juridical schema of events is as follows:
 1. Paul was released from house arrest at the end of the *biennium* described by Luke in the concluding verses of Acts because his accusers failed to come from Jerusalem to contest his appeal to Caesar (62 A.D.);

2. A short period of freedom ensued, quite possibly with a brief missionary journey to Spain;

3. The fractious leadership of the Roman Jewish community lodged charges against Paul of crimes of majesty. The Apostle was arrested; disaffected Judeo-Christians aided and abetted the Roman Jews in pursuing their case against Paul. The Apostle endured a second Roman Captivity in much harsher conditions than the first;

4. Paul was tried according to *extra ordinem* procedure, probably appearing before the Urban Prefect. He was found guilty and condemned to death. As Paul was a Roman citizen, decapitation was the indicated means of execution;

5. Paul was led outside the city walls, down the via Ostiense, and beheaded by a *speculator* (63/64 A.D.).

D) *The Apostle was buried in a columbarium very near to his locus passionis.* All the sources identify that site as just slightly off the via Ostiense, close by the Tiber, at the place where the Basilica of Saint Paul's without the Walls now stands. By the middle of the 2nd Century at the latest, a distinct *tropaeum* marked the grave and the Christian faithful were already making their way thither to pray.

III

The one thing that unites the historical Paul with the Paul of the legend is *the role of the Apostle as a model.* From the moment of his conversion on the Damascus Road till his martyrdom on the via Ostiense, some three decades later, Paul remained unswerving in his belief in the Divine Master, enduring all hardships in pursuit of his divinely-conferred mission as evangelist to the Nations. In his last tribulation, in his martyrdom, he remained, despite his age and frailty, constant, experiencing at long last that intimate communion with the world's Redeemer that he had long sought.

In his life, in his work, in his death, Paul remains a right-blessed model for all his disciples down through the ages till the end of time.

Rome, the Octave of Easter, 1993.

Bibliography

1. Reference Works

Bibles:
    English — *The Holy Bible*, Revised Standard Version, Thomas Nelson & Sons, New York, 1952
    Greek — Ἡ καινή Διαθήκη, 2nd. Edition with revised critical apparatus, The British and Foreign Bible Society, London, 1958.
    Latin — *Biblia Sacra*, Iuxta Vulgatam Versionem; adiuvantibus B. Fischer, I. Gribomont, H.F.D. Sparks, W. Thiele. recensuit et brevi apparatu instruxit R. Weber; Württembergische Bibelanstalt, Stuttgart, 1969, Tomus II.

The *Digest* of Justinian:
    Digesta — Corpus Iuris Civilis, Vol. I, Theodor Mommsen & Paul Krüger (edd.), Berlin, 1886. The re-edition with English translation used in this book is by Alan Watson (ed.) University of Pennsylvania Press, Philadelphia, 1985, in 4 volumes.

The *Liber Pontificalis*:
    L. Duchesne (ed.), *Le Liber Pontificalis: Texte, introduction et commentaire*, Ernest Thorin, éditeur, Paris, Vol. I, 1886; Vol. II, 1892; (Vol. III, 1957).

Dictionaries and Grammars:
    Arndt, William F. and Gingrich, F. Wilbur, *A Greek-English Lexicon of the New Testament and other early Christian Literature*, University of Chicago Press, Chicago, 1957. This is a translation and adaptation of Walter Bauer's *Griechisch-Deutsches Wörterbuch zu den Schriften des NT und der übrigen urchristlichen Literatur*, 4th. Edition, 1952.
    Berger, Adolf, *Encyclopedic Dictionary of Roman Law*, Transactions of the American Philosophical Society, Philadelphia, 1953.
    Kittel, Gerhard and Friedrich, Gerhard (edd.), *Theologisches Wörterbuch zum Neuen Testament*, Verlag von W. Kohlhammer, Stuttgart, 1933-1973, in 9 volumes. The English edition used in this book is by G.W. Bromiley (ed.), *Theological Dictionary of the New Testament*, Wm. B. Eerdmans Publishing Co., Grand Rapids, Michigan, 1964-1976 in 10 volumes with index.
    Lampe, G.W.H., *A Patristic Greek Lexicon*, Clarendon Press, Oxford, 1961.
    Liddell, Henry George and Scott, Robert, *A Greek-English Lexicon*, Clarendon Press, Oxford, 9th. Edition, 1940.
    Moulton, James Hope, *A Grammar of New Testament Greek*, T. & T. Clark, Edinburgh, 2nd. Edition, 1906 (Vol. I, *The Prolegomena*).
    The *Thesaurus Linguae Latinae*, Leipzig, (from) 1900.
    Zerwick, Maximilian, *Biblical Greek*, translated from the 4th. Latin edition of *Graecitas Biblica*, Rome, 1963; *reeditio*, 1982

2. Bibliography of Works cited

Adinolfi, Marco, "San Paolo e le autorità romane negli Atti degli Apostoli", *Antonianum*, Rome, Vol. 53; 1978.
Alföldy, Géza, "Tarraco", *RE. Supplementband* 15; 1978.
van Andel, G.K. *The Christian Concept of History in the Chronicle of Sulpicius Severus*, Adolf M. Hakkert, publisher, Amsterdam, 1976.
Antonelli, Ferdinando, "I primi monasteri di monaci orientali in Roma: (b). Monastero di S. Vincenzo e Anastasio ad Aquas Salvias", *RAC.*, Vol. 5; 1928.
Aus, Roger D., "Paul's Travel Plans to Spain and the 'full Number of the Gentiles' of Rom. XI,25", *Novum Testamentum*, Vol. 21; 1979.
Baillie Reynolds, P.K., "The Troops quartered in the Castra Peregrinorum", *JRS.*, Vol. 13; 1923.
Barrett, C.K., *A Commentary on the Epistle to the Romans*, Adam & Charles Black, London, 1962.
Barrett, C.K., "Pauline Controversies in the post-Pauline Period", *NTS.*, Vol. 20; 1974.
Batiffol, P., "Abdias, évêque de Babylone", *Dict.Théol.Cath.* Vol. I; 1909.
Bauman, Richard, A., *The Crimen Maiestatis in the Roman Republic and Augustan Principate*, Witwatersrand University Press, Johannesburg, 1967.
Bauman, Richard A., *Impietas in Principem: A Study of Treason against the Roman Emperor with special Reference to the First Century A.D.*, Verlag C.H. Beck, Munich, 1974.
Bayan, G. (ed.), Le Synaxaire arménien de ter Israël, *PO.*, Vol. 21; 1930.
Bayet, Charles, "Inscriptions chrétiennes de l'Attique", *BCH.*, Vol. I; 1877.
Beaujeu, Jean, "L'incendie de Rome en 64 et les Chrétiens", *Latomus*, Vol. 19; 1960.
Belvederi, Giulio, "Le cripte di Lucina", *RAC.*, Vol. 21; 1944-1945.
Benveniste, Emile, *Le vocabulaire des institutions indo-européennes*, Les Editions de Minuit, Paris, 1969.
Bleicken, Jochen, *Die Verfassung der römischen Republik*, Ferdinand Schöningh, Paderborn, 2nd. Edition, 1978.
Bovon, François, "La vie des Apôtres, traditions bibliques et narratives apocryphes", (in) *Les Actes apocryphes des Apôtres: Christianisme et Monde paien*, Labor & Fides, Geneva, 1981.
Bovon, François, "Paul comme document et Paul comme monument" (in) *Chrétiens en conflict — l'Epître aux Galates*, Labor & Fides, Geneva, 1987.
Brezzi, Paolo, "La funzione storica di Roma nel pensiero di San Paolo", (in) *Studi Paolini*, Istituto di Studi Romani, editore, Rome, 1969.
Bruce, F.F., *The Acts of the Apostles*, Wm. B. Eerdmans Publishing Co., Grand Rapids, Michigan, 1951.
Bruce, F.F., "Christianity under Claudius", *Bull.J.R.Lib.,* Vol. 44; 1961-1962.
Bruce, F.F., "St. Paul in Rome I", *Bull.J.R.Lib.,* Vol. 46; 1963-1964.
Bruce, F.F., "'To the Hebrews'; A Document of Roman Christianity?" *ANRW.* II,25.4; 1987.
Buti, Ignazio, "La 'cognitio extra ordinem' da Augusto a Diocleziano", *ANRW.*, II,14; 1982.
Cadbury, Henry Joel, "The Tradition", *BC.*, Vol. 2; 1922.
Cadbury, Henry Joel, "Roman Law and the Trial of Paul", *BC.*, Vol. 5; 1933.
Capocci, V., "Sulla tradizione del martirio di San Paolo alle 'Acque Salvie'", *Atti dello VIII° Congresso Internazionale di Studi Bizantini 1951)*; Studi Bizantini e Neoellenici 8; Rome, 1953.
Cecchelli, Carlo, "Un tentato riconoscimento imperiale del Cristo", (in) *Studi in onore di A. Calderini e R. Paribeni*, Casa Editrice Ceschina, Milan, Vol. I; 1956.
Cerfaux, L. and Tondriau, J., *Le culte des souverains dans la civilisation gréco-romaine*, Bibliothèque de Théologie III,5; Desclée et Cie., éditeurs; Tournai, 1957.

Charles, R.H., *The Apocrypha and Pseudepigraphia of the Old Testament*, Clarendon Press, Oxford, 1913.
Charlesworth, Martin Percival, "Some Observations on Ruler-Cult especially in Rome", *HTR.*, Vol. 28; 1935.
Chilton, C.W., "The Roman Law of Treason under the Early Principate", *JRS.*, Vol. 45; 1955.
Congar, Yves, "S. Paul et l'autorité de l'Eglise Romaine d'après la Tradition", *Studiorum Paulinorum Congressus Internationalis Catholicus 1961*; Analecta Biblica 17/18, Pontificio Istituto Biblico, Rome, Vol. I; 1963.
Conzelmann, Hans, *Die Apostelgeschichte*, Handbuch zum Neuen Testament 7; J.C.B. Mohr (Paul Siebeck), Tübingen, 1963.
Crook, John A., *Law and Life of Rome: 90 B.C. -A.D. 212*, Cornell University Press, Ithaca, New York, 1967.
Cullmann, Oscar, "Les causes de la mort de Pierre et de Paul d'après le témoignage de Clément Romain", *RHPR.*, Vol. 10; 1930.
Cullmann, Oscar, *Saint Pierre: Disciple-Apôtre-Martyr*, Delachaux et Nestlé, Geneva, 1952.
Cumont, Franz, "Un rescrit impérial sur la violation de sépulture", *Rev.Hist.*, Vol. 163; 1930.
Dassmann Ernst, "Archäologische Spuren frühchristlicher Paulusverehrung", *RQS.*, Vol. 84; 1989.
Delebecque, Edouard, *Les deux Actes des Apôtres*, Librairie Lecoffre/J. Gabalda et Cie., éditeurs, Paris, 1986.
De Rossi, Giovanni Battista, *Roma Sotterranea Cristiana*, Cromo-litografia pontificia, Rome, Vol. I; 1864.
De Rossi, Giovanni Battista, "Recenti scoperte nella chiesa alle Acque Salvie dedicata alla memoria del martirio dell'Apostolo Paolo", *BAC.*, Vol. 7; 1869.
De Rossi, Giovanni Battista, "Oratorio e monastero di S. Paolo Apostolo alle Acque Salvie costruiti da Narsete patrizio", *NBAC.*, Vol. 4,5; 1887.
Dibelius, Martin and Conzelmann, Hans, *The Pastoral Epistles*, Fortress Press, Philadelphia, 1977.
Duchesne, L., "Notes sur la topographie de Rome au Moyen-Age", (in) *Mélanges d'Archéologie et d'Histoire*, Paris/Rome, Vol. VI; 1886.
Dufourcq, Albert, *Etude sur les Gesta Martyrum romains*, A. Fontemoing, éditeur, Paris, Vols. I-IV; 1900-1910; Vol. V; 1988.
Dupont, Jacques, "Aequitas Romana", (in) *Etudes sur les Actes des Apôtres*, Lectio Divina 45, Editions du Cerf, Paris, 1967.
Dupont, Jacques, "La conclusion des Actes et son rapport à l'ensemble de l'ouvrage de Luc", (in) *Les Actes des Apôtres: Tradition, Rédaction, Théologie*; Bibliotheca Ephemeridum Theologicarum Lovaniensium 48; Editions J. Duculot S.A., University Press, Louvain, 1979.
Ehrenberg, Victor and Jones, A.H.M., *Documents illustrating the Reigns of Augustus and Tiberius*, Clarendon Press, Oxford, 2nd. Edition, 1955.
Erbetta, Mario, *Gli apocrifi del Nouvo Testamento*, Marietti, 1966: (Vol. II, Atti e Legende).
Fasola, Umberto M., *Pietro e Paolo a Roma: orme sulla roccia*, Vision Editrice, Rome, 1980.
Ferrari, Guy, *Early Roman Monasteries*, Studi di Antichità Cristiana 23, Pontificio Istituto di Archeologia Cristiana, Vatican City/Rome, 1957.
Ferrua, Antonio, "Iuxta coemeterium Calisti", *Rendiconti degli Atti della Pontificia Accademia Romana di Archeologia*, Vol. 20; 1943-1944.
Flamion, J., "Les Actes Apocryphes de Pierre", *RHE.*, Tome 11; 1910.
Freeborn, J.C.K., "2 Timothy 4,11: 'Only Luke is with me'", *Studia Evangelica VI*; TU. 112; Akademie Verlag, Berlin, 1973.
Frend, W.H.C., *Martyrdom and Persecution in the Early Church*, Basil Blackwell, Oxford, 1965.

Frey, Jean-Baptiste, "Les communautés juives à Rome aux premiers temps de l'Eglise", *RSR.*, Tome 20; 1930.
de Gaiffier, Baudouin, "La mort par le glaive dans les Passions des Martyrs", (in) *Recherches de Hagiographie Latine*, Société des Bollandistes, Brussels, 1971.
Greenidge, A.H.J., "The Power of Pardon possessed by the Princeps", *CR.*, Vol. 8; 1894.
Grisar, Hartmann, *Histoire de Rome et des Papes au Moyen-Age*, Desclée, de Brouwer et Cie., Paris, 1906.
Grundmann, Walter, "syn-, ktl.".*, ThWb.* Vol. 7; 1971.
Guarducci, Margarita, "I trofei degli Apostoli Pietro e Paolo", *Rendiconti degli Atti della Pontificia Accademia Romana di Archeologia*, Serie III, Vol. 55-56; 1982-1984.
Guerra, Anthony J., "Romans: Paul's Purpose and Audience with special Attention to Romans 9-11", *RB.*, Tome, 97; 1990.
Guidi, Ignazio, *"Gli Atti Apocrifi degli Apostoli nei testi copti, arabi ed etiopici",* Giornale della Società Asiatica Italiana, Florence, Vol. 2; 1888.
Hanson, Anthony Tyrell, *The Pastoral Letters*, University Press, Cambridge, 1966.
von Harnack, Adolf, *Analecta zur ältesten Geschichte des Christentums in Rom*, TU. 28,2; J.C. Hinrichs'sche Buchhandlung, Leipzig, 1905.
Hemer, Colin J., *The Book of Acts in the Setting of Hellenistic History*, J.C.B. Mohr (P. Siebeck), Tübingen, 1989.
Hengel, Martin, *Acts and the History of earliest Christianity*. SCM Press, Ltd., London, 1979.
Hitchcock, F.R. Montgomery, "Latinity of the Pastorals", *ET.,* Vol. 39; 1927-1928.
Hitzig, Hermann Ferdinand, "Custodia", *RE.*, Vol. 4,2; 1901.
Horsley, G.H.R., *New Documents illustrating Early Christianity*, The Ancient History Documentary Research Centre, Macquarie University, North Ryde, N.S.W., Australia, Vol. I; 1981.
James, Montague Rhodes, *Apocrypha Anecdota*, Text and Studies II, 3, University Press, Cambridge, 1893.
James, Montague, Rhodes, "The Acts of Titus and the Acts of Paul", *JTS.*, Vol. 6; 1905.
James, Montague, Rhodes, *The Apocryphal New Testament*, Clarendon Press, Oxford, 1924.
Jewett, Robert, *A Chronology of Paul's Life*, Fortress Press, Philadelphia, 1979.
Jones, A.H.M., "Imperial and Senatorial Jurisdiction in the Early Principate", (in) *Studies in Roman Government and Law*, Basil Blackwell, Oxford, 1968.
Jones, Donald, L., "Christianity and the Roman Imperial Cult", *ANRW.* II,23.2; 1980.
Joüon, Paul, "Divers sens de 'Parresia' dans le Nouveau Testament", *RSR.* Vol. 30; 1940.
Käsemann, Ernst, *Commentary on Romans*, SCM Press, ltd., London 1980.
Kasser, Rodolphe, "Acta Pauli 1959", *RHPR.*, Tome 40; 1960.
Keresztes, Paul, "The Imperial Roman Government and the Christian Church I: from Nero to the Severi", *ANRW.* II,23.1; 1979.
Keresztes, Paul, "Nero, the Christians and the Jews in Tacitus and Clement of Rome", *Latomus*, Brussels, Tome 43; 1984.
Kirsch, J.P., "Der Ort des Martyriums des Hl. Paulus", *RQS.*, Vol. 2; 1888.
Kittel, Gerhard, "aixmalatos, ktl.", *ThWb.* Vol. 1; 1964.
Kübler, Bernhard, "Maiestas", *RE.*, Vol. 14,1; 1928.
Lampe, Peter, *Die stadtrömischen Christen in den ersten beiden Jahrhunderten*, W.U.N.T., II,18; J.C.B. Mohr (P. Siebeck), Tübingen, 1987.
Leclercq, Henri, "Muratorianum", *DACL.*, Vol. 12,1; 1934.
Leclercq, Henri, "Paul (Saint)", *DACL.*, Vol. 13.2; 1938.
Leenhardt, Franz J., *L'Epître de St. Paul aux Romains*, Commentaire du Nouveau Testament, 2e Série, Vol. 6; Labor & Fides, Geneva, 2nd. Edition, 1981.

Leloir, Louis, *Ecrits apocryphes sur les Apôtres: Traduction de l'édition arménienne de Venise I: Pierre, Paul, André, Jacques, Jean*, Series Apocryphorum 3, Corpus Christianorum, Brepols, Turnhout, 1986.

Lindemann, Andreas, *Paulus im ältesten Christentum*, Beiträge zur historischen Theologie 58; J.C.B. Mohr (P. Siebeck), Tübingen, 1979.

Lipsius, Richard Adalbert (ed.), *Acta Apostolorum Apocrypha*, Hermann Mendelssohn Verlag, Leipzig, Vol. I; 1891.

Lopuszanski, G., "La police romaine et les Chrétiens", *AC.*, Vol. 20; 1951.

Lüdemann, Gerd, *Das frühe Christentum nach den Traditionen der Apostelgeschichte*, Vandenhoeck & Ruprecht, Göttingen, 1987.

Lugli, Giuseppe, *Itinerario di Roma antica*, Periodici Scientifici, Milan, 1970.

MacDonald, Dennis R., "Apocryphal and canonical Narratives about Paul", (in) *Paul and the Legacies of Paul*, Southern Methodist University Press, Dallas, 1990.

Maddox, Robert, *The Purpose of Luke-Acts*, Vandenhoeck & Ruprecht, Göttingen, 1982.

Martin, V. (ed.), *Apologie de Philéas*, Papyrus Bodmer XX, Bibliotheca Bodmeriana, Cologny-Geneva, 1964.

Mason, Hugh J., *Greek Terms for Roman Institutions: A Lexicon and Analysis*, American Studies in Papyrology, Vol. 13, Hakkert, Toronto, 1974.

Mattingly, Harold, *Coins of the Roman Empire in the British Museum*, London, Vol. I; 1923.

Mealand, David L., "The Close of Acts and its Hellenistic Greek Vocabulary", *NTS.*, Vol. 36; 1990.

Millar, Fergus, "The Imperial Cult and the Persecutions", (in) *Le Culte des Souverains dans l'Empire Romain*, Fondation Hardt: Entretiens sur l'Antiquité Classique 19; Vandoeuvres-Geneva, 1973.

Minear, Paul S., *The Obedience of Faith: The Purposes of Paul in the Epistle to the Romans*, Studies in Biblical Theology, Second Series 19; Alec R. Allenson, Inc., Naperville, Illinois, 1971.

Mohrmann, Christine, "A propos de deux mots controversés de la latinité chrétienne: Tropaeum-Nomen", *VC.*, Vol. 8; 1954.

Mombritius, Boninus, *Sanctuarium seu Vitae Sanctorum*, Fontemoing et Cie., éditeurs, Paris, 1910 (in 2 volumes).

Momigliano, Arnaldo, "How Roman Emperors became gods", *Ottavo Contributo alla Storia degli Studi classici e del Mondo antico*, Edizioni di Storia e Letteratura, Rome, 1987.

Mommsen, Theodor, *Römisches Strafrecht*, Dunker & Humblot, Leipzig, 1899.

Mommsen, Theodor, "Der Religionsfrevel nach römischem Recht", (in) *Gesammelte Schriften III*, Weidmannsche Buchhandlung, Berlin, 1907.

Moraldi, Luigi, *Apocrifi del Nuovo Testamento*, Unione Tipografico Torinese, Editrice, Turin, 1971, in 2 volumes.

Morin, Germain, "Codex Namurcensis", *Anecdota Maredsolana*, Maredsous, Vol. II; 1894.

Morin, Germain (ed.), "Sancti Hieronymi Presbyteri: Tractatus novissime reperti", *Anecdota Maredsolana*, Maredsous, Vol. III,3; 1903.

Moule, C.F.D., "The Problems of the Pastoral Epistles: A re-Appraisal", *Bull.J.R.Lib.*, Vol. 47; 1964-1965.

Muratori, L.A., "Fragmentum acephalum Caii, ut videtur Romani Presbyteri, qui circiter Annum Christi 196 floruit, de Canone Sacrarum Scripturarum", (in) *Antiquitates Italicae Medii Aevi*, Milan, Vol. III; 1740.

Musurillo, Herbert, *The Acts of the Christian Martyrs*, Clarendon Press, Oxford, 1972.

Nau, F.,. "Fragments d'une chronique syriaque inédite relatifs surtout à S. Pierre et à S. Paul", *ROC.*, Vol. I; 1896.

Nau, F., "La version syriaque inédite des martyres de S. Pierre, S. Paul et S. Luc", *ROC.*, Vol. 3; 1898.
Nicolet, Claude, *Le métier de citoyen dans la Rome républicaine*, Gallimard, Paris, 1976.
Nock, A.D., "The Augustan Restoration", *CR.*, Vol. 39; 1925.
Nock, A.D., "Religious Developments from the Close of the Repubic to the Death of Nero", *CAH.* Vol. 10; 1934.
O'Brien, Peter T., *The Epistle to the Philippians: a Commentary on the Greek Text*, Wm. B. Eerdmans Publishing Co., Grand Rapids, Michigan, 1991.
Paoli, Ugo Enrico, *Vita Romana*, Le Monnier, Florence, 10th. Edition, 1968.
Peeters, Paul, "Notes sur la légende des Apôtres S. Pierre et S. Paul dans la littérature syrienne", *Anal.Boll.*, Tome 21; 1902.
Penna, Romano, "Les juifs à Rome au temps de l'Apôtre Paul.", *NTS.*, Vol. 28; 1982.
Pezzella, Sosio, *Gli Atti dei Martiri: introduzione a una storia dell'antica agiografia*, Edizioni dell'Ateneo, Rome, 1965.
Pfitzner, Victor C., *Paul and the Agon-Motif*, Supplements to *Novum Testamentum* 16, E.J. Brill, Leiden, 1967.
Pherigo, Lindsey P., "Paul's Life after the Close of Acts", *JBL.*, Vol. 70; 1951.
Pietri, Charles, *Roma Christiana*, Ecole Française de Rome, Rome, Vol. II; 1976.
Platner, Samuel Ball, *A Topographical Dictionary of Ancient Rome*, L'Erma di Bretschneider, Rome, Revised Edition, 1965.
Plümacher, Eckhard, "Apokryphe Apostelakten", *RE.*: Supplementband 15; 1978.
Quasten, Johannes, *Patrology*, Spectrum Publishers, Utrecht/Brussels, Vols. I-III, 1950-1960; Vol. IV, 1986, (Angelo di Berardino, ed.).
Quinn, Jerome D., "Paul's last Captivity", *Studia Biblica III*, 1978.
Ramsay, William Mitchell, "Nicopolis", *HDB.*, Vol. 3; 1900.
Recasens i Comes, Josep Maria, *La Ciutat de Tarragona*, Editorial Barcino, Barcelona, 1966.
Reicke, Bo, "Caesarea, Rome and the Captivity Epistles", (in) *Apostolic History and the Gospel*, Paternoster Press, Exeter, 1970.
Ricciotti, Giuseppe, *Gli Atti degli Apostoli*, Coletti Editore, Rome, 2nd. Edition, 1951.
Riccobono, Salvator, *Fontes Iuris Romani Antejustiniani*, G. Barbera, editore, Florence, 1941.
Ritter, Saverio, "Il frammento muratoriano", *RAC.*, Vol. 3; 1926.
Rohde, J., "Pastoralbriefe und Acta Pauli", *Studia Evangelica V*, TU. 103; Akademie Verlag, Berlin, 1968.
Rordorf, Willy, "Die neronische Christenverfolgung im Spiegel der apokryphen Paulusakten", *NTS.*, Vol. 28; 1982.
Rordorf, Willy, "Was wissen wir über Plan und Absicht der Paulusakten?", (in) *Oecumenica et Patristica* (Festschrift W. Schneemelcher), Metropolie der Schweiz, Chambésy-Geneva, 1989.
Rougé, Jean, *Recherches sur l'organisation du commerce maritime en Méditerranée sous l'Empire Romain*, S.E.V.P.E.N., Paris, 1966.
Rougé, Jean, *Les Institutions romaines: de la Rome royale à la Rome chrétienne*, Librairie Armand Colin, Paris, 1969.
Rougé, Jean, "Néron à la fin du IVe et au début du Ve siècle", *Latomus*, Brussels, Tome 37; 1978.
Rowlingson, Donald T., "The geographical orientation of Paul's missionary Interests", *JBL.*, Vol. 69; 1950.
Ruysschaert, José, "Les documents littéraires de la double tradition romaine des tombes apostoliques", *RHE.*, Vol. 52; 1957.
Sansterre, Jean-Marie, *Les Moines grecs et orientaux à Rome aux époques byzantine et*

carolingienne, Mémoires de la Classe des Lettres, 2e Séries, Vol. 66,1, Académie royale de Belgique, Brussels, 1983 (in 2 volumes).

di S. Maria, Melchiorre, "San Paolo nella prospettiva di San Giovanni Crisostomo", (in) *Studiorum Paulinorum Congressus Internationalis Catholicus 1961*; Analecta Biblica 17/18; Pontificio Istituto Biblico, Rome, 1963.

Schlier, Heinrich, "Parresia", *ThWb.*, Vol. 5; 1967.

Schmidt, Carl, *Acta Pauli: Ubersetzung, Untersuchungen und koptischer Text* (Heidelberger koptischen Papyrushandschrift 1), J.C. Hinrichs'sche Buchhandlung, Leipzig, 2nd. Edition, 1905.

Schneemelcher, Wilhelm, "Paulusakten", (in) *Neutestamentliche Apokryphen*, E. Hennecke and W. Schneemelcher (edd.), J.C.B. Mohr (Paul Siebeck), Tübingen, 3rd. Edition, 1964; in 2 volumes.

Schneemelcher, Wilhelm, "Paulus in der griechischen Kirche des zweiten Jahrhunderts", *ZK.*, Vol. 75; 1964.

Schneemelcher, Wilhelm, "Die Apostelgeschichte des Lukas und die Acta Pauli", (in) *Gesammelte Aufsätze zum Neuen Testament und zur Patristik*, Patriarchal Institute for Patristic Studies, Thessalonica, 1974.

Schneemelcher, Wilhelm, "Die Acta Pauli — neue Funde und neue Aufgaben", (in) *Gesammelte Aufsätze zum Neuen Testament und zur Patristik*, Patriarchal Institute for Patristic Studies, Thessalonica, 1974.

Schubart, Wilhelm and Schmidt, Carl, *Acta Pauli; nach dem Papyrus der Hamburger Staats- und Universitäts Bibliothek*, J.J. Augustin Verlag, Hamburg, 1936.

Schürer, Emil, *The History of the Jewish People in the Age of Jesus Christ (175 B.C. - A.D. 135)*, New English Version revised and edited by G. Vermes, F. Millar and M. Goodman; T. & T. Clark, Edinburgh, Vol. III,1; 1986.

Serra-Vilaró, J., *Fructuós, Auguri i Eulogi: Màrtirs sants de Tarragona*, Tallers Tipogràphics, Tarragona, 1936.

Sevenster, J.N., *Paul and Seneca*, Supplements to *Novum Testamentum* 4; E.J. Brill, Leiden, 1961.

Sherwin-White, A.N., "The early Persecutions and Roman Law again", *JTS.*, Vol. 3 (N.S.); 1952.

Sherwin-White, A.N., *Roman Society and Roman Law in the New Testament*, Clarendon Press, Oxford, 1963.

Sherwin-White, A.N., *The Letters of Pliny: a Historical and Social Comnentary,* Clarendon Press, Oxford, 1966.

Smallwood, E. Mary, "The alleged Jewish Tendencies of Poppaea Sabina", *JTS.*, Vol. 10; 1959.

Solin, Heikki, "Juden und Syrer im westlichen Teil der römischen Welt", *ANRW.* II,29.2; 1983.

Spicq. C., "Saint Paul est venu en Espagne", *Helmantica*, Salamanca, Tomo 15; 1964.

Spicq. C., *Les Epîtres Pastorales*, Librairie Lecoffre/ J. Gabalda et Cie., éditeurs, Paris, 4th. Edition, 1969.

Spicq, C., "L'imitation de Jésus-Christ durant les derniers jours de l'Apôtre Paul", (in) *Mélanges bibliques en hommage au R.P. Béda Rigaux*, Editions Duculot, Gembloux, 1970.

Stern, M., "The Jewish Diaspora", (in) *The Jewish People in the First Century*, van Gorcum & Co., B.V., Assen, Vol. I, 1974.

Strathmann, Hermann, "Martys, ktl.", *ThWb.* Vol. 4; 1967.

Sundberg, A.C., "Canon Muratori: a Fourth Century List", *HTR.*, Vol. 66; 1973.

Tajra, H.W., *The Trial of St. Paul: a Juridical Exegesis of the second Half of the Acts of the Apostles*, W.U.N.T., II,35; J.C.B. Mohr (P. Siebeck), Tübingen, 1989.

Taubenschlag, Rafael, "Il delatore e la sua responsabilità nel diritto dei papiri", (in) *Opera Minora*, Panstwowe Wydawnictwo Naukowe, Warsaw, Vol. 2; 1959.
Taylor, Joan E., "The Phenomenon of early Jewish-Christianity: Reality or scholarly Invention?", *VC.*, 44; 1990.
Testini, Pasquale, *Le catacombe e gli antichi cimiteri cristiani in Roma*, Cappelli editore, Bologna, 1966.
Vega, Angel Custodio, "La venida de San Pablo a España y los varones apostólicos", *Boletin de la Real Academia de la Historia*, Madrid, Tomo 154; 1964.
Vielhauer, Philipp, *Geschichte der urchristlichen Literatur*, Walter de Gruyter, Berlin/New York, 1975.
de Visscher, Fernand, *Les Edits d'Auguste découverts à Cyrène*, Otto Zeller, Osnabrück, 1940.
Vouaux, Léon, *Les Actes de Paul et ses lettres apocryphes*, Librairie Letouzey et Ané, Paris, 1913.
Vouaux, Léon, *Les Actes de Pierre*, Librairie Letouzey et Ané, Paris, 1922.
Walaskay, Paul W., *'And so we came to Rome': The political Perspective of St. Luke*, NTS Monograph Series 49, Cambridge University Press, Cambridge, 1983.
Wikenhauser, Alfred, *Die Apostelgeschichte*, Verlag Friedrich Pustet, Regensburg, 4th Edition, 1961.
Wilckens, Ulrich, "hysteros, ktl.", *ThWb.*, Vol. 8; 1972.

Index of Passages

Old Testament and O.T. Pseudepigraphia

Leviticus
26,13   49

Psalms
7,2   92
22,21   91
35,17   92
103,19   109

Isaiah
61,1   54

2 Maccabees
7,19   181

Testament of Benjamin
4,1   98

Testament of Levi
8,2   98

New Testament

Matthew
8,11   109
10,22   97
14,12   25
18,19   147
24,9   52, 82
24,10   82
24,27   109
26,56   89
27,27   60
27,37   21
27,46   125
27,54   126
27,57-60   25
28,19   106

Mark
6,27   24
6,29   25
15,16   60
15,21   104

15,26   21
15,39   126
15,43-45   25
15,46   182
16,8   106, 109
16,15   106

Luke
4,18   54
12,11   86
13,29   109
21,14   86
21,24   54
22,15   52, 68
22,53   89
23,27   141
23,32-33   93
23,38   21
23,39   93
23,46   130
23,47   126

23,50-53	25	18,2	78
24,1	126	18,3	45
24,26	52	18,6	38
24,47	126	18,7	78
		18,12ff	139
John		18,13	11, 35
7,4	48	19,8-10	78
16,32	91	19,23ff	90
18,20	49	19,26-27	34
18,28	60	19,27	30
18,33	60	19,28	55
19,9	60	20,2	102
19,12	34	20,4	54
19,19-22	21	20,6	55
19,30	95	20,9-12	122
19,34	194	20,17-38	37
19,38	25	20,17	90
		20,24	95
Acts of the Apostles		20,25	90, 103
1,8	106	20,33-34	66
2,10	76	20,37-38	103
2,29	50	20,38	90, 108
4,13	50	21,5	108
4,29	50	21,27	90
4,31	50	21,33	43
5,39	181	22,1	86
7,10	169	22,22	36
7,29	168	22,24-29	2
7,46	182	22,25	1
7,59	130	22,27-28	174
8,2	25	23,6-10	74
9,15	91	23,11	16
12,2	23	23,18	43
12,6	43	23,29	75
12,12	55	23,34	89
12,25	55	23,35	61
13,13	55	24,5-6	35
13,25	95	24,5	124, 128
13,46	38	24,10	36, 86
13,47	106	25,8	36, 86
15,3	108	25,9	1
15,22	169	25,10-12	129
15,37-38	55	25,11	1, 13, 36, 76
16,1-3	54	25,12	16
16,21	11, 34	25,14	43, 61
16,23-34	101	25,16	86, 87
16,37-38	2	25,21	16
16,37	1	25,25	16, 75
17,7	34	26,1	86

26,2	86	*I Corinthians*	
26,23	52	3,1-2	194
26,24	86	3,2	130
26,26	50	3,3	64
26,32	75	4,17	54
27,24	16	10,10-11	54
28,15	81	15,18	181
28,16	39, 41, 42, 122	15,32	90
28,17-28	29	16,6	108
28,17-20	40	16,8-9	90
28,17	43	16,11	108
28,21	73, 76		
28,22	79	*II Corinthians*	
28,23-28	40	1,5-6	53
28,24	30	1,5	52, 70
28,25	30	1,8-10	90
28,28	38	1,16	108
28,29	30	2,4	52
28,30-31	30, 33, 39, 46	5,20	58
28,30	46	10,5	54
28,31	62	11,25	168
		12,20	64
Romans			
1,5	107	*Galatians*	
1,9-15	107	5,20	64
1,9-10	41	5,21	63
1,11-15	29		
1,14-15	41	*Ephesians*	
1,29	63, 64	1,9-10	57
2,8	64	1,15	57
5,3	53	3,1	43, 54, 57
7,23	54	3,12	50
8,18	70	4,1	43, 54, 57
8,29	71	6,19-20	57
11,25	103	6,20	43
12,13	66	6,21	58, 61
13,1-7	1, 129	6,22	58
13,4	23		
13,13	64	*Philippians*	
15,19	102, 103	1,7	59, 86
15,20-21	107	1,12-14	60
15,23-24	107	1,12	61
15,23	103	1,13	61
15,24	117	1,14	62, 63
15,28-29	108	1,15-17	63
15,28	117	1,15	168
16,2	91	1,17	86
16,7	53	1,19-23	68
16,13	104	1,23	94

1,24-26	69		*II Timothy*	
1,29-30	96		1,15	90
2,3	64		1,16-17	92
2,16	95		1,16	43
2,17	96		2,9	93
2,19-24	54		4,6-8	94
2,23	65		4,6	69, 188
2,24	65, 102		4,8	91
2,25	66		4,10-11	122, 127
2,27	66		4,10	55, 90
2,30	52		4,11	93
3,5	84		4,13	89
3,8-11	70		4,16-17	86
3,21	71		4,16	18
4,18	66		4,17	92
4,21-22	66		4,19	92
4,22	122			
			Titus	
			3,12	102
Colossians			3,13	108
1,1	54			
1,5	97		*Philemon*	
1,7	55		1	43, 54, 56
1,15-20	52		2	66
1,18	52		9	43, 54, 56
1,23	52		10	56
1,24	52, 53, 70		13	56
1,25-27	52		19	56
1,25	52		22	55, 65, 102
1,26	53		23	53, 56
4,3	53		24	55, 56, 94
4,7	61			
4,9	54, 55		*Hebrews*	
4,10-11	55		2,10	70
4,10	53		11,32-33	91
4,13	55		12,1	95
4,14	55, 94			
4,16	57		*James*	
4,18	53		1,12	97, 98
			3,14	64
			3,16	64
I Thessalonians				
2,15	185		*I Peter*	
2,17	68		3,15	86
3,2-6	54		5,4	98
3,3	53		5,8	91
			5,13	55
I Timothy			*II Peter*	
6,12-14	96		1,13-14	182

Revelation		13,2	92
2,9-11	98	13,15	12
2,10	97	20,4	12, 23

Epigraphical and Papyrological Publications

BGU
531.I.21   87
628   47, 74
917.14   51

CIL
3,13648   42
3,14187   42
6,1057.7.4 93
6,25144   152
10,820   9
13,1780   93
14,2898   9
14,3482   152

Edicts of Augustus
 (Cyrene)
2   43

IG
7,1836   9
12,(7),55.15 47

IGR
1,1294   8
3,345   9

OGIS
199.33   109
668   9
707   61

P. Amh.
66,40   91

P. Bodmer
20,1.5   88

P. Fayum
2,III.24   129
108,11   93

P. Lille
7,20   93

P. Lips.
26.11   51

P. Lond.
196,5   43

P. Oxy.
33   20
502,29-31   51
580   43
707,24   47
1242   19, 20
1242,26ff   83
2760   42

P. Ryl.
169,16   47

P. Thead,
15,19   74

SIG[3]
814   9

Christian Apocrypha: The Martyrdom of St. Paul

Acta Pauli
a). Acts of Paul
  and Thecla
2-3   93

b). Martyrium Pauli
  (Greek)
1   45, 122, 127

2	123, 128	*Historiae Apostolicae*	
3	21, 123, 128	(Ps. Abdias)	
4	124, 130	The Passion of	
5	24, 125, 130	St. Paul	157ff
6	23, 125, 131		
7	23, 126, 131		

(Armenian) 136ff

Martyrium Petri et Pauli (Armenian) 162ff

(Coptic) 137ff

Passio Apostolorum Petri et Pauli

(Syriac) 134ff

(Ps. Hegesippus) 154ff

c). P. Hamburg 121, 130
(Greek)

Passio Sancti Pauli Apostoli

d). P. Heidelberg 122, 138
(Coptic)

(Ps. Linus) 138ff

Acta Petri et Pauli
(Ps. Marcellus) 143ff

Syriac Chronicle
(fragmentum) 164ff

Christian Apocrypha: Other Passion Tales and Martyrologia

Acts of Peter
(Vercelli)

1	115
2	115
3	116
4	116
5	116
33-35	185
33	185
40	131

Acts of Thomas
169   131

Acts of Titus 122

Acts of Xanthippe, Polyxena and Rebecca   117

Martyrium S. Apollonii
45   23

Martyrium S. Polycarpi
17-18   25

Martyrologium
Ado	101, 141, 161
Notker	100, 141, 161
Rhabanus Maurus	141
Romanum	141
Usuard	100, 141, 161

Passio SS. Processi et Martiniani   100, 161

Passio S. Sebastiani
161

Legal Sources and Codices

Codex Iustinianus		48,2.7	76
3,1	74	48,3.12	44
10,19.2.1	44	48,3.14	44
13,3	74	48,4.1	4, 5, 11
		48,17.1	88
Codex Theodosianus		48,19.2	16
11,7.3	44	48,19.5	18, 74
		48,19.8	16, 93
Digesta		48,19.13	14
1,8.6	26	48,19.28	22, 24
1,12.1	15	48,20.6	24
1,12.1.10	16	48,24.1	25
1,12.1.13	15	48,24.3	25
4,4.7.12	74	49,1.16	11
4,6.10	44	49,3.1	16
11,7.2	24, 26		
12,1.40	19	*XII Tables*	
38,14.8	74	1,7	87
42,1.54.1	19		

Early Christian Writers and Sources

Ambrosiaster		381	189
In Epistolam ad			
Romanos		Benedict of Soracte	
prologus	78	*Chronicon*	
		9	153
Arnobius of Sicca			
adversus Nationes		Clement of Rome	
2,12	147	*Ep. to the Corinthians*	
		1	169
Asterius Amasenus		5	80, 167ff
Hom. 8	187	5,2	64
		5,6-7	109
Athanasius of Alexandria		5,6	75
Epistola ad		6,1	30, 127
Dracontium		7,1	96
4	113	32	169
		44,5	95
Augustine of Hippo		51	169
Epistola		55	169
153,5.14	139		
		Commodian	
Sermones		*Carmen Apologeticum*	
295,7	189	845-859	83

Cyril of Jerusalem
Catechesis
4,15	147
17,26	114

Didascalia Apostolorum
(Syriac)
24	147

Epiphanius of Salamis
adversus LXXX Haereses
(*Panarium*)
27	180
27,6	114

Eusebius of Caesarea
Chronicon
2	179, 180

Historia Ecclesiastica
2,2.6	76
2,13	147
2,22.1-2	76
2,22.4	92
2,22.6	94
2,22.7	76
2,23	180
2,25	178ff
3,1	181
3,3.5	119
3,25.4	119
4.8-9	124
5,1.44	2, 21
5,1.47	22
5,1.61	25
5,1.62	25
5,21	23
5,21.4	22
6,20	179

de Theophania
(Syriac)
4,7	183

Gregory the Great
Registri Epistolarum
14,14	152

Gregory of Tours
de Gloria Beatorum Martyrum
1,28	146
1,29	130, 194

Ps.-Hegesippus
de Excidio Urbis Hierosolymitanae
III,2	154, 155, 156

Hippolytus of Rome
Philosophumena
6,20	147

Ignatius of Antioch
Ep. to the Ephesians
4,1	171
12	170ff
13,1	171

Ep. to the Romans
2,2	110
4	170
5	22
5,1	43
6	69

Irenaeus of Lyon
adversus Haereses
1,10.2	104
3,2-3	173, 177
3,3.3	108, 109

Isidorus of Seville
Chronicon
70	148

Jerome
Epistola
65,12	113

in Isaiam Prophetam
3(130)	113
4.11(163-164)	113

Tractatus de Psalmo 96
(Series Altera)
176-183	188

de Viris illustribus
1	188
5	113, 188
12	139

John Chrysostom
Acta Apostolorum
46	128, 184

contra Oppugnatores
  Vitae monasticae
1,3	128, 184

in Epistolam ad
  Hebraeos
arg. 1,1	114

in Epistolam ad
  Romanos
2,6	186
29,3	114
30,1	114

in Epistolam secundam
  ad Timotheum
3,1	128
4	186
10,2	184
10,3	114, 128

de Laudibus Pauli
  (*Panegyrics*)
2	53
4	186
7,9	41, 114

ad Populam Antiochenum
16	186

John Malalas
Chronographia
10	26, 151

Justin Martyr
I Apology
68	124

Dialogus cum Tryphone
10	22

Lactantius
Divinarum Institutionum
4,21	178

de Mortibus Persecutorum
2	176ff
22	24

Leo the Great
Sermones
82,1	196
82,3	196
82,4	197
82,5	197
82,6	195ff
82,7	197

Macarius Magnes
Apocriticus
4,14	130, 194

Maximinus the Arian
Sermo 11   147

Michael Glycas
Annalium 3   185

Minucius Felix
Octavius
8,3-4	29

Muratorian Canon
3,5	94
34-39	111

Orosius
Historiarum adversus
  Paganos
7,6.16	78
7,7	192ff

Peter of Alexandria
de Poenitentia
  (*Epistola Canonica*)
9	175ff

Polycarp of Smyrna
Ep. to the Philippians
9	171ff

Prudentius
Peristephanon
12   189

Shepherd of Hermas
Visio 3,2   22

Sulpicius Severus
Chronicorum libri duo
2,28-29   190ff

Tertullian
adversus Gnosticos
 (*Scorpiace*)
10   83
15   173ff

adversus Iudaeos
7   104

Apologeticum
5,2   76
21   35

de Anima
51   181

de Baptismo
17   119

de Praescriptione
Haereticorum
36   172ff, 187
36,1-3   23

Graeco-Roman Writers

Aeschylus
Choephori
938   91

Antipho
6,7   87

Apuleius Madaurensis
Metamorphoseon
10,6   88

Aristotle
Politica
1302 b 4 64
1303 a 14 64

Artemidorus Daldianus
Onirocriticus
1,35   129

Cicero
de Inventione
2,17.53   4

in Verrem
II,ii,17.43   88
II,v,31.80   60

pro Caelio
63   87

pro Cluentio
93   87
175   47

pro Flacco
28,66.69 83

pro Sexto Roscio
20,55.36 74

pro Sulla
2,4   89
2,6   89

Dio Cassius
51,19   13
52,21.2   15, 16
57,19   6
60,1   42
60,6.6   77
60,17.4   3
60,28   75
63,5   10
63,12   17

63,18	17	Hyperides	
63,20	10	*pro Euxenippo*	
		31	87

Diogenes Oenoandensis
Fragmenta
2,II,11–12   69

Josephus
Antiquitates Iudaicae
2,59   93
2,74   47
13,203   43
16,41   51
17,145   43
17,300   83
18,203-204   44
18,228   92
18,235   44
20,135   83
20,195   83
20,252   83

Dionysius Halicarnassensis
Antiquitates Romanae
1,35.3   110
10,36.6   42

Q. Ennius
Annalium
17(23)   110

Epictetus
Arrian Discourses
1,1.19   129

Bellum Iudaicum
1,621   87
2,531   42
6,238   42

Euripedes
Hippolytus
422   49

contra Apionem
1,255   68
2,147   87

Ion
671-675   49

Vita
3,13   83
3,16   83

Phoenissae
390-391   49

Lucan
Pharsalia
1,45ff   10
7,541   110

Herodian
6,1.2   19

Herodotus
2,180   47
3,32   89

Ps.-Lucian
Asinus
27   54

Hesiod
Theogony
429   89

Ovid
Fasti 1,498 110

Horace
Carminum
1,12   8
1,28.26   111
1,36.4   111
3,3.8   111

Pausanias
5,26.3   96

Philo
de Cherubim
22   109

Index of Passages

de Ebrietate
152   96

de Legatione ad Gaium
44,349   19, 20

de Specialibus Legibus
1,321   49

in Flaccum
16,128-129   47
35   67
187   94

Philostratus
Vita Apollonii
4,47   111

Plato
Apologia
24 C   96
28 A   87

Respublica
557 B   49

Pliny the Younger
Epistulae
4,22   19
6,31   19
7,6.8   15
10,56   47
10,57   42
10,96   12, 22, 28
10,97   87, 124

Plutarch
Consolatio ad Apollonium
13   94

Moralia
308 D   129

Polybius
1,42.5   109
2,38.6   49
5,104.7   109
9,32.4   96

Quintillian
de Institutione Oratoria
7,2.21   87

Secundus
Sententiae
19   94

Seneca
Apocolocyntosis
10   88

de Beneficiis
3,26   6
7,5.3   47

de Clementia
1,1.9   14

Servius
Commentarius in Vergilii
Aeneidos 1,530 111

Silius Italicus
Punica
17,637   110

Strabo
Geographikon
3,5.5   110

Suetonius
Augustus
33   14, 15
51   14
52   9

Tiberius
58   6

Caligula
32   21

Claudius
14   14
15   20, 75
23   43
25   78
29   88

Nero		6,11	15
10	20	13,4	14, 17
15	20	13,8	10
16	28	14,48	6
		14,51	42
Titus		15,44	22, 28, 30, 79, 124, 191
8	6	15,68	42
		15,74	10
Domitian		16,22	11
10	21		
		Historiae	
Tacitus		1,22	83
Annales		4,42	6
1,2	12		
1,11	8	Thucydides	
1,72	5	2,96	109
3,10	14, 19	3,54.4	89
3,22	43		
3,24	14	Virgil	
3,38	14	*Aeneid*	
3,51	21	1,530	110

Index of Modern Authors

Adinolfi, M., 1,2
Alföldy, G., 104
van Andel, G.K., 191, 192
Antonelli, F., 154
Aus, R.D., 103

Baillie Reynolds, P.K., 42, 43
Barrett, C.K., 37, 86, 103, 166
Batiffol, P., 157
Bauman, R.A., 5, 6, 17
Bayan, G., 162
Bayet, C., 181
Beaujeu, J., 18,76
Belvederi, G., 161
Benveniste, E., 2
Bleicken, J., 13
Bovon, F., 84, 119, 126
Brezzi, P., 41
Bruce, F.F., 27, 37, 77, 81
Buti, I., 13,14

Cadbury, H.J., 19, 44, 112
Capocci, V., 153
Cecchelli, C., 76
Cerfaux, L. & Tondriau, J., 8
Charlesworth, M.P., 9
Chilton, C.H., 5, 7
Congar, Y., 178, 197
Conzelmann, H., 37, 42, 81
Crook, J.A., 19
Cullmann, O., 80, 81
Cumont, F., 27

Dassmann, E., 104
Delebecque, E., 50
De Rossi, G.B., 152, 154, 161
Dibelius, M. & Conzelmann, H., 102
Duchesne, L., 147

Dufourcq, A., 147
Dupont, J., 48, 87

Ehrenberg, V. & Jones, A.H.M., 8
Erbetta, M., 118, 144, 154

Fasola, U.M., 101, 102
Ferrari, G., 153
Ferrua, A., 161
Flamion, J., 144, 146
Freeborn, J.C.K., 94
Frend, W.H.C., 3, 31, 171
Frey, J.B., 41

de Gaiffier, B., 23
Greenidge, A.H.J., 13, 14
Grisar, H., 147
Grundmann, W., 71
Guarducci, M., 183
Guerra, A.J., 77, 78
Guidi, I., 137

Hanson, A.T., 90
von Harnack, A., 127
Hemer, C.J., 33
Hengel, M., 37, 39
Hitchcock, F.R.M., 3, 4
Hitzig, H.F., 43
Horsley, G.H.R., 9, 18

James, M.R., 115, 117, 118, 122
Jewett, R., 4
Jones, A.H.M., 13, 14, 18
Jones, D.L. 9, 28
Joüon, P., 48

Käsemann, E., 103
Kasser, R., 120

Keresztes, P., 28, 30, 84
Kirsch, J.P., 152
Kittel, G., 54
Kübler, B., 5

Lampe, P., 76, 181, 182
Leclercq, H., 45, 112
Leenhardt, F.J., 103
Leloir, L., 136, 144, 145, 162, 163
Lindemann, A., 131, 166, 168, 171
Lipsius, R.A., 121, 122, 143, 155
Lopuszanski, G., 93
Lüdemann, G., 111
Lugli, G., 99, 101

MacDonald, D.R., 119, 120
Maddox, R., 39
Martin, V., 88
Mason, H.J., 42
Mattingly, H., 10
Mealand, D.L., 48, 51
Millar, F., 7, 8
Minear, P.S., 79, 108
Mohrmann, C., 182, 183
Momigliano, A., 7, 8, 11
Mommsen, T., 14, 15, 31, 89
Moraldi, L., 119, 132, 151
Morin, G., 166, 168
Moule, C.F.D., 84
Muratori, L.A., 111
Musurillo, H., 39

Nau, F., 134, 135, 136, 164
Nicolet, C., 2
Nock, A.D., 7, 8

O'Brien, P.T., 59, 62, 71

Paoli, U.E., 19, 93
Peeters, E., 164
Penna, R., 83
Pezzella, S., 130
Pfitzner, V.C., 96, 97, 170
Pherigo, L., 75
Pietri, C., 139
Platner, S.B., 101

Plümacher, E., 119, 131

Quasten, J., 120, 132, 173, 175
Quinn, J.D., 166

Ramsay, W.M., 102
Recasens i Comes, J.M., 105
Reicke, B., 61
Ricciotti, G., 42, 44
Ritter, S., 112
Rohde, J., 127
Rordorf, W., 119, 130, 173
Rougé, J., 12, 105, 186
Rowlingson, D.T., 103
Ruysschaert, J., 183

Sansterre, J.M., 154
di S. Maria, M., 183
Schlier, H., 50
Schmidt, C., 121, 130., 138, 185
Schneemelcher, W., 119, 120, 131
Schubart, W. & Schmidt, C., 121
Schürer, E., 83
Serra-Vilaro, J., 105
Sevenster, J.N., 139
Sherwin-White, A.N., 12, 18, 19, 29, 43, 75
Smallwood, E.M., 83
Solin, H., 77, 78, 83
Spicq, C., 85, 89, 91, 107
Stern, M., 83
Strathmann, H., 169
Sundberg, A.C., 112

Tajra, H.W., 2, 78, 129
Taubenschlag, R., 18
Taylor, J.E., 77
Testini, P., 26, 181

Vega, A.C., 109, 112
Vielhauer, P., 116, 117
de Visscher, F., 14, 43
Vouaux, L., 118, 128, 132, 142, 144, 151

Walaskay, P.W., 38
Wikenhauser, A., 42
Wilckens, U., 52

Index of Subjects

(Supplement to the Table of Contents)

actio prima, 88ff
actio secunda, 89ff
advocatus, 18ff
aequitas, 18, 87
agon, 96
apologia, 4, 18, 87ff
appello ad Caesarem, 33, 36, 76

capitis amputatio (*decollatio*), 22, 124ff, 129ff, 133, 148, 156, 159, 173, 175, 194
castra praetoriana, 41ff, 61
civis/civitas, 1, 174
coemeterium (*Pauli*), 181ff
coercere/coercitio, 12, 15
cognitio extra ordinem, 13ff, 19, 36
consilium principis, 18ff
corona iustitiae, 91, 97ff

delator, 6, 18, 73
delegation (of Emperor's judicial power), 14ff
Demas, 55ff

Edictum de temporibus accusationum, 47, 74

imperium, 12ff, 18
interdictio, 6
ius gladii, 23
ius provocationis, 1

Lex Iulia de vi publica et privata, 2
Lex Iulia publicorum iudiciorum, 74
Luke
— *apologia pro imperio*, 38, 73
— *apologia pro ecclesia*, 38, 73, 75
— as Paul's companion, 55ff, 92ff, 122, 126ff, 131, 134ff

memorandum (judicial), 20

Nero
— divine titles of, 9ff, 35
— in apocryphal tradition, 122ff, 129ff, 134ff, 139ff, 144ff, 156ff, 163ff
— in Patristic tradition, 167, 174, 176ff, 181, 184ff, 191ff
— involvement in Great Fire, 28, 192
— legal procedure in his tribunal, 20
— persecution of Christians, 28ff, 123, 128, 133, 136, 166, 174, 192
— reluctance to try cases, 16
— revives *Maiestas* laws, 6
Nicopolis, 102

Onesiphorus, 92ff

pannicularia, 24
parresia (as a legal term), 48ff, 58
Paul
— his house in Rome, 44ff, 134
— internal exile, 168
— knowledge of Latin, 2
— legal history (prior to Rome), 34ff
— rents a *horreum*, 45, 122
Perpetua, 149, 159
Plautilla, 141, 159
Poppaea, 83
prima defensio, 18, 86ff
probare crimen, 73

religio licita, 3, 35
Roma (cult of) 9, 36

sacrilegium, 3, 5, 27
SC Turpillianum, 74

sepulcrum (*locus religiosus*), 24, 26
Simon Magus, 116, 144ff, 155ff, 158
stratopedarch, 41ff
speculator, 24, 125, 135ff, 142, 159

Tarragona, 104ff
Timothy (as Paul's companion), 54, 56, 65, 122, 126ff, 131
titulus, 21
tribunicia potestas, 13, 36

www.ingramcontent.com/pod-product-compliance
Lightning Source LLC
Chambersburg PA
CBHW070304230426
43664CB00014B/2635